The Profundity and Bifurcation of Change

The Intelligent Social Change Journey

Part IV: *Co-Creating the Future*

MQIPress (2020)
Frost, West Virginia
ISBN 978-0-9985147-8-9

The Consciousness Series

*The human experience is a neuronal dance with the Universe, with each of us
in the driver's seat selecting our partners and directing our dance steps.*

This masterpiece is inspired! As I was reading through and contemplating this wonderful Alchemy of Change, these words came to mind: The seeds have been sown, the end of the tunnel now opening to a sprouting field of light. There are people already there, young and old, all colors, all sizes, glowing in their individuation and diversity. Whiffs of thought catch our attention, and we see the wisdom in our search for truth as with conscious compassion we collaboratively create a new frame of reference for humanity. It begins here. It begins now. It begins with the Profundity and Bifurcation of Change – Barbara Bullard, Professor of Speech Communication, Orange Coast College; Reiki Master

Debra's voice rings loud and clear through this work as she reminds us the focus on knowledge, innovation and collaboration can create the platform for world peace. Debra spent her life laying the groundwork. The Profundity and Bifurcation of Change *moves us closer to achieving a world without war. We stand now smack in the middle of the Intelligent Social Change Journey, ready to take the creative leap forward. This profound book expands our understanding of possibilities, which— through attention, intention, deepening connections and the search for truth—can be turned into realities. Embrace this opportunity, capture and direct your passion toward a Golden Age for Humanity, and let's together heal the world!* – Dr. Clint Ackerman, Technical Investment Manager; Bird House Builder; and Debra Amidon's life partner and friend

Multidimensional inspiration! Part IV is an impressive work documented with very insightful aspects. It is a very timely reading on the growing Quest for Truth and Wisdom. As a very deepening mindful reading, it is addressing wisdom beyond Knowledge in several multi dimensions, including the neuroscience. Furthermore, it is guiding the reader to Intelligent Reflective Activity that will expand the creative capacity for navigating based on intelligence. In line with the book it is also an illustration of wise giving for a choice of Happiness Journeying. — Leif Edvinsson, The World's First Professor on Intellectual Capital, Lund and Hong Kong

MQIPress
Frost, West Virginia
303 Mountain Quest Lane
Marlinton, WV 24954
United States of America
Telephone: 304-799-7267

alex@mountainquestinstitute.com
www.mountainquestinstitute.com
www.mountainquestinn.com
www.MQIPress.com
www.Myst-art.com

ISBN 978-0-9985147-8-9

Man considering the Universe of which he is a unit, sees nothing but change in matter, forces and mental states. He sees that nothing really is, but that everything is becoming and changing. Nothing stands still. Everything is being born, growing, dying. At the very instant a thing reaches its height, it begins to decline. The law of rhythm is in constant operation. There is no fixed reality, enduring quality or substantiality in anything –nothing is permanent but Change. Man sees all things evolve from other things and resolve into other things; a constant action and reaction, inflow and outflow, building up and tearing down, creation and destruction, birth, growth and death. Nothing endures but Change. And if he is a thinking man, he realizes that all of these changing things must be outward appearances or manifestations of some underlying power, some Substantial Reality.

The Kybalion (1940, p. 53)

Part IV*
Table of Contents

* This book is Part IV of *The Profundity and Bifurcation of Change*, available in PDF format from www.MQIPress.net

Part IV
Tables, Figures, and Tools

TABLES

FIGURES

TOOLS

In Appreciation

Hundreds of people, named and unnamed, have contributed thousands of ideas to this book in the context of conversations and dialogues, articles and books, and quotes and stories. We are all indeed one, sharing ideas in groups and communities, face-to-face and virtual, appearing and connecting where we will, in an ever-looping creative embrace and continuous expansion toward intelligent activity.

Our deep appreciation to our co-authors, who each bring a unique focus and value to this work. These are Arthur Shelley, Theresa Bullard, and John Lewis. It is our sincere hope that each of them—who now are co-creators with us—will share this work largely in their day-to-day lives. Also, our appreciation to Donna Panucci, Maik Fuellmann, Jackie Urbanovic and Barbara Wheeler for their contributing and expanding thoughts, to poet Cindy Scott for her insights, and to Mark Boyes, who co-created the thought-provoking image in Chapter 10.

Across our consilience approach, there are a handful of authors whose work has both inspired our thinking and excited our creativity. *Life's Hidden Meaning* by Niles MacFlouer provides insights from Ageless Wisdom, just coming into our realms of understanding. Serving as an example of committed knowledge sharing, MacFlouer has hosted a weekly radio show on Ageless Wisdom since 2004! This massive and incredibly insightful body of work is available on the Internet at http://www.agelesswisdom.com/archives_of_radio_shows.htm Over the past year we have listened, reflected, associated and created connections to this work, such that it is nearly impossible to follow these connections. In this regard, we try to err on the side of over-referencing, and since there is not one specific reference, but, rather, a way of thinking, we have referenced this body of work as MacFlouer (2004-16). We encourage those who resonate with this material to explore it more fully.

In 1996, Ken Wilber wrote *A Brief History of Everything*, and his brilliance continues to emerge from that point. While we applaud his continuing search for a simple and elegant theory of everything, we would be reluctant to eliminate *any* of the rich truths and theories explored in his dozens of books. *Paths of Change* by Will McWhinney served as a baseline for exploring world views and combinations of reality in the change journey. *Spontaneous Evolution: Our Positive Future* by Bruce H. Lipton and Steve Bhaerman is inspirational and informative from the viewpoint of cell biology. Jean Houston's *Jump Time* was way ahead of its time, and is a must read for any decision-maker in today's environment, and that is all of us. And where would we be as a humanity without the brilliance and wisdom of Bohm, Cozolino, Csikszentmihalyi, Damasio, Edelman, Gardner, Goleman, Goswami, Handy, Hawkins, Kant, Kolb, Kurzweil, Laszlo, McTaggart, Polanyi, Stonier, Templeton, Tiller, Wilber, and so many others! Our appreciation to all of the contributors called out in our references, and to those who may not be in our references but whose thought has seeped into our minds and hearts in the course of living.

Our continued thanks to the professionals, colleagues and thought leaders who participated in the KMTL study and follow-on Sampler Call. These include: Dorothy E. Agger-Gupta, Verna Allee, Debra Amidon, Ramon Barquin, Surinder Kumar Batra, Juanita Brown, John Seely Brown, Frada Burstein, Francisco Javier Carrillo, Robert Cross, Tom Davenport, Ross Dawson, Steve Denning, Charles Dhewa, Nancy Dixon, Leif Edvinsson, Kent Greenes, Susan Hanley, Clyde Holsapple, Esko Kilpi, Dorothy Leonard, Geoff Malafsky, Martha Manning, Carla O'Dell, Edna Pasher, W. Barnett Pearce, Larry Prusak, Madanmohan Rao, Tomasz Rudolf, Melissie Rumizen, Hubert Saint-Onge, Judi Sandrock, Charles Seashore, Dave Snowden, Milton Sousa, Michael Stankosky, Tom Stewart, Michael J.D. Sutton, Karl-Erik Sveiby, Doug Weidner, Steve Weineke, Etienne Wenger-Trayner and Karl Wiig.

There are very special people who assisted in ensuring the quality of this work. Kathy Claypatch with Ageless Wisdom Publishers served as a conduit to assure consistency with that work; Susan Dreiband, communications expert and shaman, and Ginny Ramos, a rehabilitation counselor and Alex's daughter, who served in the role of editor; and three readers played instrumental roles in assuring consistent and understandable concepts throughout and contributing a diversity of thoughts. These are Joyce Avedisian, Edna Pasher and Denise Sumner, all knowledgeable explorers in the journey of life.

A special thanks to our families who ground us: from David to Steve, Melanie, John, Cindy, Jackson, Rick, Chris and the grandchildren that help to keep us young; from Alex to Ginny, Bill and Andrew and her long-lost new family; from Arthur to Joy, Cath and Helen; from Theresa to Barbara and Jay, as well as to Dennis H. and Gudni G. and her MMS friends and family; and from John to Mary, Shannon and Jonathan. Thank you to all our friends who support this work in so many ways, and who have supported Mountain Quest since its 2001 beginnings. And our continuing thankfulness to Cindy Taylor and Theresa Halterman, part of our MQI Team, and for our son Andrew Dean, who keeps Mountain Quest running while we play with thoughts and words and dive into the abyss of the unknown.

With Appreciation and Love, Alex, David, Arthur, Theresa and John.

Preface

As we move in and out of life situations, there are verbal cues, often conveyed by signs, that catch our attention and somehow miraculously remain in memory throughout our lives, popping in and out as truisms. Although we may not realize how true they were at the time, one of those sayings in an early office setting was: "Change. Your life depends on it!" Then, some 10 years later, a sign appearing on the check-in desk of the dental clinic on Yokosuka Naval Base, clearly referring to our teeth, read: "Ignore them, and they will go away."

So often we feel like victims, with some new challenge emerging from here or there, something interrupting our best laid plans, some stress or weight that sprouts discomfort or confusion. Yet we have a choice to be pulled along into the fray, dive into the flow and fully participate in the decisions and actions, or even to be the wave-setters, co-creating the reality within which we live and breathe.

Never in the history of humanity has the *need to change* so clearly manifested itself into our everyday existence. While the potential for catastrophic destruction has loomed over us since the mid-20th century, we are still *here*, admittedly a world in turmoil on many fronts—plagued with economic, political, eco-system, social, cultural and religious fragmentation—but also a humanity that is awakening to our true potential and power. Just learning how to co-evolve with an increasingly changing, uncertain and complex external environment, we are now beginning to recognize that it is the change available *within* our internal environment *and energetic connections to each other and the larger whole* that offer up an invitation to an incluessent future, that state of Being far beyond the small drop of previous possibility accepted as true, far beyond that which we have known to dream (Dunning, 2015).

In this work, we introduce the overarching concepts of **profundity** and **bifurcation** as related to change. Profundity comes from the Old French term *profundite* which emerges from the late Latin term *profunditas* or *profundus*, meaning profound (Encarta, 1999). Profundity insinuates an intellectual complexity leading to great understanding, perceptiveness and knowledge. There is a focus on greatness in terms of strength and intensity and in depth of thought. *We believe that the times in which we live and the opportunity to shape the future of humanity demand that each of us look within, recognizing and utilizing the amazing gifts of our human mind and heart to shape a new world.*

Bifurcation comes from the Latin root word *bifurcare*, which literally means to fork, that is, split and branch off into two separate parts (Encarta, 1999). In terms of change, this concept alludes to a pending decision for each decision-maker, each human, and perhaps humanity at large. We live in two worlds, one based on what we understand from Newtonian Physics and one based on what we don't understand but are able to speculate and feel about the Quantum Field. As change continues with every breath we take and every action we make, there is choice as to how we engage our role as co-creator of reality.

In this book, we explore very different ways to create change, each building on the former. There is no right or wrong—choice is a matter of the lessons we are learning and the growth we are seeking—yet it is clear that there is a split ahead where we will need to choose our way forward. One road continues the journey that has been punctuated by physical dominance, bureaucracy, hard competition and a variety of power scenarios. A second road, historically less-traveled, recognizes the connections among all humans, embracing the value of individuation and diversity as a contribution to the collective whole and the opportunities offered through creative imagination. This is the road that recognizes the virtues of inclusiveness and truth and the power of love and beauty, and moves us along the flow representing Quantum entanglement.

A number of themes are woven throughout this work; for example, the idea of "NOW", the use of forces as a tool for growth, the power of patterns, earned and revealed intuition, bisociation and creativity, stuck energy and flow, the search for truth, and so many more. We take a consilience approach, tapping into a deep array of research in knowledge and learning, with specific reference to recent neuroscience understanding that is emerging, pointing the reader to additional resources. And we look to psychology, physics, cell biology, systems and complexity, cognitive theory, social theory and spirituality for their contributions. Humans are holistic, that is, the physical, mental, emotional and intuitional are all at play and working together. Recognize that you are part of one entangled intelligent complex adaptive learning system (Bennet et al., 2015b), each overlapping and affecting the other, whether consciously or unconsciously, in every instant of life. As we move from science to philosophy, facts to psychology, management to art, and words to pictures, you will no doubt feel a tugging in the mind/brain, and perhaps some confusion. Such was the case for one of the authors when studying micro-economics and Shakespeare tragedies back to back! The good news is that this can result in a great deal of expansion and availability of a wide variety of frames of reference from which to process incoming information.

Through the past half a century, all of the authors have engaged in extensive research—much of it experiential in nature—which has led us to break through life-long perceived limits and shift and expand our beliefs about Life and the world of which we are a part. The advent of self-publishing virtual books has opened the door to share this learning globally. The concepts forwarded in the earlier works of all of the authors lay the foundation for this book.

While this book is quite large, it wrote itself. In the movie Amadeus (1984), when a complaint is lodged against his work saying there are just too many notes, Mozart responds that there are just exactly as many notes as are needed. In this book, there are exactly as many chapters as are needed, no more, no less. As you move through the information and concepts available in this text, we ask that you stay open to new ideas, ways of thinking and perceiving, and—using the discernment and discretion emerging from your unique life experiences—reflect on how these ideas might fit into your personal theory of the world. It is our hope that these ideas will serve as triggers for a greater expansion of thought and consciousness, which every individual brings to the larger understanding of who we are and how, together as One, we operate in the world.

To begin, we offer the following assumptions:

Assumption 1: Everything—at least in our physical reality—is energy and patterns of energy. We live in a vast field of energy in which we are continuously exchanging information, which is a form of energy.

Assumption 2: Creativity—nurtured by freedom, purpose and choice—is a primary urge of the human. Knowledge serves as an action lever for co-creating our experiences.

Assumption 3: Knowledge is partial and incomplete. Knowledge produces forces, whether those forces are used to push forward an idea that benefits humanity, or whether those forces are to push against another's beliefs and values (knowledge), which can escalate to warfare.

Assumption 4: The human mind is an associative patterner, that is, continuously re-creating knowledge for the situation at hand. Knowledge exists in the human brain in the form of stored or expressed neural patterns that may be selected, activated, mixed and/or reflected upon through thought. Incoming information is associated with stored information. From this mixing process, new patterns are created that may represent understanding, meaning and the capacity to anticipate (to various degrees) the results of potential actions. Thus, knowledge is context sensitive and situation dependent, with the mind continuously growing, restructuring and creating increased organization (information) and knowledge for the moment at hand.

Assumption 5: The unconscious mind has a vast store of tacit knowledge available to us. It has only been in the past few decades that cognitive psychology and neuroscience have begun to seriously explore unconscious mental life. Polanyi felt that tacit knowledge consisted of *a range* of conceptual and sensory information and images that could be used to make sense of a situation or event (Hodgkin, 1991; Smith, 2003). He was right. The unconscious mind is incredibly powerful, on the order of 700,000 times more processing speed than the conscious stream of thought.

The challenge is to make better use of our tacit knowledge through creating greater connections with the unconscious, building and expanding the resources stored in the unconscious, deepening areas of resonance, connecting to the larger information field, and learning how to share our tacit resources with each other.

Assumption 6: People are multidimensional, and rarely do they hold to a single belief, a consistent logic, or a specific worldview. As identified in the recent model of experiential learning (Bennet et al, 2015b), there are five primary modes of thinking, each of us with our preferences—concrete experience, reflective observation, abstract conceptualization, active experimentation and social engagement—and each of us has a dozen or more subpersonalities offering a variety of diverse thoughts and feelings that rise to the occasion when triggered by our external and internal environments (Bennet et al., 2015a). *The human experience is a neuronal dance with the Universe, with each of us in the driver's seat selecting our partners and directing our dance steps.*

Assumption 7: We are social creatures who live in an entangled world; our brains are linked together. We are in continuous interaction with those around us, and the brain is continuously changing in response. Thus, in our expanded state we are both individuated and One, bringing all our diversity into collaborative play for the greater good of humanity.

Assumption 8: We live in times of extreme change in the human mind and body, in human-developed systems, and of the Earth, our human host. Through advances in science and technology, most of what we need to learn and thrive in these times is already available. We need only to open our minds and hearts to the amazing potential of our selves.

There are still vast workings of the human mind and its connections to higher-order energies that we do not understand. The limitations we as humans place on our capacities and capabilities are created from past reference points that have been developed primarily through the rational and logical workings of the mechanical functioning of our mind/brain, an understanding that has come through extensive intellectual effort. Yet we now recognize that *knowledge is a living form of information,* tailored by our minds specifically for situations at hand. The totality of knowledge can no easier be codified and stored than our feelings, nor would it be highly beneficial to do so in a changing and uncertain environment. Thus, in this book, given the limitations of our own perceptions and understanding, we do not even pretend to cover the vast amount of information and knowledge available in the many fields connected to change. We *do* choose to consider and explore areas and phenomena that move beyond our paradigms and beliefs into the larger arena of knowing, and to move beyond the activity of our cognitive functions to consider the larger energy patterns within which humanity is immersed.

This extensive book is initially being published in five Parts as five separate books, which will be available in both kindle (from Amazon) and PDF (from MQIPress) formats. In support of the Intelligent Social Change Journey, these Parts are:

Part I: Laying the Groundwork

Part II: Learning from the Past

Part III: Learning in the Present

Part IV: Co-Creating the Future

Part V: Living in the Future

Each part has a separate focus, yet they work together to support your full engagement in the Intelligent Social Change Journey. A Table of Contents for all five parts is Appendix B. An overarching model of the ISCJ is Appendix A. This model can also be downloaded for printing at the following location: www.MQIPress.net The graphics for "Conversations that Matter" and tables related to the Intelligent Social Change Journey are also available on this site for free download.

Workshops on all five Parts of *The Profundity and Bifurcation of Change* or, specifically, on The Intelligent Social Change Journey facilitated by the authors are available. Contact alex@mountainquestinstitute.com ... arthur.shelley@rmit.edu.au ... Theresa@Quantumleapalchemy.com ... or John@ExplanationAge.com

The Drs. Alex and David Bennet live at the Mountain Quest Institute, Inn and Retreat Center situated on a 430-acre farm in the Allegheny Mountains of West Virginia. See www.mountainquestinstitute.com They may be reached at alex@mountainquestinstitute.com Dr. Arthur Shelley is the originator of *The Organizational Zoo*, Dr. Theresa Bullard is the Founder of the Quantra Leadership Academy as well as an International Instructor for the Modern Mystery School, and Dr. John Lewis is author of *The Explanation Age.* Taking a consilience approach, this eclectic group builds on corroborated resources in a diversity of fields while simultaneously pushing the edge of thought, hopefully beyond your comfort zone, for that is where our journey begins.

PART IV

Co-Creating the Future

Introduction to
The Intelligent Social Change Journey

The Intelligent Social Change Journey (ISCJ) is a developmental journey of the body, mind and heart, moving from the heaviness of cause-and-effect linear extrapolations, to the fluidity of co-evolving with our environment, to the lightness of breathing our thought and feelings into reality. Grounded in development of our mental faculties, these are phase changes, each building on and expanding previous learning in our movement toward intelligent activity.

We are on this journey together. This is very much a *social* journey. Change does not occur in isolation. The deeper our understanding in relationship to others, the easier it is to move into the future. The quality of sympathy is needed as we navigate the linear, cause-and-effect characteristics of Phase 1. The quality of empathy is needed to navigate the co-evolving liquidity of Phase 2. The quality of compassion is needed to navigate the connected breath of the Phase 3 creative leap. See ISCJ-1.

In the progression of learning to navigate change represented by the three phases of the ISCJ, we empower our selfs, individuating and expanding. In the process, we become immersed in the human experience, a neuronal dance with the Universe, with each of us in the driver's seat selecting our partners and directing our dance steps. Let's explore that journey a bit deeper.

In Phase 1 of the Journey, *Learning from the Past*, we act on the physical and the physical changes; we "see" the changes with our sense of form, and therefore they are real. Causes have effects. Actions have consequences, both directly and indirectly, and sometimes delayed. Phase 1 reinforces the characteristics of how we interact with the simplest aspects of our world. The elements are predictable and repeatable and make us feel comfortable because we know what to expect and how to prepare for them. While these parts of the world do exist, our brain tends to automate the thinking around them and we do them with little conscious effort. The challenge with this is that they only remain predictable if all the causing influences remain constant ... and that just doesn't happen in the world of today! The linear cause-and-effect phase of the ISCJ (Phase 1) calls for sympathy. Supporting and caring for the people involved in the change helps to mitigate the force of resistance, improving the opportunity for successful outcomes.

As we expand toward Phase 2, we begin to recognize patterns; they emerge from experiences that repeat over and over. Recognition of patterns enables us to "see" (in our mind's eye) the relationship of events in terms of time and space, moving us out

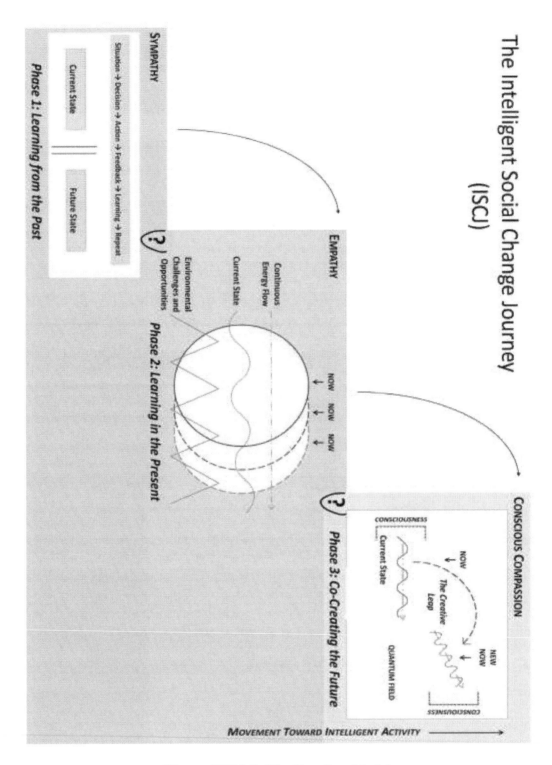

Figure ISCJ-1. *The Baseline Model.*

of an action and reaction mode into a position of co-evolving with our environment, and enabling us to better navigate a world full of diverse challenges and opportunities. It is at this stage that we move from understanding based on past cause-and-effect reactions to how things come together, to produce new things both in the moment at hand and at a future point in time.

Phase 2, *Learning in the Present*, takes us to the next level of thinking and feeling about how we interact with our world, including the interesting area of human social interactions. Although complex, the somewhat recognizable patterns enable us to explore and progress through uncertainty and the unknown, making life more interesting and enjoyable. In Phase 2 patterns grow into concepts, higher mental thought, and we begin the search for a higher level of truth. Sustainability in the co-evolving state of Phase 2 requires empathy, which provides a direct understanding of another individual, and a heightened awareness of the context of their lives and their desires and needs in the moment at hand. While not yet achieving the creative leap of the intuitional (represented in Phase 3), we are clearly developing higher mental faculties and instinctive knowledge of the workings of the Universe, which helps cultivate intuition and develop insights in service to our self and society.

The creative leap of Phase 3, *Co-Creating the Future*, requires the ability to tap into the larger intuitional field that energetically connects all people. This can only be accomplished when energy is focused outward in service to the larger whole, requiring a deeper connection to others. Compassion deepens that connection. Thus, each phase of the Intelligent Social Change Journey calls for an increasing depth of connection to others, moving from sympathy to empathy to compassion.

<<<<<<<<>>>>>>

INSIGHT: **Each phase of the Intelligent Social Change Journey calls for an increasing depth of connection to others, moving from sympathy to empathy to compassion.**

<<<<<<<<>>>>>>

The ISCJ Baseline Model accents the phase changes as each phase builds on/expands from the previous phase. As the journeyer moves from Phase 1 to Phase 2 and prepares for the creative leap of Phase 3, the mental faculties are developing, the senses are coming into balance, and there are deepening connections to others. This will feel familiar to many travelers, for this is the place where we began. The model shows our journey is a significant change of mind, body and spirit as we operate on different cognitive and emotional planes as we progress through the developmental phases. Some people are aware of the changes they are undergoing and seek to accelerate the learning, while others resist the development, hoping (perhaps somewhat naively) to simplify the way they interact with the world.

Babies are born connected, to their mothers and families, and to the larger energies surrounding them and within them. This represents Phase 3. As one author exclaimed when exploring this reversal of the Phase 1, 2 and 3 models, "This really brings it all together for me. There is something that we admire in babies that we would like to become, and this framework makes sense of that feeling." If, and when, we return to Phase 3 in the round-trip journey of life, it will be with experience in our backpack and development of the mental faculties under our cap.

Sometime around the fourth grade, as most grade school teachers will attest, the ego pokes its head out, and, through social interactions, the process of individuation has begun, with a focus on, and experiencing in, the NOW. This represents Phase 2 of our change model, a state of co-evolving. In the pre-adolescent child, intuitional connections are subsumed by a physical focus accompanied by emotional flare-ups as the child is immersed in learning experiences, interacting and learning from and with their environment.

By the time the mid-teens come around, the world has imposed a level of order and limits, with a focus on cause-and-effect. In some families and cultures this may take the form of physical, mental or emotional manipulation and control, always related to cause-and-effect. If you do that, this will happen. For others, cultural or religious aspects of expectations and punishment may lead to the cause-and-effect focus. For the mid-teen perceived as overactive and unruly in the schoolroom, the limiting forces may be imposed through Ritalin or other drugs, which may have even started at a much earlier age. Regardless of how it is achieved, learning from the past—the Phase 1 model—becomes the starting point of our lives as we move into adulthood. From this starting point, we begin to develop our mental faculties.

The Overarching ISCJ Model

To help connect the dots, we have prepared a larger version of the Intelligent Social Change Journey, which is at Appendix A. The Overarching ISCJ Model focuses on the relationships of the phases with other aspects of the journey. For example, three critical movements during our journey, consistent with our movement through the phases, are reflected in expanded consciousness, reduction of forces and increased intelligent activity. *Consciousness* is considered a state of awareness and a private, selective and continuous change process, a sequential set of ideas, thoughts, images, feelings and perceptions and an understanding of the connections and relationships among them and our self. *Forces* occur when one type of energy affects another type of energy in a way such that they are moving in different directions, pressing against each other. Bounded (inward focused) and/or limited knowledge creates forces. *Intelligent activity* represents a state of interaction where intent, purpose, direction, values and expected outcomes are clearly understood and communicated among all parties, reflecting wisdom and achieving a higher truth. We will repeat this definition where appropriate throughout the book.

<<<<<<<>>>>>>>

INSIGHT: **The ISCJ is a journey toward intelligent activity, which is a state of interaction where intent, purpose, direction, values and expected outcomes are clearly understood and communicated among all parties, reflecting wisdom and achieving a higher truth.**

<<<<<<<>>>>>>>

Immediately below each phase of the Overarching ISCJ model are characteristics related to each phase. These are words or short phrases representing some of the ideas that will be developed in each section supporting each phase. **Phase 1,** *Learning from the Past*, characteristics are: linear and sequential, repeatability, engaging past learning, starting from current state, and cause and effect relationship. **Phase 2,** *Learning in the Present*, characteristics are: Recognition of patterns; social interaction; and co-evolving with the environment through continuous learning, quick response, robustness, flexibility, adaptability and alignment. **Phase 3,** *Co-Creating Our Future*, characteristics are: Creative imagination, recognition of global Oneness, mental in service to the intuitive; balancing senses; bringing together time (the past, present and future); knowing; beauty; and wisdom.

Still exploring the overarching model, at the lower part of the graphic we see three areas related to knowledge in terms of the nature of knowledge, areas of reflection, and cognitive shifts necessary for each phase of change. For ease of reference, we have also included the content of these three areas in Table ISCJ-1.

In Phase 1, *Learning from the Past*, the nature of knowledge is characterized as a product of the past and, as we will learn in Chapter 2, knowledge is context sensitive and situation dependent, and partial and incomplete. Reflection during this phase of change is on reviewing the interactions and feedback, and determining cause-and-effect relationships. There is an inward focus, and a questioning of decisions and actions as reflected in the questions: What did I intend? What really happened? Why were there differences? What would I do the same? What would I do differently? The cognitive shifts that are underway during this phase include: (1) recognition of the importance of feedback; (2) the ability to recognize systems and the impact of external forces; (3) recognition and location of "me" in the larger picture (building conscious awareness); and (4) pattern recognition and concept development. These reflections are critical to enabling the phase change to *co-evolving*.

In Phase 2, *Learning in the Present*, the nature of knowledge is characterized in terms of expanded cooperation and collaboration, and knowledge sharing and social learning. There is also the conscious *questioning of why*, and the *pursuit of truth*. Reflection includes a deepening of conceptual thinking and, through cooperation and collaboration, the ability to connect the power of diversity and individuation to the larger whole. There is an increasing outward focus, with the recognition of different world views and the exploration of information from different perspectives, and expanded knowledge capacities. Cognitive shifts that are underway include: (1) the ability to recognize and apply patterns at all levels within a domain of knowledge to predict outcomes; (2) a growing understanding of complexity; (3) increased connectedness of choices, recognition of direction you are heading, and expanded meaning-making; and (4) an expanded ability to bisociate ideas resulting in increased creativity.

In Phase 3, *Co-Creating Our Future*, the nature of knowledge is characterized as a recognition that with knowledge comes responsibility. There is a conscious pursuit of larger truth, and knowledge is selectively used as a measure of effectiveness. Reflection includes the valuing of creative ideas, asking the larger questions: How does this idea serve humanity? Are there any negative consequences? There is an openness to other's ideas, a questioning with humility: What if this idea is right? Are my beliefs or other mental models limiting my thought? Are hidden assumptions or feelings interfering with intelligent activity?

Cognitive shifts that are underway include: (1) a sense and knowing of Oneness; (2) development of both the lower (logic) and upper (conceptual) mental faculties, which work in concert with the emotional guidance system; (3) recognition of self as a co-creator of reality; (4) the ability to engage in intelligent activity; and (5) a developing ability to tap into the intuitional plane at will.

Time and space play a significant role in the phase changes. Using Jung's psychological type classifications, feelings come from the past, sensations occur in the present, intuition is oriented to the future, and thinking embraces the past, present *and* future. Forecasting and visioning work is done at a point of change (McHale, 1977) when a balance is struck continuously between short-term and long-term survival. Salk (1973) describes this as a shift from Epoch A, dominated by ego and short-term considerations, to Epoch B, where both *Being and ego co-exist*. In the ISCJ, this shift occurs somewhere in Phase 2, with Beingness advancing as we journey toward Phase 3. Considerable focus to time and space occurs later in the book (Chapter 16/Part III).

Phase of the Intelligent Social Change Journey	ISCJ: Nature of Knowledge	ISCJ: Points of Reflection	ISCJ: Cognitive Shifts
PHASE 1: Cause and Effect (Requires Sympathy) • Linear, and Sequential • Repeatable • Engaging past learning • Starting from current state • Cause-and-effect relationships	• A product of the past • Knowledge is context-sensitive and situation-dependent • Knowledge is partial and incomplete	• Reviewing the interactions and feedback • Determining cause-and-effect relationships; logic • Inward focus • Questioning of decisions and actions: What did I intend? What really happened? why were there differences? What would I do the same? What would I do differently?	• Recognition of the importance of feedback • Ability to recognize systems and the impact of external forces • Recognition and location of "me" in the larger picture (building conscious awareness) • Beginning pattern recognition and early concept development
PHASE 2: Co-Evolving (Requires Empathy) • Recognition of patterns • Social interaction • Co-evolving with environment through continuous learning, quick response, robustness, flexibility, adaptability, alignment.	• Engaging knowledge sharing and social learning • Engaging cooperation and collaboration • Questioning of why? • Pursuit of truth	• Deeper development of conceptual thinking (higher mental thought) • Through cooperation and collaboration ability to connect the power of diversity and individuation to the larger whole • Outward focus • Recognition of different world views and exploration of information from different perspectives • Expanded knowledge capacities	• The ability to recognize and apply patterns at all levels within a domain of knowledge to predict outcomes • A growing understanding of complexity • Increased connectedness of choices • Recognition of direction you are heading • Expanded meaning-making • Expanded ability to bisociate ideas resulting in increased creativity
PHASE 3: Creative Leap (Requires Compassion) • Creative imagination • Recognition of global Oneness • Mental in service to the intuitive • Balancing senses • Bringing together past, present and future • Knowing; Beauty; Wisdom	• Recognition that with knowledge comes responsibility • Conscious pursuit of larger truth • Knowledge selectively used as a measure of effectiveness	• Valuing of creative ideas • Asking the larger questions: How does this idea serve humanity? Are there any negative consequences? • Openness to other's ides; questioning with humility: What if this idea is right Are my beliefs or other mental models limiting my thought? Are hidden assumptions or feelings interfering with intelligent activity?	• A sense and knowing of Oneness • Development of both the lower (logic) and upper (conceptual) mental faculties, which work in concert with the emotional guidance system • Applies patterns across domains of knowledge for greater good • recognition of self as a co-creator of reality • The ability to engage in intelligent activity • Developing the ability to tap into the intuitional plane at will

Table ISCJ-Table 1. *The three Phases from the viewpoints of the nature of knowledge, points of reflection and cognitive shifts.*

Cognitive-Based Ordering of Change

As a cognitive-based ordering of change, we forward the concept of logical levels of learning consistent with levels of change developed by anthropologist Gregory Bateson (1972) based on the work in logic and mathematics of Bertrand Russell. This logical typing was both a mathematical theory and a law of nature, recognizing long before neuroscience research findings confirmed the relationship of the mind/brain which show that we literally create our reality, with thought affecting the physical structure of the brain, and the physical structure of the brain affecting thought.

Bateson's levels of change range from simplistic habit formation (which he calls Learning I) to large-scale change in the evolutionary process of the human (which he calls Learning IV), with each higher-level synthesizing and organizing the levels below it, and thus creating a greater impact on people and organizations. This is a hierarchy of logical levels, ordered groupings within a system, with the implication that as the levels reach toward the source or beginning **there is a sacredness, power or importance informing this hierarchy of values** (Dilts, 2003). This structure is consistent with the phase changes of the Intelligent Social Change Journey.

<<<<<<<◇>>>>>>>

INSIGHT: **Similar to Bateson's levels of change, each higher phase of the Intelligent Social Change Journey synthesizes and organizes the levels below it, thus creating a greater impact in interacting with the world.**

<<<<<<<◇>>>>>>>

With Learning 0 representing the status quo, a particular behavioral response to a specific situation, Learning I (first-order change) is stimulus-response conditioning (cause-and-effect change), which includes learning simple skills such as walking, eating, driving, and working. These basic skills are pattern forming, becoming habits, which occur through repetitiveness without conceptualizing the content. For example, we don't have to understand concepts of motion and movement in order to learn to walk. Animals engage in Learning I. Because it is not necessary to understand the concepts, or underlying theories, no questions of reality are raised. Learning I occurs in Phase 1 of the ISCJ.

Learning II (second-order change) is deuteron learning and includes creation, or a change of context inclusive of new images or concepts, or shifts the understanding of, and connections among, existing concepts such that meaning may be interpreted. These changes are based on mental constructs that *depend on a sense of reality* (McWhinney, 1997). While these concepts may represent real things, relations or qualities, they also may be symbolic, specifically created for the situation at hand.

Either way, they provide the means for reconstructing existing concepts, using one reality to modify another, from which new ways of thinking and behaviors emerge.

Argyris and Schon's (1978) concept of double loop learning reflects Level II change. Learning II occurs in Phase 2 of the ISCJ.

Learning III (third-order change) requires thinking beyond our current logic, calling us to change our system of beliefs and values, and offering different sets of alternatives from which choices can be made. Suggesting that Learning III is learning about the concepts used in Learning II, Bateson says,

> In transcending the promises and habits of Learning II, one will gain "a freedom from its bondages," bondages we characterize, for example, as "drive," "dependency," "pride," and "fatalism." One might learn to change the premises acquired by Learning II and to readily choose among the roles through which we express concepts and thus the "self." Learning III is driven by the "contraries" generated in the contexts of Learning I and II. (Bateson, 1972, pp. 301-305)

<<<<<<<<>>>>>>>

INSIGHT: **There is a freedom that occurs as we leave behind the thinking patterns of Phase 2 and open to the new choices and discoveries of Phase 3.**

<<<<<<<<>>>>>>>

Similarly, Berman (1981, p. 346) defines Learning III as, "an experience in which a person suddenly realizes the arbitrary nature of his or her own paradigm." This is the breaking open of our personal mental models, our current logic, losing the differential of subject/object, blending into connection while simultaneously following pathways of diverse belief systems. Learning III occurs as we move into Phase 3 of the ISCJ.

Learning IV deals with revolutionary change, getting outside the system to look at the larger system of systems, awakening to something completely new, different, unique and transformative. This is the space of *incluessence*, a future state far beyond that which we know to dream (Dunning, 2015). As Bateson described this highest level of change:

> The individual mind is immanent but not only in the body. It is immanent in pathways and messages outside the body; and there is a larger Mind of which the individual mind is only a sub-system. This larger Mind is comparable to God and is perhaps what people mean by "God," but it is still immanent in the total interconnected social system and planetary ecology. (Bateson, 1972, p. 465)

Table ISCJ-2 below is a comparison of the Phases of the Intelligent Social Change Journey and the four Levels of Learning espoused by Bateson (1972) based on the work in logic and mathematics of Bertrand Russell, and supported by Argyris and Schon (1978), Berman (1981), and McWhinney (1997).

■■■ i

Phase of the Intelligent Social Change Journey	Level of Learning [NOTE: LEARNING 0 represents the status quo; a behavioral response to a specific situation.]
PHASE 1: Cause and Effect (Requires Sympathy) • Linear, and Sequential • Repeatable • Engaging past learning • Starting from current state • Cause and effect relationships	**LEARNING i:** **(First order change)** • Stimulus-response conditioning • Incudes learning simple skills such as walking, eating, driving and working • Basic skills are pattern forming, becoming habits occurring through repetitiveness without conceptualizing the content • No questions of reality
PHASE 2: Co-Evolving (Requires Empathy) • Recognition of patterns • Social interaction • Co-evolving with environment through continuous learning, quick response, robustness, flexibility, adaptability, alignment	**LEARNING II (Deutero Learning)** **(Second order change)** • Includes creation or change of context inclusive of new images or concepts • Shifts the understanding of, and connections among, existing concepts such that meaning may be interpreted • Based on mental constructions that depend on a sense of reality
[Moving into Phase 3] **PHASE 3: Creative Leap** (Requires Compassion) • Creative imagination • Recognition of global Oneness • Mental in service to the intuitive • Balancing senses • Bringing together past, present and future • Knowing; Beauty; Wisdom	**LEARNING III: (Third order change)** • Thinking beyond current logic • Changing our system of beliefs and values • Different sets of alternatives from which choices can be made • Freedom from bondages **LEARNINNG IV:** • Revolutionary change • Getting outside the system to look at the larger system of systems • Awakening to something completely new, different, unique and transformative • Tapping into the large Mind of which the individual mind is a sub-system

Table ISCJ-Table 2. *Comparison of Phases of the ISCJ with Levels of Learning.*

An example of Learning IV is Buddha's use of intuitional thought to understand others. He used his ability to think in greater and greater ways to help people cooperate and share together, and think better. Learning IV is descriptive of controlled intuition in support of the creative leap in Phase 3 of the ISCJ, perhaps moving beyond what we can comprehend at this point in time, perhaps deepening the connections of sympathy, empathy and compassion to unconditional love.

How to Best Use this Material

This book has, quite purposefully, been chunked into five smaller books, referred to as Parts, which are both independent and interdependent. Chunking is a methodology for learning. The way people become experts involves the chunking of ideas and concepts and creating understanding through development of significant patterns useful for identifying opportunities, solving problems and anticipating future behavior within the focused domain of knowledge. Figure ISCJ-2 shows the relationship of the Parts of this book and their content to the Intelligent Social Change Journey. *Remember*: the ISCJ is a journey of expansion, with each Phase building on—and inclusive of—the former Phase as we develop our mental faculties in service to the intuitional, and move closer to intelligent activity. As such, one needs to experience the earlier phases in order to elevate to the upper levels. Early life experiences and educational development during these earlier stages create the foundation and capacity to develop into higher levels of interactions and ways of being.

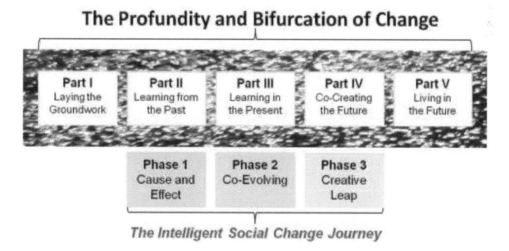

Figure ISCJ-2. *Relationship of Parts and Phases of the ISCJ.*

While many different ideas have been introduced in the paragraphs of this Introduction to the Intelligent Social Change Journey, you will discover that all of these ideas are addressed in depth during the course of this book, and each Part is inclusive of tools, references, insights and reflective questions provided in support of your personal learning journey. We also cross-reference, both within the Parts, and across all of the Parts.

This is a journey, and as such *the learning is in the journey*, the reflecting on and application of the learning, not in achieving a particular capability or entering the next Phase at a specific point in time. Similar to the deepening of relationships with others, the growth of understanding and expansion of consciousness takes its own time, twisting and curving forwards and backwards until we have learned all we can from one frame of reference, and then jump to another to continue our personal journey. That said, we suggest that those who are impatient to know the topics within this book, but reluctant to read such an extended text, jump to Chapter 11/Part III, which provides readiness assessment statements and related characteristics reflecting the high-level content of this book.

For your reference, the Overarching ISCJ model can be downloaded for printing in A3 format at www.MQIPress.net The corresponding author may be reached at alex@mountainquestinstitute.com

PART IV

Co-Creating the Future

Introduction to Part IV

All experiences in life offer the potential for developing higher order patterns, and thus taking on larger meaning. In other words, development of the higher mental faculties through experience occurring in the physical, emotional and mental perspectives is in service to the intuitional. It is through these perspectives that we create a platform for the creative leap, and it is through these perspectives that we develop the consciousness that helps us hone our intuition as a tool for co-creating our future.

Phase 3 of the Intelligent Social Change Journey (see Figure IV-1) builds on the understanding of cause and effect gained in Phase 1, the recognition of patterns and development of conceptual thinking experienced in Phase 2, and the deepening of relationships with others as we expand from sympathy to empathy and reach inward toward compassion. Note that multiple phases can be, and are, engaged simultaneously such that there is a back and forth, never negating a previous phase, rather growing and expanding from it, either consciously or unconsciously and, as Phase 3 is engaged, moving into a state of conscious compassion and consciously-controlled intuition.

As we move toward co-creating our future—which builds on learning from the past and co-evolving with the present—the basic dynamics of change move from a grounding in the mental faculties and engaging creative imagination, to opening up to intuitive thought, that is, achieving the ability to tap into the intuitional plane at will. This is where risk becomes a burden and a choice, and once released, the tool of forgetting comes into play. Eccles and Nohria (1992, p. 178) say, "Knowing when one's knowledge is no longer useful is the beginning of wisdom." While we may not entirely forget (see Chapter 20/Part III), if we are to continue to find higher truths, we must be able to let go of prior knowledge to make way for new learnings. As we discovered in Chapter 20/Part III, the very best way to avoid attending to a memory is to have a stronger, more significant memory replace it.

Let's explore that concept a bit deeper. Consistent with the phrase *use it or lose it*, forgetting and unlearning take the form of *lack of use*, that is, no focus, attention or thought, then no neuronal firings. Of course, when we are told *not* to think of something, that "something" is the first thing in our mind! However, that something can be laid aside when a more significant concept, thought and feeling has pre-empted it. This happens when stronger connections are made to the more significant

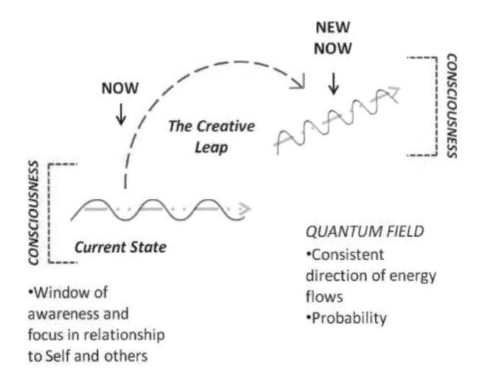

CHARACTERISTICS: *Creative imagination;* Recognition of global Oneness; Mental in service to the intuitive; Balancing senses; Bringing together past, present and future; Knowing; Beauty; Wisdom

Figure IV-1. *Phase 3 of the Intelligent Social Change Journey.*

concept in terms of relating to and connecting with a large number of other thoughts (sense-making), a higher level of emotion (passion, excitement, joy), and a conscious focus on this new concept. Regardless of age, the best mental exercise is new learning, acquiring new understanding and knowledge, and doing things that you have never done before (Amen, 2005).

As part of our evolving learning system, memories and the emotional tags that gauge the importance of those memories become part of an individual's everyday life. Emotions and mood play a prominent role in learning, or what Christos (2003) calls the laying down of memories. However, consciousness also plays an important role in the learning experience. "We seem to have to become conscious of something before we can learn it properly" (p. 40).

We simultaneously live in several worlds as we learn to become the co-creators that we are. Still somewhat captured by the limitations of our cause and effect model, it is difficult to fully unleash our natural creative juices. As Peat (1988, p. 38) describes,

> The linear chain of causality and the predictive power of mathematical equations have dominated science for so many generations that it is now difficult to see what room there can be in the Universe for freedom, novelty, and creativity.

Just learning how to co-evolve with an increasingly changing, uncertain and complex external environment can be difficult. The difficulty comes in recognizing that it is the change available *within* our internal environment *and energetic connections to each other and the larger whole* that can best offer up an invitation to an incluessent future. Such incluessent future is that state of Being far beyond the small drop of previous possibility accepted as true, far beyond that which we have known to dream (Dunning, 2015). Our very existence—or what we perceive as our existence—is opening to unique possibilities as we transition from the relatively known and therefore comfortable existence of Newtonian physics to the unknown potential of Quantum. From the Quantum perspective, *the direction of our very thoughts and intentions become responsible for our reality*. This is a big responsibility.

This shift in thinking is bombarding us from many directions. From neuroscience, we now understand that we are not victims of our DNA, that it is, rather, how DNA is expressed that largely determines our future health. As if that's not enough, we are beginning to understand the power of our thoughts and feelings and their impact on every aspect of our lives, internally and externally. Evidently, we have to take responsibility for *who* we are as well as *who we are becoming*.

When organizations develop a *vision* of the future, that vision is generally developed as a noun with descriptive adjectives. A popular approach is to think of the world in *telecological* terms, that is, as being *directed toward a future goal* (Carroll, 2016). What we have begun to understand in the unfolding of this book is that reality—whether perceived in terms of past, present or future—is not a fixed state, but an ever-shifting and changing process of perceiving and learning. So, while a future vision serves as a useful tool for our imagination, it is more about the consistency of our thoughts, feelings and actions with the *direction we are heading* than about achieving a specific state. Accompanied by intelligent activity, painting the vision and setting goals *do* help head us in the same direction and *can* serve as tools to keep us on track. Consistency of direction increases the probability of a creative leap occurring.

<<<<<<<◇>>>>>>>

INSIGHT: **While a future vision serves as a useful tool, its value is more about the consistency of our thoughts, feelings and actions with the direction we are heading than about achieving a specific state.**

<<<<<<<◇>>>>>>>

Since the future is somewhat dependent on the non-rational acts of human beings, it has the potential to be affected by events and factors that are *not* linked to the past and cannot be anticipated. As the mental faculties of humanity develop through the co-evolving phase of change, the ability of the brain expands to work within its own space-time domains. This is the ability that futurists use to bring many years of future events into a current thought pattern. For example, Loveridge (1977) identified three space-time domains which are generally used today to think about the future: conceptual, perceptual and physical. The *conceptual* space-time domain is spatial and holistic thinking, having no existence except to the individual and going out of existence when the individual stops thinking in that mode. While the *perceptual* space-time domain is also specific to the individual, it has to do with an individual's *perception and experiencing* of the external environment, that is, using our thoughts and feelings to arrange objects and close feedback loops in sequential tasks such as writing and speech. The *physical* space-time domain is related to the external world and is public, acting in and on the world, providing many ways of measuring time.

When we look back at technological growth and computing power over the past several thousand years, we realize that growth is not linear; it is exponential. As Mulhall (2002, p. 28) describes:

> [I]t took many millennia to get from counting on cave walls to counting with manual analog computers. From manual computers to mechanical ones took several centuries; from mechanical to electronic ones, several lifetimes; and from integrated circuit computing to self-taught computers, less than a generation. Appreciating this rise in computing power … is central to understanding the potential for technology leaps.

This is why scientists and technologists such as Ray Kurzwell (1999) have extrapolated on this more than exponentially increasing timeline to tout that the *Singularity* is near. The Singularity is that time when machines become more intelligent than their human creators, an era where machines can carry on by themselves and brains are enhanced by neural implants. Mulhall (2002) feels that the point of Singularity requires a vital scientific discussion and, indeed, that it may very well foreshadow our next evolutionary stage. Humans have always been in a hurry to supersede themselves. Recognition of these leaps in technological change can help prepare us for a future where new ways of being and acting may or may not appear connected to evolutionary approaches.

The question becomes: Are we on the road to developing a human-generated super intelligence or opening to a human-connected superconsciousness, or perhaps both? In 1993 computer scientist Vernor Vinge published a paper entitled "The Coming Technological Singularity: How to Survive in the Post-Human Era". In this work Vinge (1993) identifies ways that superior intelligence might arise, including through developing a human-technology network of colleagues and associates; using biological means such as neural implants, genetic modification or chemical inputs; via self-aware computers such as HAL; and, potentially, a spontaneous "wake up" of super intelligence occurring in networks.

Before launching into the chapters related to Phase 3, we provide the **Introduction to the Intelligent Social Change Journey** (ISCJ), which was primary in *The Profundity and Bifurcation of Change Part I.* The ISCJ is a journey toward intelligent activity, which is a state of interaction where intent, purpose, direction, values and expected outcomes are clearly understood and communicated among all parties, reflecting wisdom and achieving a higher truth. (If you have read previous Parts, you may wish to jump directly to the following chapter.)

It is with all this in mind that we move into Phase 3 of the Intelligent Social Change Journey, where we consciously choose to tap into energies beyond our perception of self, but of which we are a part, to become the co-creators that we are. In Part IV, we explore:

Chapter 22: Learning Points Along the Path. New perceptions and ways of thinking create new words and concepts, or new ways of interpreting old concepts. This chapter touches on concepts that emerge as we move toward conscious compassion, Phase 3 of our Intelligent Social Change Journey. Concepts presented here include: consilience; divination, prediction and forecasting; empathy, givingness, happiness, harmony, inclusiveness, nobility, presence, serendipity, symmetry and symbiotic thinking, synchronicity, synergy and thought forms.

Chapter 23: Co-Creating Frames of Reference. What does it mean to co-create our reality? Recognizing that just as each and every individual is unique, the realities we create individually and collectively are unique, this chapter explores multiple perspectives on self-creating reality. These include taking a literary perspective, a living-system perspective, a consciousness perspective, a scientific perspective, and a spiritual perspective. We explore the sense and meaning behind the quote: "As mind pursues reality to its ultimate analysis, matter vanishes to the material senses but may still remain real to the mind."

Chapter 24: Knowledge and the Search for Truth. The discovery of truth is the greatest virtue in the journey of mental development. The very concept of knowledge is concerned with truth. However, just as knowledge is incomplete and context sensitive and situation dependent, truth is a living, dynamic concept. This chapter addresses truth as a quality of reality. It then focuses on the current misinformation explosion, exploring the relationship of perception and propaganda, and the power of brainwashing.

Chapter 25: Attention and Intention. Attention and intention are tools of self, laying the web for interaction with the world in which we interact. Managing both concepts is necessary to balance current priorities with future opportunities and guide your Intelligent Social Change Journey.

Chapter 26: The Mental Fabric. The abilities to control our attention, remember, abstract and reason are what sets the human apart from other animals. This chapter dives deeply into thought, which is a combination of choices, connecting those choices to other choices previously made, and affecting further choices by limiting or reducing those choices. Development of our mental faculties has been the hallmark of humanity to date. We explore the movement from lower mental thought (logic) to higher mental thought (concepts) and their relationship in today's environment. Finally, we bring in the roles of theory and heuristics.

Chapter 27: Moving into Wisdom. The highest part of mental thought is wisdom, which represents completeness and wholeness of thought. Wisdom occurs when activity matches the choices that are made and structured concepts are intelligently acted upon. This chapter explores wisdom from several frames of reference. We then provide an example of wisdom in terms of mental discipline.

Chapter 28: Tapping into the Intuitional. Building towards the creative leap, we explore intuition in terms of earned intuition and revealed intuition, bringing in findings from recent neuroscience research. Controlled intuition is introduced, and the Field of ideas as the collective unconscious is explored.

Chapter 29: Exploring Creativity. We first ask: From whence does creativity come? Then we look at what we have discovered from neuroscience in terms of creativity before modeling the relationships among information, knowledge, creativity and innovation.

Chapter 30: The Creative Leap. Finally, we take a close look at the creative leap, the "punctuated equilibrium" aspect of Phase 3 of the Intelligent Social Change Journey.

We begin.

Chapter 22
Learning Points Along the Path

SUBTOPICS: CONSILIENCE ... DIVINATION, PREDICTION AND FORECASTING ... EMPATHY ... GIVINGNESS ... HAPPINESS ... HARMONY ... INCLUSIVENESS ... NOBILITY ... PRESENCE ... SERENDIPITY ... SYMMETRY AND SYMBIOTIC THINKING ... SYNCHRONICITY ... SYNERGY ... THOUGHT FORMS ... FINAL THOUGHTS

FIGURE: **22-1**. STOPPING BY THE "CO-ING" UNIVERSITY FOR A BIT OF CO-LEARNING. **22-2**. COOPERATION AND COLLABORATION IN ALL WALKS OF LIFE CREATE SYNERGY, AND MOVE US CLOSER TO INTELLIGENT ACTIVITY.

TOOL: 22-1. PREDICTING THROUGH PATTERN DISCOVERY. **22-2**: CHOOSING HAPPINESS.

Following the phases of change, humanity began its long learning journey toward today with simple cause-and-effect related actions. As we shift gears to focus on Phase 3 of the Intelligent Social Change Journey, it makes sense to explore ideas that have emerged during the course of this change journey, ideas that began the conceptual and developmental expansion necessary for spontaneous change.

This chapter contains but a sprinkling of the conceptual shifts that could be included. While choosing some of our favorites that are making a difference in our personal and professional lives, we touch on concepts of growing significance today in preparation for ushering in a new level of conscious thought. See Figure 22-1. Each concept can be related to the physical, emotional, mental and spiritual planes, and the correlating senses of each of those planes and the balancing of our senses across those planes.

We talk about these concepts alphabetically and, while certainly affected by our experiences which reside in the past, they all represent approaches, states or conditions that happen in the NOW and have large implications for understanding the future. The learning points included below are: consilience; divination, prediction and forecasting; empathy, givingness, happiness, harmony, inclusiveness, nobility, presence, serendipity, symmetry and symbiotic thinking, synchronicity, synergy and thought forms.

While these concepts interweave through all the Phases of the Intelligent Social Change Journey, they are very supportive of the social aspect of our journey, the "co-ing" introduced in Chapter 14/Part III, and the co-creating of Chapter 23. As you read through these concepts, try to remember when each concept was new to you,

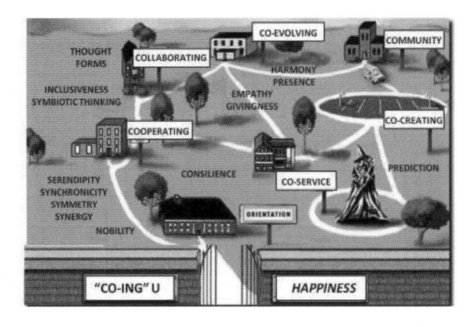

Figure 22-1. *Stopping by the "Co-ing" University for a bit of co-learning.*

recalling how you felt about it then, and how you feel about it now. There is so much growth occurring in each of us, and we rarely take the time to realize that *is* occurring and to honor the self that is developing through this growth. So, as we continue this journey, take a moment to appreciate your self.

Consilience

Since it is humans that separate knowledge into different domains, not nature, it is easy to resonate with E. O. Wilson's work on consilience, the bringing together of two or more disciplines, or when two or more inductions drawn from different disciplines come into agreement (Wilson, 1998). This book takes a consilience approach, tapping into a deep array of research in knowledge and learning, with specific reference to recent neuroscience understanding, and looking to psychology, physics, cell biology, systems and complexity, cognitive theory, social theory and spirituality for their contributions.

Taking a system's perspective, limitations and challenging problems often derive from our inability to rise above the tendency to categorize and specialize in separate disciplines. While disciplines are convenient artificial constructs that may be effective within their boundaries, they can also be limiting by their frame of reference and accepted procedures and practices. Of course, limitations can happen within a discipline as well as across disciplines. An example of such a limitation within a discipline was the dominance of behaviorism on learning research in the 20th century. As David Kolb (1984, p. 2) posited, "In the overeager embrace of the rational, scientific, and technological, our concept of the learning process itself was distorted first by rationalism and later by behaviorism."

By looking across fields, it may be possible to see interactions and possibilities that are not obvious within individual disciplines. An example in the authors' research would include past beliefs regarding adult learning that have been shown to be false through neuroscience findings. Our interests are in looking across fields to enhance understanding and find new ways of achieving objectives. Howard Gardner calls this *synthesis*, what he considers the human ability to knit together information from disparate sources into a coherent whole. This is an important human capability. Gardner (2006) notes that the Nobel prize-winning physicist Murray Gell-Mann believes that the mind most at a premium in the 21st century will be the mind that can synthesize well. As Gardner contends,

> The ability to knit together information from disparate sources into a coherent whole is vital today. The amount of accumulated knowledge is reportedly doubling every two or three years (wisdom presumably accrues more slowly!) Sources of information are vast and disparate, and individuals crave coherence and integration. (Gardner, 2006, p. 46)

In today's global world where we have recognized the power of social interaction, synthesis is taking on an expanded meaning to include bringing people together to share and integrate their thoughts, honoring individuation as value to collective collaboration.

<<<<<<<<<>>>>>>>

INSIGHT: **Synthesis, the ability to knit together information from disparate sources into a coherent whole, is a powerful important human capability**.

<<<<<<<<<>>>>>>>

As a working definition, consilience means a "jumping together" of knowledge through the linking of facts and fact-based theory across disciplines to create a common groundwork of explanation (Wilson, 1998). Wilson quotes Whewell as saying in an 1840 synthesis of *The Philosophy of the Inductive Sciences* that, "The Consilience of Induction takes place when an Induction, obtained from one class of facts, coincides with an Induction, obtained from another different class" (Wilson, 1998, p. 8).

When taking a consilience approach, each field or discipline provides a different perspective, each has a contribution to make, and each has its own way of solving problems and validating findings. In addition, each discipline may hold a specific primary frame of reference. Although individuals in various fields may be studying the same general phenomena, their frame of reference will influence what is considered valid data or acceptable conclusions.

As systems become more complex, their behavior and characteristics change, requiring different (or multiple) approaches to understanding (Bennet & Bennet, 2004; Wilson, 1998). Thus, there is also the phenomena of emergence of hybrid disciplines. Examples are evolutionary psychology, cognitive psychology, neurobiology and functional medicine (Wilson, 1998).

Consilience can be challenging, particularly as in the example of a focus on experiential learning, when one discipline leans toward the "hard" sciences (such as neuroscience) and others lean toward the "soft" sciences (such as psychology and education). In addition, each field of study may have a different ontology as well as epistemology while simultaneously having an impact on the other. For example, Blakemore and Frith (2005), both cognitive neuroscientists, and Byrnes (2001), a professor of human development, agree that knowledge of the brain and how it learns will undoubtedly have an impact on education. Blakemore and Frith (2005) offer that there is almost no literature on the connection between the brain sciences and education. This perception may, however, be due to a lack of awareness in the educational field of some of the available research.

In 1959, Snow (1959/1993) wrote about the two cultures of science and humanism, identifying many aspects of their differences as well as the importance of their interdependence. While there has historically been a divide between the natural sciences on the one hand and the social sciences and humanities on the other hand, Snow also believes that, "Nothing fundamental separates the course of human history from the course of physical history, whether in the stars or in organic diversity" (Wilson, 1998, p. 11). The issues we face as a humanity require that we bring our knowledge of the humanities and natural sciences together, erasing their boundaries to produce a clearer view of reality (Wilson, 1998). The National Research Council (2000) suggests that the growth of interdisciplinary inquiries and new kinds of scientific collaboration have begun to make the path from basic research to education practices somewhat more visible, if not yet easy to travel.

Divination, Prediction and Forecasting

Let's briefly differentiate these terms. Divination is a seeking of knowledge in an attempt to foretell the future, the direction of things, identifying forces and creatively acting with or on those forces. Prediction is concerned with exactness, that is, in time, nature and the magnitude of future events. "I am going to predict what item is behind that closed door." Conversely, forecasting deals very much with uncertainty and conjecture, offering a spectrum of possibilities. This is closer to the Quantum concept, where all that is possible exists behind a closed door until the door is opened and what is behind it is observed.

<<<<<<<<>>>>>>>>

INSIGHT: ***All that is possible*** **exists behind a closed door until the door is opened and what is behind it is observed.**

<<<<<<<<>>>>>>>>

We acknowledge MacFlouer's (2004-2016) focus on the expansion of Quantum theory[22-1] as helping us understand a subtle but significant point that surfaces in the wording of this insight. When this insight was initially written, it said "...where all possibilities exist behind a closed door until the door is opened ...." This wording insinuates *things already in existence* waiting behind the door, much like the television game shows where you have doors A, B and C, each with something already existing waiting behind it. Taking into account human preferences, etc., you can calculate the probabilities of choosing the specific thing you would like to have behind the door you choose (perhaps a car or Caribbean vacation) versus, say, a vacuum cleaner or a hair treatment that exists behind the other two doors. Indeed, this has been our historic understanding of probability theory. However, the wording "... where *all that is possible exists* behind a closed door ..." has an inclusiveness that *points to the phenomenon of emergence, or creation.* Prior to opening the door, what is behind that door is *potential,* energy waiting to be transformed to thought, energy that can be engaged in the process of co-creation.

At several points within the course of this book we have introduced the term "incluessence", which was a term coined by Jo Dunning (2014) to describe that which is beyond our ability to dream or imagine. We would contend that from a Quantum viewpoint this is the state behind the door which is not yet open. It is in the instant of the opening that new energies are available, new thought forms emerge and/or are attracted and coalesce, and "all that is possible exists", inclusive of that which we could not previously conceive as possible. If this sounds related to the concept of the Quantum jump or the creative leap, then we are sharing this learning together. What could not have existed from our previous frame of reference, now is possible from a new frame of reference, that is, a door has opened and "all that is possible" is a different state before we open the door and after we open the door.

In both the East and the West, divination has been a tool to explore the future since antiquity. Divination can be thought of as the imagination tapping into the unconscious side of a situation, perceiving forces and then creating ways to deal with those forces. It "involves a combination of analysis and intuition that normal thinking usually keeps apart. This process values imagination and creativity. It shifts the way you make decisions." (Ritsema & Karcher, 1995, p. 11)

<<<<<<<◇>>>>>>>

INSIGHT: **Divination is the imagination tapping into the unconscious side of a situation, perceiving forces and creating ways to deal with those forces.**

<<<<<<<◇>>>>>>>

There are many systems of divination or insight that can serve as a way of developing intuition. For example, there are various systems of astrology (Western, Vedic, Chinese, Real-Sky, Mayan), numerology, human design, gene keys, Tarot decks, etc. While they all work, certain ones will resonate more than others for certain individuals. This resonance is based on the symbolism and framework used that makes most intuitive sense to the user such that the user tunes their awareness into it more consciously, training their mind to those symbols. These tools then become a vehicle for gaining insight into things to which we might otherwise be blind.

The Kabbalah, or the Tree of Life, and its various symbolic correspondences of numbers, letters, sounds and archetypes is at the foundation of many divination tools in Western Mystical Traditions. It is a both a mathematical and geometric system of organizing information and archetypal patterns in a way that adapts itself well to a Western way of thinking. In Kabbalah, using something like Tarot is not for divination, but rather for using the archetypal imagery of the cards to create a window or bridge into the unconscious and/or a mirror to the self. The unconscious works in symbolism and imagery well, so this is a way to train our conscious mind to the language of the unconscious. We meditate upon the images/symbols, build them up in our mind, recreate the inner landscape, and then "walk through the door" into that imagery using our creative imagination. This is called *Pathworking* and is best documented in the books by Paul Foster Case (Case, 2009, 2008, 2007; Clark and Forbes, 2013).

The *I Ching* (the Book of Change) is the oldest divinatory system to have survived from the past. Through the use of symbols, seekers are able to connect with forces that govern the world. (Symbolic representation is introduced as a Knowledge Capacity in Chapter 19/Part III.) As Ritsema & Karcher (1995, p. 14) describe the *I Ching,*

> The *I Ching* … puts its users in a position to create and experience their own spirit as a point of connection with the forces that govern the world. It is this imaginative power that was elaborated, re-interpreted and defined throughout later Chinese history to the basis of philosophy, morals and ethics. It is a way to connect with the creative imagination that underlies all systems and creeds. Thus, the *I Ching* serves as a manual and sourcebook for Jung's archetypal forces. It asks the general question: How can I creatively act with the forces shaping this instant of time?

Bayesian Inference is an early mathematical approach to predicting the future based on probability theory. Bayes was a Presbyterian minister and amateur mathematician who lived in the early and middle part of the 18th century. He was interested in how humans judge the reliability of information. He developed a method of calculating probabilities that was modified whenever new information was acquired. This led to the development of Bayesian statistics, which has become more powerful with computers crunching big data. Bayes' method begins with *prior odds*, that is, estimating the relative probabilities of A versus B. Then, as new information (X) becomes available, you calculate the likelihood of X being true if A is true and if B is true. Now, the relative probabilities of A and B are re-estimated taking into account a Likelihood Ratio, that is, the likelihood of X if A is true divided by the likelihood of X if B is true. This whole process is repeated whenever new information is acquired (Devlin & Lorden, 2007).

It is important to recognize that in predicting the future prior beliefs matter. As Carroll (2016, p. 79) says, "Bayes Theorem allows us to be quantitative about our degrees of belief, but it also helps us keep in mind how belief works at all." Each of us has developed an inner mapping of reality, the way the world works, and a personal theory and beliefs of how to operate in this world. Yet, as we now recognize, all knowledge is incomplete. We are continuous learners in a continuously changing environment that is becoming more and more complex. Nonetheless, our experiences and the associations of our mind bring us to our current starting point for living life.

In the 1980's, Davis (1996) developed a framework he described as *Future Perfect*. The framework was based on a simple syllogism, that time, space and mass are the basic dimensions of the known Universe, and that everyone and everyone's business is part of that Universe. These resources can be exploited and manipulated for better or for worse. Linking these universal abstract truths to specific business applications—and asking a lot of questions along the way—changes our thinking. (See Chapter 14/Part III on Time and Space.)

<<<<<<<<>>>>>>>>

INSIGHT: **Time, space and mass are the basic dimensions of the known Universe, and everyone and everyone's business is part of that Universe.**

<<<<<<<<>>>>>>>>

By 1996, when Davis (1996, p. 231) reviewed and updated his model, he ended, "When management treats time, space, and no-matter as resources rather than as roadblocks, our methods of organization will no longer be lagging behind, at the end." In making this shift to "no-matter", Davis was acknowledging the shift to a Knowledge Economy, that is, with information (an infinite intangible) the major fuel for the new economy and knowledge the principal product of this fuel.

Although there are limits to growth in finite resources, **there are no limits to learning, the ultimate renewable resource** [emphasis added] … The more information you add to a finite resource, therefore, the more valuable it becomes. (Davis, 1996, p. 114-115)

Since 1996 we understand the difficulties as well as the advantages of information overload. With this in mind, we would shift Davis' words from "the more valuable it becomes" to "the more potential value is created." Nonetheless, Davis' framework, and others working in this field who were heading the same direction, looked into the future and *moved us toward an understanding of the organic nature of organizations and the co-evolving model of change.*

With knowledge-based companies in full swing, the predictions of sociologist Michael G. Zey (2000) jump from innovations in biotechnology, computing, robotics, medicine, energy development and space technology to the exploration of gene therapy and decoding of the human genome, next generation robots and smart machines, space tourism and fusion-based energy. He identifies four powerful new forces that are changing the way we live: biogenesis, cybergenesis, species coalescence and dominionization. Placing humanity at the threshold of what he refers to as the Expansionary Age, he visions a *Humaniverse*, which is *the emergence of human consciousness and human intelligence that is happening today.* He calls this an historical event:

> … the human race's capacity to vitalize, bring life, order, creativity, and novelty to everything it touches, sets the world on a complete new evolutionary trajectory. Moreover, the world now possesses an entity, the human species, that could develop the tools to save the Universe … (Zey, 2000, p. 216).

We agree with Zey that, ultimately, it is *human will* that will determine the shape and direction of the Universe, a Universe that we are actively creating. As Zey (2000, p. 258) concludes, we have entered "the most magnificent period imaginable—the future is an act of love. It will also be the most challenging in human history—the future is an act of will."

<<<<<<<◇>>>>>>>

INSIGHT: **Ultimately, it is human will that determines the shape and direction of the Universe, a Universe that we are actively co-creating.**

<<<<<<<◇>>>>>>>

This brief glance at divination, prediction and forecasting suggests that the human mind is quite capable of—in the NOW and based on the past— focusing thought toward exploring the future. As introduced in Chapter 2/Part I, a significant aspect of the mind/brain is its capability to continually make sense of its environment and anticipate what's coming next. Part of knowledge is anticipation of the future. As Buzsaki states,

... brains are foretelling devices and their predictive powers emerge from the various rhythms they perpetually generate ... The specific physiological functions of brain rhythms vary from the obvious to the utterly impenetrable. (Buzsaki, 2006, p. viii)

In other words, *our behavior is closely related to our capacity to form accurate predictions.* This perspective is reinforced by the neuroscientist Rudolfo Llinas who considered predicting the outcome of future events as the most important and common of all global brain functions (Llinas, 2001). The sense of movement of the body provides a simple demonstration of the need—and power—of anticipating the future. Imagine walking down a staircase and accidentally missing a step, recognizing the surprise one has when beginning to fall (Hawkins, 2004). Since for thousands of years survival has depended upon humans being capable of anticipating their environment and taking the right actions to survive, perhaps it should be no surprise that that capability has come through the evolution of the brain. As Damasio explains,

...survival in a complex environment, that is, efficient management of life regulation, depends on taking the right action, and that, in turn, can be greatly improved by purposeful preview and manipulation of images in mind and optimal planning. Consciousness allowed the connection of the two disparate aspects of the process—inner life regulation and image making. (Damasio, 1999, p. 24)

Planning as a human capability is discussed in detail in Chapter 16/Part III.

****

TOOL 22-1: Predicting through Pattern Discovery

Pattern thinking was introduced in Chapter 17/Part III. Understanding patterns is one way to predict change. In *Thinking in the Future Tense*, James (1996, pp. 47-68) said that patterns evolve through six processes. Exploring the landscape through each of these lenses can aid creativity and promote innovation. These are briefly described below.

APPROACH (1): EXTENSION. Observe a known phenomenon, imagine how it could be expanded, and the implications of that expansion. For example, when a new-sized iPhone comes out, what accessories are needed? With electromagnetic sensitivity growing, what protection products would help these individuals?

APPROACH (2): ELABORATION. This is the process of changing an existing product or service. James (1996, p. 63) points out: "Elaboration is the best way to capitalize on an already established pattern or trend." For example, Disney expanded his entertainment and product focus to include building resorts, broadening his focus and expanding the impact of his products.

APPROACH (3): RECYCLING. This is the process of taking an old product and recycling it for a new generation, or as a point of nostalgia for an older generation.

APPROACH (4): PATTERN REVERSALS. These are hesitations or momentary interruptions in forward movement. "When we push too far in one direction, there is a tendency for whatever we are pushing to snap back. Veggie burgers somehow create a demand for steak houses." (James, 1996, p. 66) This is a human anomaly. When you push too hard in one direction, the other direction is perceived as less available and therefore more desirable.

APPROACH (5): STRANGE ATTRACTIONS. These are unpredictable and odd combinations of patterns or trends, much like the strange attractors in chaos theory. An example is techies putting crystal on their computers to ground them. These unusual combinations can excite the mind.

APPROACH (6): CHAOS. Chaos theory cautions us to stay open to the unlikely, improbable and unpredictable. As James (1996, p. 68) notes, "Chaos theory is the science of process, the knowledge of what is becoming, not what is or will remain. Our minds and our business are not always systems in balance: they are always in process."

****

Empathy

Cozolino (2006, p. 203) calls empathy a hypothesis that we make based on a combination of visceral, emotional and cognitive information, a "muddle of resonance, attunement, and sympathy." Kohut (1984) says empathy is objectively trying to experience the inner life of another. Riggio (2015) describes three different types of empathy: (1) a cognitive-based form called *perspective-taking*, that is, seeing the world through someone else's eyes; (2) literally feeling another's emotions, a *personal distress* caused by "emotional contagion"; and (3) recognition of another's emotional state and feeling in tune with it, what is called *empathic concern*.

Empathy—part of a continuum based on an increasing depth of connection—is required in order to co-evolve in a dynamic environment, Phase 2 of the Intelligent Social Change Journey. The movement through this journey is from sympathy to empathy to compassion, and, for most humans sometime in the future, to unconditional love. (See Chapter 33/Part V.)

Interestingly enough, from a neuroscience viewpoint, the physiological basis for empathy is so inherent in brain function that it has been extensively documented in scientific experiments with other tested primates. For example, Masserman (1964) reported that in a study of rhesus monkeys when one monkey pulled a chain for food, a shock was given to that monkey's companion. The monkey who pulled the chain refused to pull it again for 12 days, that is, the primates would literally choose to starve themselves rather than inflict pain on their companions. de Waal (2009) feels that *empathy is nature's lesson for a kinder society*.

A key proponent of empathy is feeling, and Riggio (2015) thinks that in reality we all have some level of each type of empathy. However, it is when the boundaries between self and the other blur, and the inner states of the other are assumed to be identical with the self, that empathy is replaced by what Cozolino (2006) calls identification or fusion, lacking perspective and an awareness of boundaries. This is an important point. Empathy cannot take over individuation. There is a balance needed. This balance is discussed further in terms of compassion in Chapter 35/Part V. See also the discussion of "givingness" below.

Although the neurobiology of empathy is still in its early development (Augustine, 1996), the insula—described as the limbic integration cortex lying beneath the temporal and frontal lobes—appears to "play an important role in both the experience of self and our ability to distinguish between ourselves and others" (Cozolino, 2006, p. 206). Beyond basic sensations, the left insula is involved in the evaluation of eye gaze direction, the response to fearful faces, and the observation of facial expression of the other (Carr et al., 2003; Kawashima et al., 1999). Further research has found that the insula mediates the extreme limits of emotions, ranging from severe pain to passionate love (Andersson et al., 1997; Calder et al., 2003).

<<<<<<<<◇>>>>>>>>

INSIGHT: **The movement from sympathy to empathy to compassion reflects the increasing depth of connection necessary to move through the three phases of the Intelligent Social Change Journey**.

<<<<<<<<◇>>>>>>>>

Cozolino (2006) says that the insula cortex and anterior cingulate link hearts and minds and that this is best demonstrated when watching others experience pain. These two regions become activated either when we experience pain, or when a loved one experiences pain. The degree of activation of these two structures has been shown to correlate with measures of empathy (Singer et al., 2004; Jackson et al., 2005). Thus, whereas the insula cortex has played a small role in the history of neurology and neuroscience up until this point, it appears to have a bright future as a central component of the developing social brain (Cozolino, 2006, p. 208).

These findings suggest that through feelings there is an active link between our own bodies and minds and the bodies and minds of those around us. Thus, the feelings that we each perceive in the course of our daily living may be affected by, *or even belong to*, those around us.

With this understanding, we are now in a position to think conceptually, that is, understand the patterns that emerge through emotive thinking, recognizing the differences and similarities in emotional reactions between ourselves and others and among all living things. This understanding leads to exploring the "why" of actions based on the feelings of the actors. As can be seen, empathy, as with all feelings and emotions, supports development of the mental faculties (see Chapter 24 on the Mental Fabric of our Mind). Acting effectively on empathy requires development of the higher mental mind (concepts, the recognition of patterns). It is not just *what* you do, but *how others will respond to what you do* that supports taking right actions.

Empathy is included in the discussion of compassion in Chapter 35/Part V.

Givingness

Giving is a universal opportunity. Regardless of your age, profession, religion, income bracket, and background, you have the capacity to create change. - Laura Arrillaga-Andreessen, Philanthropist, Educator and Author

Givingness is a way of caring, a way of loving. By virtue of definition, at different levels, sympathy, empathy, compassion and unconditional love (all part of the continuum detailed in Chapter 33/Part V) are connected to the desire to help, the desire to give, the desire to serve. While this desire is commendable, it is critical that any service provided be accompanied by a high vibration in terms of thought and emotion. For example, when you are feeling discomfort from observing another person in a needy situation and you decide to help them from this place of discomfort, there is no lasting value for two reasons. First, you are not in "alignment" with your self, so you have little to give. Second, paying attention to their need *amplifies* their need. Helping from a position of strength means that you are in alignment with their *success* when you offer assistance, not in alignment with the problem (January 11, 2017, daily quote from Abraham-Hicks Publications). See the discussion of motives in Chapter 7/Part II and the discussion of attention and intention in Chapter 25.

As we move through life, "giving" opportunities are ripe. There are people on the street corner asking for help; family members and friends in trouble; not-for-profit groups looking for donations; groups of children running after tourists begging. It is so easy to ignore them, write a quick check, or throw some change in a bucket, and then dismiss them. Yet, *giving is an art* that must be cultivated to achieve *wise* giving, which was introduced in Chapter 4/Part I. It is about paying it forward, that is, loving someone enough that you can help them learn to be more loving of themselves and others.

<<<<<<<<>>>>>>>

INSIGHT: **Giving is an *art* that must be cultivated to achieve *wise* giving.**

<<<<<<<<>>>>>>>

Consider for a moment the thoughts and feelings that go through you as you toss your change into a bucket in the following scenarios: (1) A young musician playing in the park with his violin case open. You pause and listen. He's quite good, and, you toss your change (or dollars) in to encourage him. (2) Without you asking, a middle-aged man aggressively cleans your windshield as you stop at a light, then holds out his hand for money. (3) An older woman pushes her way to the front of the check-out line in a store, then turns to the person behind her to ask for money when she discovers she doesn't have enough to pay for her cigarettes. (4) A middle-aged woman in the hospital parking area approaches you to ask if you can help with gas money. She points to an older man and young child in a nearby car and explains she had to rush him to the hospital early that morning, but doesn't have enough gas to get back home.

Most of us would be inclined to help in situations (1) and (4), but not in situations (2) and (3). In situation (1), the young musician is sharing his talent and you are listening, thus there is an informal value exchange. Further, your contribution has a clear potential for paying it forward. In situation (4), the context of the situation supports the request for assistance, and while there is certainly the potential that this story is a fabrication, there is a strong likelihood that it is real. Thus, you will go with your gut feel. You are in a small way assisting a person who is assisting another person in need, a pass-it-on situation.

Conversely, in situation (2) the individual is counting on your feeling of guilt, that he has performed an act for which he is owed a payment, despite the fact that you did not ask him to do so. He is attempting to manipulate you. By responding to this manipulation, you not only enable him to continue this behavior, but you also create a negative force within yourself by knowing that you are being manipulated. In situation (3), this is a woman who clearly feels entitled, while showing little concern for others. If you give in this situation you are enabling the woman while, as in situation (2), creating negative forces within yourself. (Forces are discussed in detail in Chapter 3/Part I.)

Thus, we have a model for wise giving. This is giving where the recipient is participatory, either immediately (as an exchange or partnering) or in the future (pass-it-on). From your point of view the act of wise giving may be paying-it-forward. Wise giving was introduced in Chapter 3/Part I as an important element of a relationship that can help reduce forces, with the object to *reduce forces over the long term by cooperating and sharing with others the amount of energy they need in the short term*. The example provided was that of lending a hand with a difficult task that requires more than one person; or providing a short-term loan to get through a rough spot, which is then repaid in some way as promised; or the sharing of knowledge, effort or material objects in an equitable relationship. On the other hand, unwise giving can help produce selfishness in others, thereby *producing* forces. Unwise giving can be characterized as taking care of other's issues and problems without their participation. For example, paying someone's debt without them learning from the experience, thereby repeating it again and again or building a dependency on you such that they cease their own creativity and growth, giving away their freedom and personal power. Think about this carefully. While you *think* you are helping this individual, over the long-term you are hurting them. If the lessons of life are not learned, they are repeated; participation in resolution of issues that emerge in life is essential for learning to take place.

Giving is always of ourselves. To give is to present, provide or deliver something to someone. The Collins dictionary and dictionary.com both include a reference to *voluntarily* doing so, although this is not mentioned in Merriam-Webster, Macmillan or Cambridge, leading dictionary references. We contend that if what you are giving is not of yourself, then it is not giving. We cannot give to others that which is not ours (MacFlouer, 2004-16).

<<<<<<<<>>>>>>>

INSIGHT: **If what you are giving is not of yourself, then it is not giving.**

<<<<<<<<>>>>>>>

Happiness

Happiness is a choice. As Templeton (2002, p. 216) says, "The way we choose to see the world creates the world we see!" From our neuroscience learnings, we know that this is true. (See the discussion of positive thinking in Chapter 9/Part II). So, then, *happiness is not the product of events, but rather how we respond to events*, and that is a choice.

The "happiness formula" forwarded in positive psychology (Haidt, 2006), is H = S + C + V, that is, happiness is equal to "your biological set point (S) plus the conditions of your life (C) plus the voluntary activities (V) you do" (Haidt, 2006, p. 91). Of course, as voluntary, V includes intentional activities. Note that the biological set point is also impacted by physical choices such as what and how much you eat and physical and mental exercise as well as natural hormonal levels, etc. Further, the "conditions of your life" have a great deal to do with how you choose to *perceive* the conditions of your life. See Chapter 19/Part III on the emotions as a guidance system.

Happiness is not a state of being, for it cannot be static when generated by a verb (a person), nor could it sit still in a changing, uncertain and complex environment. It is a by-product. In *What All the World's A-Seeking*, written in 1897 by Ralph Waldo Trine, he says:

> A corollary of the great principle already enunciated might be formulated thus: **there is no such thing as finding true happiness by searching for it directly** [emphasis added]. It must come, if it comes at all, indirectly, or by the service, the love, and the happiness we give to others. So there is no such thing as finding true greatness by searching for it directly. It always, without a single exception, has come indirectly in the same way, and it is not at all probable that the great eternal law is going to be changed to suit any particular case or cases. Then recognize it, put your life into harmony with it, and reap the rewards of its observance, or fail to recognize it and pay the penalty accordingly, for the law itself will remain unchanged. **Life is not, we may say, for mere passing pleasure, but for the highest unfoldment that one can attain to, the noblest character that one can grow, and for the greatest service that one can render to all mankind** [emphasis added]. In this, however, we will find the highest pleasure, for in this the only real pleasure lies.

As introduced in Chapter 16/Part III, Baird and Nadel (2010) describe the "full involvement of flow" as a state of natural happiness. Thus happiness, a state of mind or feeling characterized by inner peace, love and joy, is part of the flow of life, **not an inward flow, but *an outward flow***. As Martin Luther King, Jr. spoke, "Those who are not looking for happiness are the most likely to find it, because those who are searching forget that the surest way to be happy is to seek happiness for others." Robert J. McCracken agreed as he wrote, "The most infectiously joyous men and women are those who forget themselves in thinking about others and serving others. Happiness comes not by deliberately courting and wooing it, but by giving oneself in self-effacing surrender to great values." John Marks Templeton shortened this to say, "Happiness pursued eludes; happiness given returns." (Templeton, 2002, p. 273) (See the discussion of flow as the optimal experience in Chapter 18/Part III.)

<<<<<<<◇>>>>>>>

INSIGHT: **True happiness cannot be found by searching for it directly; if it comes, it is by the service, love and happiness that we give to others.**

<<<<<<<◇>>>>>>>

A Harvard Grant Study followed 268 male Harvard undergraduates from 1938-1940 for 75 years, collecting data at regular intervals on aspects of their lives. The study was focused on exploring the secrets of a happy and purposeful life. Vaillant (2012), the psychiatrist who directed the study from 1972 to 2004, says that while it may be obvious that love is key to a happy and fulfilling life, there are two pillars of happiness. "One is love," he writes. "The other is finding a way of coping with life that does not push love away."

The Harvard study provided a number of insights. First, it's about more than money and power. There is a larger picture, and the older we grow the more we appreciate that picture. Second, we can all become happier regardless of how we begin life. One participant started with pretty bleak prospects for life, yet wound up being one of the happiest. He said he spent his life searching for love. Third, connection is essential. "Joy is connection" says Vaillant (2012). **The more areas in your life you can make connection, the better**" [emphasis added]. Strong relationships were found to be a high predictor of life satisfaction, and feeling connected at work was more important than the amount of money being made. Fourth, the perspective you get from challenges can make you happier. Examples cited were Mother Teresa, who had a terrible childhood and painful inner spiritual life but a "highly successful life by caring about other people" and Beethoven, who's connection to music helped him cope with misery.

****

TOOL 22-2: Choosing Happiness

Happiness is a choice. The foundational concepts that support this tool are: (A) There is a spot of happiness to be found in almost every situation; and (B) We have the ability to create happiness through our thoughts and actions.

STEP (1): Look and find the spot of happiness in the situation. This may be peripheral to the situation at hand; for example, perhaps no one was hurt in an accident; or your health may be intact despite the situation; or recognize the situation as a learning experience (all situations do have the potential for learning, even if only learning that you don't want to repeat them); or you can be happy that the experience is over.

STEP (2): Treat yourself to something you enjoy. This might be as simple as a hot fudge Sunday, a new outfit, a book or movie.

STEP (3): Do something for someone else. Surprise a loved one with a gift; give a financially struggling employee a raise; participate in a "house building" experience for someone in need; write an inspiration poem or short story and share it with your friends and neighbors. The possibilities are endless. Think of those you know—and those you don't know—and do an act in service to others. (See the discussion of "wise-giving" earlier in this chapter.)

****

Laughter, supporting health and productivity, has the capacity to glide an individual and group into happiness. Along the path of life, one of the authors had a colleague who had one of those loud, joyful bursts of laughter, accompanied with a big smile, which periodically emerged in her conversations. There was no way you couldn't respond in like manner, and you always felt good after the conversation. Even the writing of this brings a smile. Laughter is contagious.

Embracing laughter as a universal language, in cooperation with United Kingdom application developers Platoon and Made in Space, Israeli artist Eyal Gever originated a competition called "#Laugh" to create an application that can generate a digital 3D sculpture *based on the sound of laughter*. Gever said to CNN representatives, "Lately, the world seems to be dominated by racism and the rise of right-wing politics. Laughter is something we can all do, and that unifies us." And, as Pequenino (2016) captures, "According to the artist, laughter reminds people that there is beauty in humanity." (See Chapter 33/Part V on the harmony of beauty.) The winning design from this competition, selected through social media online voting, is to be sent into space and 3D printed on the International Space Station (ISS). The sound of human laughter will be the first 3D art printed in space!

Bliss is a form of extreme happiness. For at least the older authors, the phrase *follow your bliss* is one that emerged in inspirational speeches as well as in everyday conversations, fiction books and movies. It's a phrase that bears surfacing again today. **Follow your bliss.**

Harmony

To harmonize is to bring into harmony, bring into agreement, adjusting differences and inconsistencies. In music it is the mixing of melodies and chords to create pleasing sounds. An example of harmony is beauty, a consistency and pleasing arrangement of parts (Dictionary.com, 2016). (See the discussion of the harmony of beauty as a short-cut to expanded consciousness in Chapter 33/Part V.)

Harmony deals with multiples, that is, in terms of its usage in music, it began historically describing the sounds of combined voices produced by more than one person singing at the same time. Accordingly, Kostka et al. (2013, p. xi) define harmony as "the sound that results when two or more pitches are performed simultaneously. It is the vertical aspect of music, produced by the combination of the components of the horizontal aspect." There are two important learnings for us from this definition.

First, that individual tones alone do not create harmony, rather **it is the combination of tones**. Kostka et al. (2013) specifically describe the combination of these tones, saying that the soprano and tenor line are the most melodic, with the actual melody in the soprano, the tenor following for awhile, then bringing in a figure of his own. While the bass is less melodic, it is also strong and independent, and the alto, the least distinctive, adds the tones that fill out the harmonic line. Thus, harmony in the sense of people and organizations (or countries) is *an inter-weaving, the working together such that there is an overall sense of well-being and beauty.* Harmony would appear to emerge with intelligent activity, *a state of interaction where intent, purpose, direction, values and expected outcomes are clearly understood and communicated among all parties, reflecting wisdom and achieving a higher truth.*

Second, harmony is not created in an instant of time, rather it is produced through the combined *movement* of the musical tones. As Kostka et al. (2013, p. xi) state, "Although this book deals with harmony and with chords, which are little samples taken out of the harmony, you should remember that musical lines (vocal or instrumental) produce the harmony, not the reverse." This reminder is a good one. Harmony is produced by social interaction over time. While it may be punctuated by chords (events), it is the movement of the social interaction that produces the harmony. This makes sense. So often we are reminded that it is the journey of life that is important. And when we achieve an important personal or professional milestone, we find it is just part of a larger flow towards something else, and so forth.

<<<<<<<◇>>>>>>>

INSIGHT: **People create harmony through the combined movement of working together such that there is an overall sense of well-being and beauty.**

<<<<<<<◇>>>>>>>

It is quite easy for an individual "melody" to go off on its own, an independent horizontal line with little attention to the resulting (vertical) chords, which would most likely result in the build-up of forces, or dissonance, as one melody battled with another for dominance. This is actually the case in some 20th century music! The opposite case is where the melody is totally subsumed by a focus on the chords, or events, resulting in an absence of flow and loss of the melodic line (and harmony). In other cases, some voices just double the melody, offering no additional value or individuation. As can be seen, we can learn much about human behavior from exploring the harmony of music!

In the Native Hawaiian *Lokahi* tradition, balance and harmony represent the seamless unity and interconnectedness of all things. This is a reference to the concept of supernal harmony, with supernal meaning heavenly, celestial or spiritual (alphaDictionary, 2016). The *Lokahi* Triangle as a tool is introduced in Chapter 30, which is focused on balance.

Inclusiveness

We have right in front of our eyes the Universal model for inclusiveness, the Earth with whom we live. The Earth is an amazingly rich planet, with a high diversity of living organisms and inorganic forms, an example of what *Urantia* (1954, p. 1222) describes as "*exquisite repleteness* of the all-inclusive nature of the Universe" [emphasis added].

Yet, somehow, it's easy to forget that Universal lesson when focusing on our organizations and day-to-day life. Recognizing the value of diversity, forward-thinking leaders around the world have worked to bring diversity into their organizations. However, this is not enough. Inclusiveness is far more than diversity of gender, race or culture (David, 2014). As Riordan (2014) points out, "while many organizations are better about creating diversity, many have not yet figured out how to make the environment inclusive—that is, create an atmosphere in which **all people feel valued and respected and have access to the same opportunities** [emphasis added]."

David (2014) says it's about shifting our mindset. "What matters most is a fundamental mindset that embraces every person as an individual and helps them bring who they are—both their backgrounds and their opinions—into the workplace." She suggests the following practices: becoming aware of biases, creating a shared identity, and being attentive to emotions.

In Phase 2 of the Intelligent Social Change Journey we begin to recognize the amazing power of diversity in terms of thought and action, and the contribution of diversity to the bisociation of ideas that leads to innovation. To move fully into the flow co-evolving in a global world, it is necessary to release any remaining barriers or forces attached to the illusion of separation. This does not negate the power of individuation; rather, it elevates its significance. Only through individuation can Oneness expand and grow (see the discussion of individuation in Chapter 4/Part I and the discussion of Oneness in Chapter 36/Part V).

<<<<<<<>>>>>>>

INSIGHT: **Releasing the illusion of separation does not negate the power of individuation; rather, it elevates its significance.**

<<<<<<<>>>>>>>

Nobility

Nobility represents a human being's highest virtue, *doing the best each human can do at a particular point in time*. The concept of nobility provides an excellent descriptive term for doing our best in a situation that is relative, that is, situation dependent and context sensitive. Thus, every human being has the capability of acting nobly.

The linking of nobility and virtue has occurred throughout the history of man. For example, an oil-on-canvas ceiling painted for the Palazzo Manin, Venice, by Giovanni Battista Tiepolo is entitled "The Triumph of Virtue and Nobility Over Ignorance" (circa 1740-50). Virtue and Nobility, female and male, respectively, are vanquishing ignorance. A poppy leaf that is falling through the sky refers to the "sleep of the mind." Bats represent the refusal of ignorance to see the light of knowledge and wisdom (Norton Simon Museum, 2016). Virtue and Nobility are winning.

In terms of knightly chivalry, nobility conveyed the importance of supporting one's convictions at all times. This was especially important when no one else was watching. Similarly, Smith (1986) believes that Aristotle's conception of nobility—tied to goodness and virtue—is quite realistic. He supports Aristotle's stance that **political life can be justified only when it is related to some level of human flourishing and good character.** This is an important learning lesson for those who politically seek to serve.

While we often attach the term "nobility" to aristocrats, people with privilege and rites of birth, the foundational intent is that of *possessing high moral ideals or revealing excellent moral character* (*Encarta*). Thus, when associated with knowledge and the actions based on that knowledge, the characteristic of nobility represents good character, which is extensively detailed in Chapter 34/Part V.

Presence

Without presence we would become our environment. We are chameleons, and brilliant at imprinting what we see and bringing it into our own energy. When we are conscious, we are present. While presence and consciousness are interrelated, the idea of presence in this discussion goes beyond an awareness of the NOW to include deep listening and moving beyond the way we've done things in the past, that is, it brings with it the freedom of choice. Senge et al. (2004) see presencing as a core capability of the future, a way to access the living fields that connect us and *that which is seeking to emerge*. These living fields are, in the larger sense, what we have referred to as the Noosphere, the Zero Point Field, the Quantum Field or the God Field. The concept of connecting to "that which is seeking to emerge" is certainly consistent with the Quantum Field as a probability field containing all possibilities.

Senge et al. (2004) introduce seven capacities that are foundational to see, sense and realize these new possibilities: suspending, redirecting, letting go, letting come, crystalizing, prototyping and institutionalizing. Each of these capacities enable various activities, which serve as a gateway to the next capacity. This theory has become more popularly known as the *Theory of U*, which was introduced as a change strategy in Chapter 8/Part II.

This idea of "letting come" is the process of *allowing*, whose importance cannot be overemphasized. As the adage goes, we are often our own worst enemies. As we realize the power of the mind/brain in terms of thought and feelings in the process of co-creating, we do not want to interject barriers to our desired progress forward. Presencing opens us to receiving and learning. As is forwarded in the January 08, 2017, daily quote from Abraham-Hicks Publications, "Over time, your appreciation for the question will become equivalent to your appreciation for the answer, and your appreciation for the problem will become equivalent to your appreciation for the solution. And in your newfound ease with what-is, you will find yourself in the state of allowing what you truly desire."

Presencing is not an individual concept, but rather considers the individual as a living system that is of the whole. In other words, there is a sense of social identity present. In the discussion of time and space in Chapter 16/Part III, we talk about the relationship of objects, space and time, which are quite interdependent on each other. In the context of the mind, this would mean *consciously* showing up, being aware of our inner connections to the larger Field.

Serendipity

Serendipity is the art of finding what we are not seeking, *yet perhaps what we need or want*. It is the interweaving of chance into our lives ... or is it?

In a recent article on serendipity, Kennedy (2016) asks: How do we cultivate the art of finding what we're not seeking? She provides the example of Steve Hollinger who, in 2008, developed a throwable videocamera, which took the shape of a baseball that was equipped with gyroscopes and sensors. This baseball (called Squito) could be tossed into a crawlspace to provide nonhuman visual perspectives of the world.

The term serendipity is traced back to English author Horace Walpole who, in the mid-1700's while researching a coat of arms, stumbled upon an exciting tidbit of information. He coined the word serendipity to represent the discovery of something for which we were not searching. The more formal definition is luck that takes the form of finding valuable or pleasant things that are not looked for (*Merriam-Webster*, 2016).

In the mid-1900's Dr. Sandra Erdelez, a University of Missouri information scientist, studied 100 people to discover how they created—or failed to create—their own serendipity. She discovered that these individuals fell into three groupings: (1) non-encounterers, who did exactly what they set out to do and didn't look beyond that tasking; (2) occasional encounterers, who "stumbled" into occasions of serendipity; and (3) super-encounterers, who purposefully explored random texts, hoping to find treasures in odd places. Erdelez felt that *believing* you were a super-encounterer helped you be one, possessing "special powers of perception, like an invisible set of antennas, that will lead you to clues" (Kennedy, 2016). This is consistent with neuroscience findings. (See also the discussion on co-creating our reality in Chapter 23.)

In the 1960's, reporter Gay Talese published a book titled *New York: A Serendipiter's Journey*, which "traced the perambulations of feral cats, cataloged shoeshine purveyors, tracked down statistics related to the bathrooms at Yankee Stadium and discovered a colony of ants at the top of the Empire State Building" (Kennedy, 2016). This work breathed new life into the concept of serendipity.

Thus, the super-encounterers, or serendipiters, dive into the unknown in search of the unknown, a *highly creative act*, and discover something new and different and yet related to them, an expression of self. Clues emerge when least expected from unexpected places. Through these clues, serendipiters are imagining their way around impossible issues to discover groundbreaking solutions. As Kennedy (2016) sums up: "The journey will be maddening, but the potential insights could be profound: One day we might be able to stumble upon new and better ways of getting lost."

Symmetry and Symbiotic Thinking

Symmetry is proportional or balanced harmony, and is tightly linked with the concept of beauty. It is the exact correspondence of form on opposite sides of a centerline or point (*American Heritage Dictionary*, 2006). As Weyl (1952, p. 5) says, "Symmetry, as wide or as narrow as you may define its meaning, is one idea by which many through the ages have tried to comprehend and create order, beauty, and perfection." As order, beauty and perfection, symmetry moves far beyond the idea of art, and is woven into the disciplines of mathematics and physics, architecture and building, and many other fields where categorization and classification are involved. The principles of symmetry penetrate every level of life (Wade, 2006).

Wade says that symmetry is simultaneously a mundane and mysterious area of study. He offers that, "In itself symmetry is unlimited ... symmetry principles are characterized by a quietude, a stillness that is somehow beyond the bustling world; yet, in one way or another, they are almost always involved with transformation, or disturbance, or movement" (Wade, 2006, p. 1).

Two common characteristics of symmetry are *congruence* and *periodicity*. Congruence refers to similar patterns and periodicity refers to regularly repeating patterns. Two different aspects of congruence are rotation and reflection. For example, a simple rotation occurs when a pattern is laid out in a circle around a central point. Symmetries abound in our everyday lives. For example, a butterfly's wings or the patterns in a quilt.

Amazingly, four fundamental features can be used to describe any symmetrical pattern! As Conway and Burgiel (2008, p. 27) note, "It is a remarkable fact that wonders, gyrations, kaleidoscopes and mirrors suffice to describe all the symmetries of any pattern whatsoever." Gyrations have repeating points around a circle; kaleidoscopes are symmetries defined by reflections; miracles occur when a pattern from one side is reflected by a pattern on the other side but does *not* go through a mirror line; and wonders are patterns that don't present the other three aspects, sort of a "catch all the rest" kind of category.

As introduced in Chapter 17/Part III, symmetry plays an important role in patterns and in the physical world. Nature is fond of doing things in the most economical and efficient way. As short forms of larger patterns, symbols help facilitate thinking about symmetry, and can help us recognize simpler solutions to issues and situations. Symbolic Representation is a Knowledge Capacity introduced in Chapter 21/Part III.

The idea of infinite symmetry is appealing. This would insinuate that we know much more about the Universe than we know that we know. A popular saying in spiritual circles is, "As above, so below" which also says, "As below, so above." This means that if we can understand the models of life within our context, we have the keys to understanding higher-order patterns beyond our cognizance. While sounding like a paradox, as we discover more and more about the human mind/brain, and as we touch the thought of Quantum, the idea of infinite symmetry opens the doors to expanding our understanding of the Universe.

In our attempt to understand the wholeness of a topic, we are usually led to the idea of systems thinking. This extension of cause-and-effect thinking shows us that effects provide a feedback loop into the next cause, helping us to understand that what we call an "effect" is actually *part* of the next "cause." From the lens of symmetry, we move from *systems* thinking to *symbiotic* thinking when we realize that the very concept of "cause" cannot *exist* without the concept of "effect." This deeper relationship is not from causality, but from existence.

Would the concept of "day" exist if not also for the concept of "night?" Would we have a need for the term "summer" if not also for the term "winter?" In the physical Universe, we find that since there is such a thing as "matter" that there is also "antimatter." The very existence of a thing or idea *requires* the existence of something else. We see this same pattern play out in the Chapter 16/Part II discussion of time and space, noting that space cannot exist without objects, and objects must be enclosed by space. Does lightning just travel downward? With symbiotic thinking, we would understand that if there is a reaching down then there is also a reaching up, and indeed modern photography has captured the phenomenon of upward streamers.

As we develop our symbiotic thinking, we see that "supply and demand" is not just a single business concept, but two concepts where each exists because the other exists. We now view the old and new testaments of the Bible not as a contradiction but as a completion, since grace (new) cannot exist without law (old). And we begin to understand the nature of Quantum physics where two states must exist at the same time; for example, consider the famous thought experiment of Schrodinger's cat, which is both alive and dead. Things that don't make sense using systems thinking begin to make sense using symbiotic thinking.

<<<<<<<>>>>>>

INSIGHT: **Things that don't make sense using systems thinking begin to make sense using symbiotic thinking**.

<<<<<<<>>>>>>

In our efforts towards co-creating the future, with symbiotic thinking there is reason to expect that our individual ideas cannot exist without also a larger consciousness which seeks to incorporate our ideas. The need to create cannot exist without the need to receive that which is created; and we begin to see that *there really is no creating without also co-creating*. (See Chapter 23 on co-creating our reality.) Yet we also understand that we should expect a degree of resistance that may push against what we are creating. This was introduced in Chapter 3/Part I, which explores the forces we act upon.

Synchronicity

Synchronicity can be thought of as a coincidence of events that seem related, yet with no obvious connection one to the other. The term synchronicity was first used in the sense of a *meaningful occurrence happening in time* in the work of the psychologist Carl Jung. In the first chapter of Jung's (1952) work titled "Synchronicity: An Acausal Connecting Principle", Jung notes that "modern physics has shown natural laws to be statistical truths and the principle of causality to be only relatively valid, so that at the microphysical (i.e., subatomic) level there can occur events which are acausal" (Main, 1997, p. 18). He also questioned whether acausal events could be demonstrated at the macrophysical level.

Evidence in support of this was provided by Rhine in experiments that revealed statistically significant correlations between events **even though there was no causal relationships between those events**. Jung saw the synchronicity principle—that a meaningful coincidence is connected by simultaneity and meaning—as "the absolute rule in all cases where an inner event occurs simultaneously with an outside one" (de

Laszlo, 1958, p. 261). The conclusion by Jung was that *time and space become relative under certain conditions, and even appear to be transcended.*

An early researcher looking into the nature of life's coincidences was Paul Kammerer, an Australian biologist who investigated coincidences and unexplained clusterings of events. Over a number of years at the turn of the century, Kammerer collected data and looked for clusters in time through careful statistical analysis. From this work, Kammerer hypothesized that random events fall together into clusters just as asteroids drift together in space under the influence of gravity (Kammerer, 1919).

In his book, which speaks to synchronicity as the bridge between matter and mind, Peat (1988, p. 16) suggests that synchronicity "arises out of the underlying patterns of the Universe rather than through a causality of pushes and pulls that we normally associate with events in nature." This is the acausal principle of Jung, which suggests that there are inherited characteristics in the brain prefigured by evolution. This links the individual with the history of the species. Never before a part of the consciousness of the individual, the collective unconscious "is that portion of the psyche which can be differentiated from the personal unconscious by the fact that its existence is not dependent upon personal experience" (Hall & Nordby, 1973, p. 39).

This is also the causal connection proposed in the Pauli principle. Wolfgang Pauli, a physicist and early contributor to the field of Quantum Mechanics, is best known for his exclusion principle, which complements Heisenberg's Quantum mechanics. Pauli argued that at the Quantum level nature engages in an abstract dance—with electrons, protons, neutrons and neutrinos engaging in an antisymmetric dance and mesons and photons of light engaging in a symmetric dance, keeping particles of the same energy apart from each other (Peat, 1988). This is not the result of force or any specific act of causality, "rather it arises out of the … abstract movement of the particles as a whole" (Peat 1988, p. 16).

Certainly, a causal explanation can be argued for all events and behaviors, and biological connections can be made as well. So, while causality certainly has a role to play, *it is only part of the change picture.* For example, in the 18th century, David Hume concluded that causality could not be placed on a strictly logical footing, that is, because A follows B in one instance or in all similar instances of which we are aware, this does not mean that A will always follow B. He called this belief in causality a habit of the mind based on repeated historical precedent. As Hume (1978) says, "We have no other notion of cause and effect, but that of certain objects, which have been always conjoined together … We cannot penetrate into the reason of the conjunction." (See Chapter 7/Part II on Looking for Cause and Effect.)

<<<<<<<◇>>>>>>>

INSIGHT: **While causality certainly has a role to play, it is only part of the change picture. This is where synchronicities can bridge the gap between mind and matter.**

<<<<<<<◇>>>>>>>

While agreeing that when forces are well defined and time flows freely the concept of causality does not present problems, this is not the case as complexity increases.

> … as science probes deeper into the Universe of internal flows and dynamic unfoldings, of subtle influences and intersecting time scales, then causal chains can no longer be analyzed and reduced to linear connections of individual events so that the very concept of causality begins to lose its power. (Peat, 1988, p. 42)

Since mental events are not dependent on causality, this is where synchronicities can bridge the gap between matter and mind (Peat, 1988). Indeed, as has been shared throughout this book, the human mind is an associative patterner, continuously creating knowledge for the moment at hand, triggered by internal and external stimuli yet not necessarily part of a linear chain of causality. We are engaged in a continuous process of unfolding patterns.

<<<<<<<◇>>>>>>>

INSIGHT: **We are engaged in a continuous process of unfolding patterns.**

<<<<<<<◇>>>>>>>

From complexity theory we understand that emergence is a global property of a complex system that results from the interactions and relationships among its agents, and between the agents and their environment (Bennet & Bennet, 2004; 2013). Systems can also generate responses that are not proportional to the action taken. We say a system possess nonlinearity when a small action may generate a very large outcome—or a large action may have very little effect on the system. Further, meaningful patterns can emerge from an instable and chaotic system.

The concept of self-synchronization (the self arrangement of actions in time, space and purpose to produce maximum relative effect at a decisive place and time), whether applied to an individual or a larger group of individuals, and, when coupled with interoperability (the ability to work together) and orchestration of means (the ability to act in concert in a timely manner), is consistent with the definition of intelligent activity. For example, as one of the tenets for Network Centric Warfare to achieve self-synchronized forces and actions, it is defined as: a clear and consistent understanding of command intent; high quality information and shared situational awareness; competence at all levels of the force; and trust in the information, subordinates, superiors, peers, and equipment (Alberts & Hayes, 2005). In other words, *it is dependent on measures that guide but do not dictate details.*

From another frame of reference, Senge et al (2004, p. 160) say that perhaps "synchronicity is simply what it feels like, from our personal vantage point, to be part of a field knowing itself and to be taking action informed by the whole." Sheldrake (1989) asserts that this is not extraordinary, but rather that synchronicity is a natural feature of a living system. From the viewpoint of experience over our collective years of life, we agree.

Synergy

No doubt this is a concept that you have known in the past. Synergy is that something more that emerges from the coming together of two or more elements in a complex adaptive system, with the result of producing more than the sum of the parts of the system. This is a tool of creation, the condition that drives the bursting forth of ideas. Whether we are conscious of it or not, we all have been a party to this experience.

<<<<<<<◇>>>>>>>

INSIGHTS: **Synergy is a tool of creation, the condition that drives the bursting forth of ideas.**

<<<<<<◇>>>>>>>

An example of synergy in the organizational setting is created through unity and shared purpose, which serve to integrate organizational activities, enabling the mobilization of resources to gain the synergy of complementary talents and to coalesce personnel resources to meet surge requirements. By synergy in this context, we mean the working together of two or more people when the results are greater (and usually different) than the sum of their individual talents. See Figure 22-2.

If all parts of an organization are kept informed and up to date on the overall direction of the organization, the autonomous units can then respond rapidly, collectively and collaboratively, without the often-seen confusion over what is wanted or needed, or why. When an organization is behaving intelligently it is similar to the conscious mind working intentionally, using its unconscious experience, its incoming information, and its full capability to focus on the task at hand to create a synergy of thought and action (Bennet and Bennet, 2004).

Figure 22-2. *Cooperation and collaboration in all walks of life create synergy, and move us closer to intelligent activity.*

Thought Forms

The material world is an effect, not a cause. Change occurs from the inside out. As the Dalai Lama says so beautifully, "In order to change conditions outside ourselves, whether they concern the environment or relations with others, we must first change within ourselves" (Epstein, 1995, p. ix).

Change begins with thought, then energy follows thought and becomes thought forms. Thus, thoughts and images have a profound creative and motivating power within human consciousness, with the mind controlling energy and building form. These are not physical forms, rather "energy complexes on the subtle levels of reality that are analogous to physical things. They are forms made of emotional-mental matter" (Besant & Leadbeater, 1999, p. xx thought forms).

<<<<<<<◇>>>>>>>

INSIGHT: **The material world is an effect, not a cause.**

<<<<<<<◇>>>>>>>

As produced on our mental and emotional planes, thought forms are sent out into the environment where they attract sympathetic vibrations, that is, those who resonate with the thought being produced. This can be difficult to accept for those who suffer from the Cartesian dichotomy between matter and mind and want to bring everything to the physical level. Even bringing it to the physical, we now understand from neuroscience findings the power of the mind/brain and that our thoughts actually change the structure of the physical brain as well as impacting all of our human systems! Further, we now recognize that we are in continuous two-way communication with all those around us. Our thoughts are permeable and porous (Sheldrake, 1995). See Chapter 24 for more depth on this topic.

Each thought that is definite has a double effect, producing both a floating form and a radiating vibration. Each thought form differs in both density and quality. In analyzing the qualities that have significance for the meaning of the thought form, Besant and Leadbeater (1999) have identified color, shape and distinctness of outline. Color has to do with the emotional quality of the thought; form has to do with the intent of the thought; and distinctness of outline has to do with the degree of concentration of the thought. The radiating vibration is a complex one, with every rush of feeling associated with thought producing a permanent effect.

Interesting examples are thought forms built by music. While sound is often associated with color, it also produces form. As Besant and Leadbeater (1999, p. 67) describe:

> Some such forms are very striking and impressive, and naturally their variety is infinite. Each class of music has its own type of form, and the style of the composer shows as clearly in the form which his music builds as a man's character shows in his handwriting. Other possibilities of variation are introduced by the kind of instrument upon which the music is performed, and also by the merits of the player. The same piece of music if accurately played will always build the same form ...

Lower mental thought forms diminish the capacity for higher thought forms to function, and increasingly have an effect on an individual's ability to create higher thought forms. This is because thought forms linked through logic limit the ability to perceive the larger truth of conceptual thinking. (See Chapter 24.)

In their book on *Thoughtware*, Kirby and Hughes (1997) assert that if you change an organization's thinking, the organization will change itself. This is based on the belief that behavior is rooted in thought and that people's thinking and collective interactions drive organizational performance. *Thought and the thought forms produced through thought are directly related to behaviors and actions.* As Kirby and Hughes (1997, p. 193) describe, thinking and action are "synonymous and integral at the point of change."

Thought forms are further discussed in Chapter 28.

Final Thoughts

As these concepts were identified and expanded by authorial explorers and put into words, the readers of those words found a way of expressing, understanding and sharing their experiences. In Chapter 11/Part II, The Change Agent's Strategy, part of the strategy moving from Phase 1 to Phase 2 of the ISCJ was to *share new ideas, words and behaviors*. It was suggested that thinking in new ways demands new words, or putting old words together in new ways, to communicate new thinking; and that those new words (or combinations of old words) drive new behaviors, and, in turn, new behaviors drive new thought and words. This is consistent with what Hugh Blair identified: *thought and language act and re-act upon each other*.

These concepts and words have been waiting, slowly expanding in our hearts and minds, for their time to move into full conscious awareness, and these are just representative of the larger set supporting human experience and expansion. You know them. They are at your fingertips, awaiting the ripeness of time as we move closer to the fork in the road, the Bifurcation.

Questions for Reflection:

How many of these have you proactively included in the way that your approach life?

Are you learning through iterative development loops in the course of your journey?

Am I able to employ symbiotic thinking to understand the wholeness of a topic?

Chapter 23
Co-Creating Frames of Reference

SUBTOPICS: OUR GREATEST CO-CREATION ... WHAT DOES IT MEAN TO CO-CREATE OUR REALITY?
... MULTIPLE PERSPECTIVES ON SELF CO-CREATING REALITY ... *FROM THE LITERARY PERSPECTIVE ...
FROM A LIVING SYSTEM PERSPECTIVE ... FROM A CONSCIOUSNESS PERSPECTIVE ... FROM A SCIENTIFIC
PERSPECTIVE ... FROM A SPIRITUAL PERSPECTIVE ...* FINAL THOUGHTS

Reality is essentially subjectively unknowable, existing as an image, perception, perspective or belief generated by an individual, a group or a society. Knowledge acquired from the external world comes through our senses, usually the result of physical, psychological and social interactions of our minds and bodies with an external world, or a perceived external world. Consciousness, because of its central role in our ontology, also plays a crucial part in shaping and filtering our epistemology. The physical characteristics of our brains, together with the emergence of language and higher-order consciousness, act as both filters and interpreters of the external world. However, no matter how much we know or think we know, the best we as evolutionary products of that world *can* know is a qualified reality, a reality limited by both our individual embodiment and our space-time location. Further limited by our genetic heritage, our developmental morphology, chance events and our external environment, the best we can hope for is a qualified understanding of ourselves and of our reality. "As mind pursues reality to its ultimate analysis, matter vanishes to the material senses but may still remain real to the mind." (*Urantia*, 1954, p. 1228)

Nevertheless, consciousness, supported by our unconscious mind/brain and bootstrapped through social collaboration, is the only resource available to observe, create and comprehend our existence. It is also the experiential lens through which we must look to interact with other beings and with the physical world. This lens is reminiscent of Plato's allegory of shadows in the cave.

According to Plato, all living beings in the sensible world are but imperfect copies of eternal forms residing in the world of Ideas…the world accessible to our senses is akin to the world of shadows experienced by the men in the cave. It is merely an imperfect manifestation of a perfect world—the world of Ideas, illuminated by the Sun of intelligibility. (Thuan, 2001, p. 300-301)

Another interpretation of a perfect world would be one in which everything in the Universe is exactly as it should be. What else could it be if we eliminate personal morality and accept the sentence as meaning that nature and the Universe work as they do, independent but consistent with rocks and beetles and humans. Perhaps as Plato opined, it is only man that separates himself from nature and thereby creates the fuzziness and imperfections he then perceives. Does a true world of eternal and immutable ideas exist where mathematical relations and perfect geometrical structures reign supreme? The doctrine of physical realism states that reality exists independent of our own existence and that we can have knowledge of this reality through scientific research, at least in principle (Omnes, 1999, p. 216). While some of the mathematical laws of physics have the same form throughout space, from the current scientific viewpoint there is no theory of everything (in spite of book titles and some hype), and modern science continues to create more questions than answers where epistemology is concerned. As Omnes describes, the evolution of scientific investigation has been one of increasing use of formalism, in both mathematics and physics (Omnes, 1999, p. 84-155). Recognizing that mathematics is often referred to as the science of patterns, it is interesting to speculate that scientific progress and the growth of our individual understanding of a qualified reality have given more credence to the concept that reality is made up of patterns. Patterns are defined as relationships and structures in time, space or both. See Chapter 17/Part III.

In the final analysis—and consistent with Edelman's (1989) theory—our ideas, thoughts and feelings are made up of patterns of neuronal firings, connections and weights. Many feel that everything in the Universe is connected to everything else, and the laws of physics support that hypothesis through the mathematical formulation of gravity and electromagnetism. If the connectivity is supported by science and intelligence exists via patterns of forces, what possibilities are there for the existence of the collective unconscious, souls, spiritualism, and other widely held phenomena? Science, religion and spirituality are not so far apart as was commonly believed. Neither the Universe nor Nature come in bits and pieces. It seems that we humans are the only ones that chop them up for our own convenience.

<<<<<<<◇>>>>>>>

INSIGHT: **Neither the Universe nor Nature come in bits and pieces. It seems that we humans are the only ones that chop them up for our own convenience**.

<<<<<<<◇>>>>>>>

However, we can *choose* to break through the limitations of the past, and take advantage of potential possibilities. Since we are each unique and create our own version of the world through thinking, learning, growing and social exchange, we may be able to reach far beyond our present capabilities and minimize the qualified part of our qualified reality, eventually making our reach far overshadow our embodied capability. We are all part of an amazing playing field of creation. As Lipton (2009, p. 107) describes, "We can realize that humanity is operating on a unified field of dreams, and we can rejoice that the field is a playing field, not a battlefield." Thus, a requirement of creation is indeed the ability to dream.

McTaggart, author of *The Field: The Quest for the Secret Force of the Universe*, shows that, technically, physical reality doesn't exist. McTaggart says that the Zero-Point Field, what is perceived as empty space, is "an ocean of microscopic vibrations in the space between things—a state of pure potential and infinite possibility." She continues, "Particles exist in all possible states until disturbed by us—by observing or measuring—at which point, they settle down, at long last into something real" (McTaggart, 2002, p. xvi-xvii). In 1925, when the principles of Quantum mechanics were adopted by physicists, Astrophysicist Sir James Jeans wrote:

> The stream of knowledge is heading toward a non-mechanical reality; the Universe begins to look more like a great thought than like a great machine. Mind no longer appears to be an accidental intruder into the realm of matter … we ought rather hail it as the creator and governor of the realm of matter. (Henry, 2005, p. 29)

In 1993, Goswami clearly stated his convictions that the one reality of which mind and matter are both an integral part is not based on material realism. He proposed that this one reality is based on monistic idealism, monistic as opposed to dualistic, and idealism because ideas and our consciousness of those ideas are the basic elements of reality. Goswami (1993, p. 11) adds, "Note that the philosophy does not say that matter is unreal but that the reality of matter is secondary to that of consciousness, which itself is the ground of all being—including matter." Thus, consciousness is the Field in which everything—including material reality—exists. This is consistent with our understanding of the Quantum Field.

Supportive of our role as co-creators of reality, Csikszentmihalyi (1993, p. 216) says,

> In order to make sense of the stimuli that bombard our senses, our nervous system has learned to bundle up information in manageable chunks, so that we are not overwhelmed by a mass of discrete details … Our minds, in reflecting on what we see, endow these images with separate identities, identities they have only in our imagination. This is the process of *reification*, by which we attribute reality to mental constructs.

Examples provided by Csikszentmihalyi include the mental construction of what we call the "ocean" or "sea", although in reality each body of water is just a large number of water molecules made up of hydrogen and oxygen. Similarly, particles of air appear to be the "sky" and the surface of our planet is the "Earth".

<<<<<<<<◇>>>>>>>

INSIGHT: **Consciousness is the Field in which everything—including material reality—exists.**

<<<<<<<<◇>>>>>>>

Our Greatest Co-Creation

We are not abject observers in the path of life, we are co-creators, with the very act of observing capable of changing the outcome of activity. And for each of us, **the greatest creation in this life is that of our self**; and, for the fortunate ones who traverse the road to intelligent activity, the expanded expression of *Self*. This is a journey of discovery, growth and choice, with knowledge triggering ideas, and ideas begetting ideas. The only limits imposed on us are our own, the limits of our creative imagination, the mental faculties we develop, and the consistency of our choices and actions.

Walsch (2009) says that there are six things that create our reality in this physical experience called life. These are events, data, truths, thoughts, emotions and experience. When any of these elements change, then our reality changes. Thus, if we want to change our experience, we can purposefully change one of these elements and our reality will change!

We can proactively create our self to be something more than we are, and as we act accordingly the environment around us will respond. Concurrently, as the environment within which we interact changes, we can create ourselves to be something different, to whatever level needed or desired. Our freedom to think and create offers the opportunity for amazing diversity and infinite possibilities.

This freedom to create does not equate to control. As we move through life expanding our understanding of self, we become aware of a new reality. In this larger reality we are co-creating, the need to control is an illusion as well as an impossibility, and the need to create is not dependent upon the need to control. Rather than control others, it is beneficial to ourselves and the larger whole to help others in any way necessary to learn to control themselves; and we don't need to control others to be in control of ourselves. Nor do we need to control others—or anything else—to be creative (MacFlouer, 2004-16). See the discussion in Chapter 3/Part I of control as a force.

Feelings, thoughts and mental images serve as the medium of exchange for creating our reality, what is called neural plasticity, the ability of neurons to change their structure and relationships, depending on environmental demands and personal decisions and actions (Bennet et al., 2016b). Recall that the brain is the physical structure of atoms and molecules and the mind is the totality of neuronal patterns within this physical structure, that is, patterns of neurons, their connections (synapses) and the strength of those connections. It is exciting to note that this complex, interwoven and interdependent system that is the mind/brain/body is continuously changing, never exactly repeating a pattern!

<<<<<<<<>>>>>>

INSIGHT: **One person's reality is another's perception.**

<<<<<<<<>>>>>>

Recognizing the plasticity of the mind/brain, we begin to understand that what we focus on heavily impacts the co-creation of our reality. There is a feedback loop between our thoughts and the structure of the brain, an interdependence and self-organization such that each influences the other (Bennet et al, 2015b). This impacts our everyday thoughts and actions, the way we interact with others and the way we do business. For example, while certainly failures need to be acknowledged and addressed, the old method of focusing on failure gives way to an appreciative inquiry model that pushes us to discover what is good and working, and focus and expand from that point of understanding. This means putting less focus and energy on problems and much more focus and energy on solutions.

What Does It Mean to Co-Create Our Reality?

As a child, co-creating our reality may mean getting a stomachache from eating too many jelly doughnuts on a Saturday morning shopping jaunt with dad. As a teenager, it may mean getting a report card that reflects the effort (or lack of) you've put into your homework. As an expectant mother or father, it may mean the looming responsibility of parenthood. But, as the years pass and the self experiences more of life, the concept of co-creating our reality becomes far richer and far more meaningful.

As you read these words, the information you are receiving is not an attribute of the letters or words themselves. The **print** on this page is not information, it *transmits* information. The letters and words on this page are symbols, which have learned and agreed-upon meanings connected with them. This is why Symbolic Representation is such an important Knowledge Capacity (see Chapter 21/Part III). Similarly, when we speak to each other the actual sounds in the form of words *convey* information. Though thoughts and feelings may also be communicated, they are quite different things than the words themselves.

Our feelings, thoughts and mental images are derived through a sense of knowing, a deep personal, subjective sense that an idea or thought is important and, when connected with other ideas or thoughts through associative patterning, insights and understanding of both ourselves and our surrounding world emerge. Knowing, or having knowledge of, has the same relationship to what is often called objective reality as that of subject and object (Bolles, 1991) discussed in Chapter 4/Part I. Knowing is to *perceive or understand* as fact or truth while objective reality is *composed* of facts or truths, a state or quality of being real, or that which is perceived as existing independently of ideas concerning it. Of course, that can never entirely be the case. The frame from which we understand objective reality is always limited by our personal experiences, beliefs and knowledge.

The word "limits" is often perceived in a negative connotation, but this is not necessarily the case. When referring to ideas, the limits imposed by defining our ideas within a framework help us develop a deeper understanding within that bounded domain, assist in the sharing of that understanding, and spur on the emergence of new ideas, some even beyond the framework in which they are presented. In other words, limits can offer the opportunity for learning and the emergence of new ideas. A dramatic example of the value of limits can be found in the use of information technology. By placing limits (such as standards and protocols) on information technology, we are able to achieve broader interoperability among different technologies, giving more people access to more data and information.

<<<<<<◇>>>>>>

INSIGHT: **Setting limits by defining our ideas within a framework helps us develop a deeper understanding within that bounded domain, assists in the sharing of understanding, and spurs on the emergence of new ideas.**

<<<<<<◇>>>>>>

In like manner, the symbiotic relationship between knowledge and what we perceive as *objective* reality can be highly productive by allowing our creative imagination and *subjective* knowledge to expand and play with ideas that may then extend our knowledge of objective reality (Emig, 1983). For instance, Einstein imagined he was riding on a light wave as he developed the general theory of relativity—which changed the way all of science understood the Universe. It is the imagination of artists that creates a painting with the potential of expanding hundreds of viewer's understanding and appreciation of the world. For example, consider Leonardo da Vinci's portrayal of *The Last Supper* painted on the wall of the refectory of the Convent of Santa Maria delle Grazie in Milan. The variety of reactions in the faces and body movements of the disciples captured by Leonardo have intrigued and inspired viewers and writers since the beginning of the 16th century. From a new objective reality, viewers often discern more about themselves and their own subjective reality, with the newly discovered subjective often being very different from the artist's original intent or experience.

Simultaneously, what we perceive as objective knowledge can serve as a framework upon which subjective reality can play. For example, when Darwin's theory of evolution became widely known to the public, it caused many people to change their self-image and shook the basic foundation of their very existence. The concept of Darwinian Evolution created such strong subjective feelings that repercussions can still be felt today. The mind that can use this interplay between multiple realities has the capability of extending both their subjective knowledge *and* understanding of objective reality, if indeed such a thing exists.

Today, we live in a world where thoughts and ideas are spurred onward by an almost exponentially increasing amount of data and information accessible to everyone. In both our personal and professional lives, we have become adept at responding to and anticipating change. The very act of change may create a new reality requiring new values and perspectives of life. While we clearly recognize the importance of the individual—of self—in creating and sharing feelings, thoughts and mental images to bring about and apply new knowledge, thinking about ways we create our reality can move us from a reactive role to a proactive role, fully embracing the power of self. An important first step in harnessing this power is to understand the different perspectives and theories about how we as humans create our reality.

Multiple Perspectives on Self Co-Creating Reality

Just as each and every individual is unique, the realities we create individually and collectively are unique. As von Forester (1977, p. 108) posits,

> The new paradigm recognizes that there is not just one reality; rather, we must recognize that there are many realities … The reality of a Navajo, the reality of a multimillionaire, the reality of a slum dweller, are quite different realities. Cognition is the computation of just such *a* reality.

To help build a deeper understanding of the relationship of self and the perceived external environment, we will explore different frames of reference from which we assume the role of co-creator as we engage in a continuous loop of acting and learning. Depending very much on our perception, these frames of reference are foundational to how and what we create in our reality. We will briefly look at the following perspectives: Literary, Living System, Consciousness, Scientific and Spiritual. A word of caution as we begin this exploration. As in all human constructs provided to facilitate understanding, while the discussions are representative of these perspectives they are not the perspectives themselves. As ever, the map is not the territory.

From a Literary Perspective. The relationships among thought, language and behavior have been explored throughout man's history. The power of knowledge in the form of writing is evident in early records describing the role of the *Overseer of All the King's Works* in ancient Egypt. This Overseer, who directed the massive labor force required to build a pyramid, was a scribe. His palette and papyrus scroll were the symbols of his knowledge and of his authority, and bureaucratic lists and registers were the tools of political and economic power (Silverman, 1997, p. 90). Literature was prized because of its influence over others, and brought fame to the scribe. In short, knowledge, demonstrated by writing, was considered an authority, whether it took the form of literature, a medical recipe or a list. Whatever was written (as symbols) was considered truth, or reality.

In 1784 Hugh Blair identified a clear, close alliance between thought and language, with the spoken/written word sometimes responsible for the clarification of thought, and the clarification of thought sometimes responsible for the improvement of the word. In his words, *thought and language act and re-act upon each other mutually* and *by putting our sentiments into words, we always conceive them more distinctly.* How do I know what I mean until I hear what I am going to say? So the story goes. While tying this close connection, it is clear that Blair (2015) believes the conception of thought remains *prior in time and importance* to language.

Later theorists (Brown, Black, Bloomfield, Skinner and Quine) regarded language as a major form of behavior, a significant entity in its own right. Language as behavior is very much in contrast with language as a subordinate feature in the process of communication. In 1982, a writing text contended that *the freedom to act upon the world and to construct reality is both the aim and the process of education* (*Writing*, 1982). This implies that language is a powerful, if not unique, way of constructing reality and acting on the world. A number of well-known and well-published authors would agree. They describe the writing process—that is, interacting with pen and paper or, in more recent years, keyboarding—in the following words:

Francoise Sagan: "For *Bonjour Tristesse* all I started with was the idea of the character, the girl, but nothing really came of it until my pen was in hand. I have to start to write to have ideas …."

James Thurber: "I don't believe the writer should know too much where he's going. If he does, he runs into old man blueprint – old man propaganda."

Truman Capote: "But in the working-out, the writing-out, infinite surprises happen. Thank God, because the surprise, the twist, the phrase that comes at the right moment out of nowhere, is the unexpected dividend, that joyful little push that keeps a writer going."

William Faulkner: "Sometimes technique charges in and takes command of the dream before the writer himself can get his hands on it … It [*As I Lay Dying*] was simple in that all the material was already at hand."

Gertrude Stein: "It will come if it is there and you will let it come, and if you have anything you will get a sudden creative recognition. You won't know how it was, even what it is, but it will be creation if it came out of the pen and out of you and not out of an architectural drawing of the thing you are doing …"

(Excerpts from Cowley, 1958)

In more prosaic terms, every act of writing is an act of creating, interacting with the medium in the environment to create symbols external to self, a release of the unconscious reality into public view. As Lakoff and Nunez note in their book, *Where Mathematics Comes From*, and as now a basic understanding:

> Perhaps the most fundamental, and initially the most startling, result in cognitive science is that most of our thought is unconscious – that is, fundamentally inaccessible to our direct, conscious introspection. Most everyday thinking occurs too fast and at too low a level in the mind to be thus accessible. … We all speak in a language that has a grammar, but we do not consciously put sentences together word by word, checking consciously that we are following the grammatical rules of our language. To us, it seems easy: We just talk, and listen, and draw inferences without effort. But what goes on in our minds behind the scenes is enormously complex and largely unavailable to us. (Lakoff and Nunez, 2000, p. 27)

From a Living System Perspective. Autopoiesis is a term with Greek derivation that means self-production. The main argument of the theory is that living systems are created and reproduced in an autonomous, simultaneously open and closed self-referential manner. This means a porous boundary, where some things can come in and others are warded off. An example would be the intake and processing of food versus the rejection of foreign matter. Autopoiesis assumes everything the living system needs for self-production is already in the system (Maturana & Varela, 1987).

In epistemological terms, autopoietic systems are considered to contain their own knowledge since the system is the observer of external events. The subject/object relationship was introduced in Chapter 4/Part I. External events, such as clouds, people, buildings, etc., are all part of the individual's experience and the interpretation and description of these events are the results of the *relationships* established between our previous experience and our perceptions. From an autopoietic viewpoint, it is impossible to step out of the individual and see ourselves as a unit in an environment because what the individual sees as the external environment is still part of his experience and by no means lies outside the interface that, in theory, separates the knower from the known.

If our reality cannot be separated between ourselves and the external world, then within our own minds what we perceive and create and believe is reality. Therefore, when we actively create new realities within ourselves, they become "the" reality upon which we act, anticipate and analyze. From this internal reality, and the forthcoming actions, comes behavior in the external world that then creates a perceived reality in the minds of others. Thus, the possibility of diffusion of our own individual reality to others becomes realized, and a significant external reality can be created through wide-spread commonality of interpretation.

From a Consciousness Perspective. The permanency of form, or reality, is an illusion, since all consciousness is a process of change. Consciousness is a process in which thoughts, images and feelings are constantly evolving. Its major characteristics are unity, optimum complexity and selectivity. Unity is necessary to make the time flow of thoughts, images and feelings coherent. Optimum complexity allows the processing of divergent signals from within the individual and from the external environment. Selectivity limits the incoming signals to those that are essential to survival or interest. What this means is that when you get incoming information from the senses, you take that information and mix it with your memories of thoughts, feelings and images related to that incoming information (the associative patterning process). The brain's ability to integrate these forms is what is called the remembered present (Edelman, 1989). The process we call consciousness is a continuous sequence of these remembered presents and the understanding of their connections and relationships to each other and our self. (See Chapter 5/Part I for an in-depth treatment of consciousness.)

Studies from consciousness would agree with autopoiesis in that when we receive external information, since we immediately compare it with what is already in our memory, it is the combination of these two, coupled with our own belief and value systems, that yields what we perceive as reality, an integrated mental scene. That means the individual mind participates in the creation of its own reality.

From a Scientific Perspective. From the view Newtonian physics, scientific inquiry assumes the existence of an objective, external reality that can be studied, understood and tested through empirical methods. Although science recognizes the potential subjectivity of individual perceptions and observations, where possible, particularly in the domains of physics and chemistry, it has built into its methodology protection mechanisms that minimize or eliminate subjectivity in areas of concern to science. Through the process of creative construction of models and theories of objective reality, filtered by empirical testing and public dialogues and debate, the best estimate of objective reality is created. While this objective reality is not "the" objective reality, it is self-consistent and for each area of its applicability it has been highly effective, leading to great advances in technology and a deeper understanding of our world and our Universe.

Under these working assumptions, to some extent an individual's perception of reality can influence that reality predominantly through the psychological impact that belief has on the individual's actions. Through these actions, then, the external reality can be influenced, and therefore a self-fulfilling prophecy may be possible (Davis, 1997).

While science recognizes that individuals have different subjective realities as explained by autopoiesis and numerous psychological studies, these differences in reality do not preclude understanding the objective reality in the hard sciences. However, there are significant open questions in several areas related to the observer's impact on that objective reality.

While Quantum physics is shifting all that was previously learned in science, there is still so little we understand, and many other fields of science have not yet taken into account what we do understand. This is not surprising since it challenges the questions at the core of our very existence. And, as Carroll (2016, p. 171) points out, although our understanding of Quantum mechanics at a fundamental level is not finished, "... there is nothing we know about it that necessarily invalidates determinism (the future follows uniquely from the present), realism (there is an objective real world), or physicalism (the world is purely physical)." Change can be difficult regardless of the direction from which you look!

What we are beginning to understand is that the Quantum Field is a probability field, and, consistent with the treatment throughout this book, that *all that is possible exists*. (See the discussion of divination in Chapter 22.) Further, we know that there is a relationship of thought to this Field, and that consciousness emerges when enough thought is heading the same direction (MacFlouer, 2004-2016). Much like the hierarchical structure of neuronal patterns in the human mind/brain, there are hierarchical relationships in the Quantum Field, with the qualities of self-organization and self-creation. Thus, consciousness itself creates more consciousness, and has the ability to, at the level of the hierarchy where it is focused, affect the direction of energy flows in the Field. When enough thought is focused in the same direction, a shift in the Field occurs.

From the viewpoint of cell biology and the discoveries related to the new field of Epigenetics—the study of the mechanisms by which the cell environment influences gene activity—we now know that we are not victims of our genes. It is the way genes are expressed that determine their strength in our lives, and that involves choice. As Lipton says, we now know that we are not frail bio-chemical machines controlled by genes, but rather "powerful creators of our lives and the world in which we live." Further, we have discovered that the cells of the body are controlled through receptor and effector proteins—a set of antennas, that appear on the outer membrane of the cell. Thus, Lipton (2005) sees consciousness as a simulation information field. This has huge impact for the human as co-creator.

From a Spiritual Perspective. Like the words in this book, the objects around us that make up our environment are symbols that transmit a reality with a learned, and agreed-upon, meaning. The true information is not in the object any more than thought is in words and letters. Both words and objects are methods of expression. When you speak words, and though they may express more or less your feelings, they are not your feelings. There is a gap between our thought and our expression of thought. This gap is particularly visible when we consider how often each of us begins a sentence, and don't know exactly how it's going to end. We create the thought and the language as we go along. This same gap occurs between our thoughts, feelings and mental images and the creation of objects (in space) and events (in time).

Spirituality sees the continuous creation of our physical environment as a method of communication and expression, with the self in the role of co-creator. Feelings, thoughts and mental images are translated into physical reality. Feelings play a significant role in this process. The intensity of a feeling, thought or mental image is an important element in determining subsequent physical materialization; feelings— often linked to thoughts and mental images—largely build that intensity. If your mind works with high intensity, and you think in vivid mental emotional images, these are swiftly formed into physical events. We form the fabric of our experience through our beliefs and expectations, which are not *about* reality, but *are reality itself* (Roberts, 1994). This is the power of intent introduced in Chapter 25.

Final Thoughts

Because we have addressed our roles as co-creators from a diversity of frameworks does not mean that each of these frameworks is separated from the other. Quite to the contrary. As forwarded in Chapter 6/Part I, we've finally reached the understanding as humans that we are holistic. Our preferences dictate our focus, but these frameworks interact, just as the energies within us interact to create an individual, and just as people in an organization interact to create a business, and just as organizations around the world interact to create a global economy.

Interestingly, just as our thoughts and feelings and perceptions encourage success, the ability to accomplish our goals, our misperceptions can threaten survival. As Lipton 2009, p. 26) acknowledges, "Almost all of us have unknowingly acquired limiting, self-sabotaging misperceptions that undermine our strength, health, and desires." Perceptions are beliefs, and the nature of our perceptions greatly influence our lives. For example, consider the placebo and nocebo effects. The placebo effect is a sense of benefit arising solely from the knowledge that treatment has been given (Encarta, 1999); the nocebo effect is a sense of illness or a toxic condition arising solely from the knowledge of exposure to same (Lipton, 2009). One study dealt with Japanese children who were allergic to a poisonous plant. One leaf labeled as poisonous was rubbed on the children's forearm, and another leaf that looked the same but was labeled as non-poisonous was rubbed on the other forearm. As expected, the majority of the children developed a rash on the arm rubbed with the leaf labeled poisonous and had no reaction to the non-poisonous leaf. However, what the children did not know is that the two leafs had been purposefully mislabeled! The children had broken out in a rash because of their perception that the non-toxic leaf was poisonous (Ikemi & Nakagawa, 1962).

Ultimately, the answers to the nature of reality are to be found through an inner journey into ourselves, through ourselves and through the world we know. It is human imagination and creativity that is constantly creating the reality in which we live (Edelman & Tononi, 2000). Each and every one of us has observed or been a part of this great creativity, which always seems greater than our physical dimension with its perceived objective reality. This joy of creativity flows though us as effortless as our breath; and each of us uses this flow of creativity to create a unique reality, different from any other individual.

<<<<<<<<>>>>>>>>

INSIGHT: **The joy of creativity flows though us as effortless as our breath; and each of us uses this flow to create a unique reality, different from any other individual.**

<<<<<<<<>>>>>>>>

In summary, the literary perspective is that language is a powerful way of constructing reality and acting on the world. The living system and consciousness perspectives agree that the individual mind does participate in the creation of reality, and in autopoiesis a diffusion of individual reality to others can be realized. The hard science perspective, based on Newtonian physics, is that while there is an objective reality, parts of external reality can be understood and influenced, and therefore a self-fulfilling prophecy may be possible. However, Quantum theory, and discoveries in cell biology, have opened up new possibilities for the human as co-creator. The spiritual perspective, which now appears to reflect the possibilities of Quantum thinking, is that all reality is a result of feelings, thoughts and mental images, and reality emerges dependent on the intensity of those feelings, thoughts and mental images.

Regardless of the perspective that is part of an individual belief set, it is clear that we as humans are involved in the creation of the reality in which we live. Perhaps the idea of co-creation would be more descriptive in the following context: The self is continuously learning from that which is perceived as its environment, and using this learning to act on reality, which we are simultaneously co-creating. Because realities are continuously being created and recreated by human beings, individually and collectively, they are part of our evolutionary system of constant change. And, as a friend often reminds, *we've got to quit playing small.*

Questions for Reflection:

What is your perspective for co-creating your reality? Are you open to include the perspectives of others?

Are you able to see differences of opinion as potential opportunities or does that lead to conflict?

How often do you deliberately change your own lens in order to gain an alternative perspective?

Can you create a higher truth by combining a range of perspectives?

Chapter 24
Knowledge and the Search for Truth

A good path has no ruts.
A good speech has no flaws.
A good analysis uses no schemes.
(Wing, 1986, passage 27)

SUBTOPICS: SURFACE, SHALLOW, DEEP ... TRUTH AND CONSCIOUSNESS ... MISINFORMATION AND DISINFORMATION ... PERCEPTION AND PROPAGANDA ... FORMS OF PROPAGANDA ... BRAINWASHING ... FINAL THOUGHTS

FIGURES: **24-1**. LEVELS OF TRUTH AS FORWARDED BY WALSCH (2009) ... **24-2**. AS WE MOVE TOWARD INTELLIGENT ACTIVITY, THE RELATIVITY OF TRUTH DECREASES AND THE TRUTH BECOMES A HIGHER-ORDER PATTERN ... **24-3**. MOVEMENT FROM PHYSICAL CONTROL TO PROPAGANDA.

TOOLS: 24-1. TRUTH SEARCHING ... 24-2. RHYTHM DISRUPTOR

The very concept of knowledge is concerned with truth. Recall our functional definition of knowledge is *the capacity (potential or actual) to take effective action.* The definition forwarded by Plato, which is still used by many people today, is knowledge as *justified true belief.* In other words, if someone *believed* something was true, and could justify their belief and demonstrate that it was true, then that person had knowledge. This definition served humanity well in beginning a conversation around knowledge, and the definition we use today is built on this early conversation. However, today we realize that humans act on more than beliefs—that our very thoughts and the focus of those thoughts move us to act—and that not only our beliefs but our underlying values and other mental models emerging from experiential learning promote our actions. The word "effective" in our functional definition of knowledge relates both to the "truth" of knowledge in terms of meeting an anticipated outcome, and our understanding of relativity, that is, that knowledge is relative to the context and situation at hand. This functional definition also adds the concept of "potential", acknowledging the value of education and learning in preparing us to take effective action in the future. This, of course, is why we invest a great deal of capital in sending our children to college and trade schools, to gain knowledge that prepares them for the *ability to take effective action in the future.*

As introduced in Chapter 4/Part I, even concepts which can provide a higher level of truth than single events are continuously shifting and changing. At least from our human perspective, **there are no absolute truths**. When a new situation occurs where a concept that was previously considered as truth does not fit, then a larger concept exists that encompasses that concept, and our job is to find that higher level of truth. Since humans operate from a place of yearning to know the truth, when prompted by insecurity, our mind often *does* embrace "absolute truths" in an attempt to develop internal stability. This may take the form of a set of rules or beliefs, deference to an external authority, or a repeatable pattern of past events. However, as Cooper (2005, p. 42) reminds us,

> Truth is a living, dynamic awareness that grows in its meaning and value as our consciousness expands. Trying to rigidly define absolute truth causes separation from the world and judgment of the world. It does not allow our threshold of consciousness to grow and change. It does not allow the continuous and steady development of unconditional love through the acceptance and understanding of ALL things created in the Universe.

Thus, as an experiential learner in the school of life, absolutes do not serve us.

Further, in our shifting reality and because we are both individuated and complex adaptive systems, an apparent truth and an imagined truth may accompany the actual truth (for the moment at hand). Walsch (2009) likens these to three levels of reality, that is, we can experience things at the level of distortion (imagined truth), the level of observation (apparent truth) or the level of ultimate truth (actual truth) which, of course, is subject to all of the discussion in this chapter.

Using Walsch's terminology, Figure 24-1 visually displays the levels of truth.

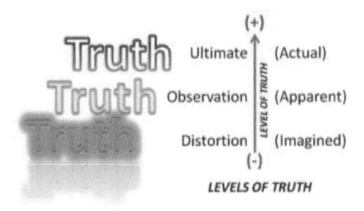

Figure 24-1. *Levels of truth as forwarded by Walsch (2009).*

Thus, truth is a changing target and, as a quality of reality, is relative to our self (experiences, beliefs, values, etc.) and the amount of information that has been garnered, which, like knowledge, is at some level context sensitive and situation dependent. We will address this further below. Since *we* are continuous learners and the *situation* in which we find ourselves is continuously changing, new knowledge is always emerging and we, as co-creators, are continuously changing our way of seeing and interacting with the world. As truth seekers, being human carries with it a huge responsibility, with the individual ability to discern higher truths impacting all those with whom we interact. We begin our exploration of truth by first expanding our understanding of knowledge.

Surface, Shallow, Deep

While this material was briefly introduced in Chapter 2/Part I, we believe it will benefit the reader to review it in the context of this chapter. It is helpful to consider knowledge in terms of three levels: surface knowledge, shallow knowledge and deep knowledge. The analogy built upon here is that of exploring the ocean. A pontoon or light sail boat catching the wind skims rapidly across the waters without concern for that which lies below in the water; as long as whatever lies below does not come to or affect the surface, it is of little concern to forward movement. Note there would still be the impact of surface perturbations such as storms, other boats, etc. For any boat moving in shallow waters, more attention (and some understanding) is required of what is beneath the surface, dependent on the ballast, to ensure forward movement. Not only is an understanding of depth necessary, but also the underwater currents.

In deep waters—engaged over longer periods of time—safety and success require a proven vessel, an experienced captain, a thorough understanding of oceanography, a well-honed navigation system sensitive to current flows and dangers of the ocean, and a well-developed intuition sensitive to deep water terrain, weather patterns, currents and so forth. Carrying the metaphor a bit further, whether surfing or moving through shallow or deep waters, a certain amount of skill is involved, although these also require somewhat *different* skill sets. The metaphor deals with the *level of involvement with what is below the surface*, that which is hidden from sight. Further, as a ship moves into deep waters there is increased reliance on experience and intuition as unforeseen perturbations affect the situation.

Because surface knowledge is continuously changing in response to a changing, uncertain and complex environment, the element of truth is also changing. For example, directions on how to get to someone's house are dependent on road repairs, added traffic lights, changing landmarks, traffic, etc. Because context is so important to understanding shallow knowledge, it may be difficult to discern the level of truth, which is critical to the next actions you take. For example, is the source of your information trustworthy? How will you determine the truth of this information? How was the information shared with you? Did you understand it correctly? When did this event happen? Note that since knowledge is defined as the capacity to take effective action, if this information supports effective action from the viewpoint of the user, then it is Knowledge (Informing). If it does not support effective action from the viewpoint of the user, then it remains information. Note that personal intent plays a large role in what is determined knowledge from the viewpoint of the user. For example, from their viewpoint the executors of the 9/11 disaster had "good" knowledge.

In an organizational setting, shallow knowledge emerges (and expands) through interactions as employees move within and through the processes and practices of the organization. For example, organizations that embrace the use of teams and communities facilitate the mobilization of knowledge and the creation of new ideas as individuals interact in those groups. While the level of truth in shallow knowledge may be greater than surface knowledge, nonetheless, shallow knowledge is also highly sensitive to gossip and propaganda since this is the realm of social knowledge. Propaganda will be further discussed below.

Because deep knowledge is largely conceptual—based on the patterns emerging from multiple events—its level of truth is generally higher and longer lasting than surface or shallow knowledge. However, the development of deep knowledge is not an easy task. It takes an intense and persistent interest, focus and dedication to a specific area of learning, knowledge and action. An individual must "live" with their field of expertise and at the same time focus on the details and contexts of specific experiences. Asking questions and analyzing what went right, what went wrong and why leads to uncovering relationships and patterns that, over time, become the bedrock of expertise, that is, deep knowledge. Gathering relevant information and chunking it builds up a wide range of higher-order patterns that support conceptual thinking (see Chapter 26) and provides models to draw upon when encountering a new or unusual situation.

Since we are continuous learners, each learning experience can build on its predecessor by broadening the sources of knowledge creation and the capacity to create knowledge in different ways. When an individual has deep knowledge, more and more of their learning will build up in the unconscious. In other words, in the area of focus, knowledge begets knowledge. The more that is understood, the more that can be created and understood, and the better qualified we are to judge the level of truth of this knowledge in various situations.

Deep knowledge can also be a limiting frame by choice or by focus., and it potentially carries with it the perceptual burden of ownership. This is because it becomes our point of reference to the world, complete with its self-constructed set of mental models and beliefs. (See Chapter 20/Part III on stuck energy.) Since knowledge is a capacity, continuously emerging in individuals and social settings in response to a shifting, changing environment, no one can own or control knowledge.

Deep knowledge does not represent a perfect state of interaction, that is, intelligent activity. In fact, an inherent difficulty with deep knowledge is communicating it and having others understand it. Because of this difficulty, a separation often occurs between the expert and the user, with the ever-present danger that the "expert" ceases to interact with others and the environment, bounding the domain. When this happens, the expert may perceive his/her self *as* the knowledge instead of the creator and user of knowledge. This behavior is reinforced by others' reliance on the expert. *Being* the knowledge can lead to pushing, directing or ordering—and perhaps even controlling—others' actions because of a perceived superiority. Further, when an expert is cut off from the environment, there is a diminishment of situational and experiential learning related to that environment, which eventually leads to a lack of effectiveness, with a lowering of the level of truth no matter how good the knowledge was previously perceived to be.

Truth and Consciousness

Truth is locally structured thought connected to the lower mental thought of logic, which can be connected to examples in the world. Conceptual in nature and mentally constructed, *truth is not discovered; it is created.* At any given time, we can take a truth and compare it against a related aspect of existence and determine whether something will likely pan out (MacFlouer, 2004-16).

As we now begin to understand, in our everyday lives, truth is a relative value, subjective and, like knowledge, highly context sensitive and situation dependent. While truth, the highest virtue in the mental world, has the ability to reduce forces, since it is a variable changing and growing over time, it can only be *effectively used during a limited period of time.* Over time, dynamic differences cause forces to develop, and old truth becomes conceptually and logically wrong. Thus, there is an inverse correlation between the amount of relativity and the amount of truth in a concept. The less relativity, the more truth; the more truth, the less relativity. See Figure 24-2.

Truth is also highly contingent on an individual's level of consciousness and level of perception. Perception is considered the result of using the senses to acquire information about a situation or the surrounding environment; the impressions, attitudes and understanding about what is observed (Encarta, 1999). Since each individual is unique, both in terms of physical, mental, emotional and spiritual makeup, and in terms of experiences, individual perceptions also vary. For example,

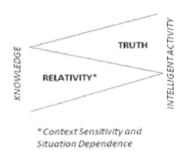

Figure 24-2. *As we move toward intelligent activity, the relativity of truth decreases and the truth becomes a higher-order pattern.*

the value of truth—whether subjective, operational, hypothetical or intellectual—is dependent on its meaning *as translated by individual perception*. As Hawkins explains,

> The legitimacy of any of these is dependent upon the context of a given perceptual level. Truth isn't functional unless it's meaningful and meaning, like value, relies on a unique perceptual field. Facts and data may be convincing at one level and irrelevant at another. (Hawkins, 2002, p. 283)

An excellent example is the shadows on the wall of Plato's cave. This well-known allegory relates the story of slaves who live within the confines of a cave, chained such that they are facing a wall and can only see shadows moving on the wall, shadows that become their reality. When one slave escapes and sees the outside world, and realizes that their entire view of the world is wrong, he goes to tell the other slaves. They reject the idea and defend their current reality. This is the timeless struggle with change, when it conflicts with our worldview.

When truth is meaningful, it is functional, which is also dependent on an individual's intellectual level and ability for abstraction. "To be operational, truth must not simply be 'true' but knowable; yet each level of truth is unknowable to the levels below it …" (Hawkins, 2002, p. 283). Thus, all truth, at least in the physical/emotional/mental planes which are the focus of this book, is dependent on the individual perceiving that truth. The power of perception is discussed further below.

Reflect on the levels of consciousness introduced in Chapter 5/Part I. As Hawkins (2002, p. 271) describes: "At the lower levels of consciousness, propositions are accepted as true even when they're illogical, unfounded, and express tenets neither intellectually provable nor practically demonstrable." For example, people are convicted of crimes they did not commit because of their cultural heritage and being in the wrong place at the wrong time, and murder can occur based on the belief of the justice of revenge.

Exploring the decline of the level of truth in the world's great religions, Hawkins (2002) states that there is a greater vulnerability to misinterpretation when the creed is more dualistic. The split between belief and action in dualism causes a disorientation of levels of truth. "When this occurs, the spiritual essence can be confused in translation into physical expression. Thus, the conceptual Christian Soldier (of the spirit) becomes, through a distorted 'literal' translation, a self-justified battlefield killer" (Hawkins, 2002, p. 274-75). The downfall of lofty spiritual teachings is based on their misinterpretation by those with lower consciousness. (See Chapter 5/Part I on Hawkins' levels of consciousness.) Further, Hawkins believes that "process of perverting truth through a failure of discernment is responsible for providing the vehicle for the decline in the world's great religions", noting that those religions with a level of consciousness below 500 (the level of Love) preach love, but don't practice it. This same phenomenon occurs among political parties.

<<<<<<<<>>>>>>>

INSIGHT: **When truth is linked with fact, it becomes as relative as knowledge, both context sensitive and situation dependent.**

<<<<<<<<>>>>>>>

While intuitively we know that love and truth are in relationship, what is that relationship? In fairytales, we read about the endurance of true love to separate the concept of a short event and a lifetime event, or in relationship to faith we think in terms of eternal and unconditional love (agape). When discussing the wonder of love in Chapter 19/Part III, we introduced the irrevocable connection between love and freedom, that is, love grows and is born of the understanding of another, it cannot be willed or demanded. Understanding, while subjective, is born of truth, comprehension and appreciation of a thought, an event or a person.

Because truth is structured, it can be discerned in comparison to another truth and can be given a relative value regarding the level of truth, that is, a mathematical representation of how much a conceptual truth is true in a specific example. And because truth is relative, over time we are able to recognize situational value and determine contradictions.

Through conceptual thinking our higher mental senses tell us when truth is not truth by recognizing forces moving in a different direction. This occurs through identification of examples that do not fit into a concept. Along with the ability to determine the level of truth of an example, conceptual thinking brings with it a fuller level of consciousness, that is, an *understanding of the relationships* among concepts and examples. **As the source of facts, science provides the backbone for the discovery of truth.** Mind cannot operate without facts. "They are the building blocks in the construction of wisdom which are cemented together by life experience"

(*Urantia*, 1954, p. 1222). Nowhere is this clearer than when we act on our knowledge. As explained in *Urantia* (1954, p. 1222):

> The expansion of material knowledge permits a greater intellectual appreciation of the meanings of ideas and the values of ideas. A human being can find truth in his inner experience, but he needs a clear knowledge of facts to apply his personal discovery of truth to the ruthlessly practical demands of everyday life.

Recall the words of a television private investigator: "The facts and nothing but the facts." Thus, as forwarded, **the mental is in service to the intuitive**. Through science, we develop a more thorough understanding of the physical Universe and are provided the tools to act on the world.

<<<<<<<◇>>>>>>>

INSIGHT: **Science provides the backbone for the discovery of truth. Through science, we develop a more thorough understanding of the physical Universe and are provided the tools to act on the world.**

<<<<<<<◇>>>>>>>

****

TOOL 24-1: TRUTH SEARCHING

Since truth deals with what is generally believed or considered "facts" in a particular context or focused on a particular situation, the search for truth is a search for examples of the level of truth currently known.

STEP (1): Clearly define the truth which you are affirming (Truth A).

STEP (2): Understand the context and/or situation clearly from which this truth is emerging (Situation/Event A). In this stage, it is important to engage both logical *and* conceptual thinking; logic is lower mental thinking and concepts, as patterns, are higher mental thinking.

STEP (3): Search for other situations or events that reflect similar patterns (Situations/Events B, C, etc.). For each situation or event, *ask*: Is Truth A also true in this situation or event?

STEP (4): Determine the *level of truth* of Truth A. If Truth A is true in every situation and/or event you have identified, then, for the present, you can be confident of its truth value in Situation A. If Truth A *does not* work in one or more of the events and/or situations you identified, then reconsider the value of Truth A in Situation A.

STEP (5): For any event/situation identified where Truth A does not work, first ensure the event/situation has a similar pattern of activity. If so, then reflect on how Truth A might be changed in order to become true in both Situation A and in this new event/situation. Continue with this process until you discover a truth that works in *all* of the events/situations you have identified or can identify that reflect similar patterns to Situation/Event A.

NOTE: While your personal beliefs may be difficult to circumvent, your body will often indicate that this is the case. A *cognitive dissonance* can occur when considering two beliefs which are in conflict with each other. To help mitigate the possibility of cognitive biases and the injection of hidden assumptions, *vericate* your findings with others in your network. *Verication* is the process of consulting a trusted ally, that is, someone with expertise in the domain of knowledge in which you are truth searching. There is considerable discovery power in engaging groups of minds in truth searching.

Almost always, new ideas emerge from a negative insight, that is, recognition that the current theoretical body of knowledge is insufficient to explain a current situation. This requires discarding previous beliefs and theories in preference to a new or expanded conceptual truth. An example is Einstein's early paper on relativity, published at age 26 in 1905. In this paper Einstein had to break away from the concept of absolute space and time so that he could accept the general principle of Maxwell's equations for electromagnetism, which are the symmetries that correspond to special relativity (Gell-Mann, 1994). (See Tool 4-1: Humility, Chapter 4/Part I).

****

Misinformation and Disinformation

The information explosion has enabled a misinformation explosion. In this context, we take misinformation to simply mean information that misinforms. Recall from Chapter 2/Part I that all knowledge is imperfect and/or incomplete since knowledge is continuously shifting and changing in concert with our environment, the demands placed upon us, and our response to that environment. Even knowledge that has been effective in one instant of time serves only as information in another instant of time, *even when applied in the same or a similar situation.* Thus, systems filled with data and information are also filled with misinformation, distorting the search for truth.

<<<<<<<◇>>>>>>

INSIGHT: **The information explosion has enabled a misinformation and disinformation explosion.**

<<<<<<<◇>>>>>>

Disinformation coming from many different sources also abounds. While the term disinformation appears to include *intent* of deception, Miniter (2005) reminds us that people's motives are impossible to test. So, he describes disinformation as that which is widely believed, yet *probably false.* This makes sense. The very concept of disinformation gains power if there is an element of uncertainty regarding the level of truth.

Let's further explore the sources of disinformation. First, there are honest errors upon which myths are built. An example is the concept "survival of the fittest" which was taken out of context, and in a later publication corrected by Darwin (1998, p. 110) to read: "Those communities which included the greatest number of the most sympathetic members would flourish best and rear the greatest number of offspring." However, few people read or remember the correction.

Some errors are simply mistakes, misquotes or misattributions. Some information is partial, confusing or ignoring details and context such that what is provided cannot be understood. As seeming facts that become part of conventional wisdom yet are probably false (Miniter, 2005), myths often become or promote memes. A meme is an idea, behavior pattern, or piece of information that is passed on, again and again, through the process of imitation such that it takes on a life of its own (Blackmore, 2000). Memes may or may not reflect the original intent of an idea. They act as replicators of information (that may become knowledge) as they spread throughout groups of individuals. The role that memes play in learning comes from their capability to retain the memory because of their sound and meaning. Of course, learning only occurs if their meaning and relevance is understood by individuals within the group. This means that for memes to spread they need to relate to the culture, attitudes, expectations and interests of the group. Learning can be greatly enhanced by the effective choice and use of memes throughout the communication process. Because they are symbolic, people using similar memes, together with common syntax and semantics, can understand each other much more effectively and rapidly, thereby more easily creating social networks which facilitate the transmission of information and the creation of knowledge (Bennet & Bennet, 2007). Memes become stronger (more memorable) when they are delivered in connection with an emotional event that engages the feelings of the listener/participant. A well-known example of a meme is the U.S. Army's slogan for many years: Be all you can be!

A second source of disinformation is official spin, that is, selective partial information released by "those in charge" that favorably situates an event. This can be a destructive and controlling force when used by people in positions of power. A third source of disinformation is that spread by foreign sources. The media may pick up dubious information and run with it, or they may be misled by foreign websites and releases. A fourth source of disinformation is connected to historical amnesia. History easily vanishes from media memory, and dates of events are often confused in the rush to be the first to reveal breaking news (Miniter, 2005). A fifth source of disinformation is leaks, which may or may not contain a level of truth. These are generally on purpose, with a personal agenda behind the leak.

Sensing the truth in others can occur in conjunction with higher-level communication skills such as empathy coupled with reflection. When we sense untruth in ourselves or others, forces are created. For example, consider the force between mental thinking and non-mental thinking when limited funding is being allocated and the choice is between a research study and an emotional plea to act now and take a chance. While we can mentally sense when things are not heading in the same direction, calling emotions into play adds an element of confusion, creating force. As MacFlouer (2004-16) forwards, the total value of truth (T) minus the value of untruth (U) equals force (F), that is,

$$T - U = F \quad or \quad T - (t_1 + t_2 + t_3, \text{etc.}) = F$$

Truth has value; untruth *reduces the ability of thought to control energy*, so thinking becomes more difficult. Exposure to untruth reduces the structure of our thinking and reduces our senses. *The greater our exposure to untruths, the lower our ability to sense those untruths*. An example is the continuous pattering of a politician. When people become used to untruths, they are not in a position to hear truth, that is, they cannot discern it. One strategy to move toward intelligent communication with such individuals would be to share partial truths, slowly increasing their receptivity to the truth. If you have empathy and the ability to think ahead, you can consider how another person is going to respond *prior* to communicating, and determine the level of truth to share.

Perception and Propaganda

Recall that perception is our impressions, attitudes and understanding about what we observe. What we are aware of, what we observe, is a product of the threshold through which we focus, that is, consciousness (see Chapter 5/Part I). We can change internal mechanisms in order to affect external reality. For example, an artist will see things that a lawyer will not, and vice versa. Further, as we learn about our emotions, we can affect our personal feelings—bringing about personal change—by changing our perception. For example, when an individual perceives themselves as fat, they are continuously comparing themselves to others. When an individual recognizes their personal beauty, whether outward or inward, individuation and contribution become more significant than comparison. Recall the power of perception introduced in Chapter 19/Part III on using emotions as a guidance system.

Perception can also be impacted by external forces. For example, because Fashion magazines use incredibly skinny models week after week, year after year, many individuals with normal body weight perceive themselves as fat. So, individuals are susceptible to social trends. Further, repeated bombardment of ideas also has a heavy impact, such that even initially recognized untruths become partial truths which may, for an individual or society over time, become truths. Further, as introduced above, the mixture of truth and untruth clogs our filters such that we lose the power of discernment.

With freedom of thinking and choice comes the need for discernment and discretion in recognizing truth, and a good understanding of the broader ramifications of decisions. To discern is to have the ability to see the unobvious, to distinguish between two or more things, to have good taste and judgment (Encarta, 1999). Phase 2, the co-evolving phase of change, is still heavily linked to a cause and effect model based on an advanced mental understanding of patterns and relationships among elements of the complex adaptive systems of which we are a part and in which we facilitate change. Yet, it also is a space where third-order thinking can arise, and it takes courage to choose whether to be a part of something larger or to assert one's individuality—a "choice between conventionalizing and differentiating the path of change. The differentiating choice calls for the courage to commit to oneself. It is the belief that allows one to let go of the maintained worldview, that is, one's story, in search of a new one … **the courage to see and courage to act (or change)** [emphasis added]" (McWhinney, 1997, p. 225-6). The courage to act, along with the knowledge of how to act, is the self empowerment at the end of the AUBFOE sequence in the individual change model (see Chapter 6/Part I).

Unfortunately, youth and innocence can be quite susceptible to propaganda and manipulation. This is immortalized in the words of poet Cindy Scott (2016) in her verse titled *Innocence*:

Oh, for the innocence of the heart,
So vulnerable to manipulation,
Gullible to charismatic intellectuals,
That fill the lamb with jubilation.

The naive trust the knowledgeable schemer,
Sitting upon a visionary's imagined throne,
Giving enlightenment with the jaded word,
Asking the susceptible to give all they own.

Simple minded, unsuspicious of the teachings,
Impervious to how vulnerable they may be.
Unpretentious in receiving information,
Believing and accepting what they see.

Propaganda is a group of ideas or statements, often false or exaggerated, that are spread with intent, to help or hinder a cause, a political leader, a government, etc. (Merriam-Webster, 2016). It is a mode of **power and control through information**. Note that while the information associated with propaganda may or may not be true, it is selectively engaged and spread to accomplish a hidden agenda, highly questionable as to level of truth for the situation at hand. Thus, the knowledge created from propaganda does not lead to intelligent activity

<<<<<<<>>>>>>>

INSIGHT: **Because it is selectively engaged and spread to accomplish a hidden agenda, the knowledge created from propaganda does not lead to intelligent activity.**

<<<<<<<>>>>>>>

As an element of information warfare, in today's global environment, propaganda has no visible and definable fronts; it is not geographically localizable and is ubiquitous, that is, everywhere simultaneously (Stocker, 1998). This is the dark side of globalization. Further, because of fragmentation in small bites and wide-spread dispersal at every level of society, it is intangible and can be difficult to recognize. These small bites are of a nature such that they often morph into memes, catching on and becoming part of a larger myth.

The threat is so real that governments around the world focus resources on mitigating disinformation and propaganda. For example, in December 2016, on his way out of office, U.S. President Barack Obama signed the 2017 National Defense Authorization Act (NDAA) into law. Buried within this $619 billion military budget was the Countering Disinformation and Propaganda Act, a provision that established a national anti-propaganda center in the State Department. This Global Engagement Center is tasked with recognizing, understanding, exposing and countering "foreign state and non-state propaganda and disinformation efforts aimed at undermining United States national security interests." The law also grants non-governmental agencies the tasking to help "collect and store examples in print, online, and social media, disinformation, misinformation, and propaganda" that is directed toward the US. and its allies, as well as to help "counter efforts by foreign entities to use disinformation, misinformation, and propaganda to influence the policies and social and political stability."

While this bipartisan bill received overwhelming support in both Houses, and it may well provide some awareness to citizens in terms of disinformation distributed across the Internet, countering disinformation and propaganda can prove quite difficult without leaning too far over the other direction, that is, **pushing out disinformation and propaganda that favors the organization and those it supports**. This potential has become a reality in many parts of the world.

This has happened before. As early as 1971 Lewis Powell, a former U.S. Supreme Court justice, designed a campaign to counter what he called an attack on the American free enterprise system. This report called for generating resources, directing government policy, and molding public opinion. It included specific methods that could be used by corporations to silence those who showed hostility to corporate interests in "the college campus, the pulpit, the media, the intellectual and literary journals." In other words, curtail dissenters and remove freedom of speech. This document went so far as to call for pro-corporate judges on the bench, and utilizing think tanks to direct "ideological assaults against government regulation and environmental protection" to a mass audience (Hedges, 2016). What is even more difficult to fathom is that, according to Ellen Schrecker, an author and historian of McCarthyism, this campaign was implemented and *unbelievably successful*. This assault on knowledge included campaigns calling for defunding of the humanities in public schools and universities as well as public broadcasting and the arts. As Schrecker describes,

> The humanities were eviscerated. Vocational training, including the expansion of the study of finance and economics in universities, replaced disciplines that provided students with cultural and historical literacy, that allowed them to step outside of themselves to feel and express empathy for the other. Students were no longer taught how to think, but what to think. Civic education died. A grotesque kind of illiteracy ... was celebrated. Success became solely about amassing wealth. The cult of the self, the essence of corporatism, became paramount. (Hedges, 2016)

This attack on the American mind—and on the minds of those around the world—continues today as people, both knowingly and unknowingly, allow their leaders to make decisions without accountability. Whether the Global Engagement Center in the U.S, and other organizations charged with similar missions, *are beneficial or harmful* to the citizens of their countries and people of the world is up to those citizens. Ultimately, the only way to cease being a pawn in another person's game is to expand our own awareness, learning and consciousness, connecting with others of like mind and heart, sharing our thoughts, and collectively and collaboratively acting on those thoughts. (See Figure 32-1 in Chapter 32/Part V in support of "Conversations that Matter" focused on the balance between freedom and the need for societal/governmental controls.)

Forms of Propaganda

While physical force still has pockets of activity in our world, as technologies have opened larger avenues of communication, propaganda has increasingly become the method of choice for controlling the larger population and gaining power. Taking power by force wastes energy, with forces concurrently having the ability to diminish power. This old way of using force certainly works up to a point, and then has consistently through history been recognized and defeated.

In today's information environment, there are two primary forms of propaganda: (1) the shifting of cause and effect and (2) the strategic weaving of untruth and truth, creating layers of lies. See Figure 24-3.

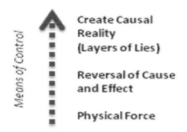

Figure 24-3. *Movement from physical control to propaganda.*

The shifting of cause and effect is the most common. Power—at least for a time (you can fool some of the people all the time, all the people some of the time, but not all the people all the time)—has been achieved through making effects look like they are causes, which provides the ability to distort reality and create false beliefs. Take for example, the promise of communism. The *effect* is some limited giving (example, food on the table and the promise of better times) leading to power transfer from the people to the government. The effect becomes the cause and people believe that communism is the reason they have food. Another example of reversal is when people try to take something for nothing by getting people to relinquish their power. When truth is compromised, the mental capability shrinks. It is easier to convince people of untrue things, thus becoming easier to manipulate and control them. The more often this occurs, the less ability the victims have to discern the truth. Concomitantly, as people relinquish power, the understanding of what they are doing is lost and their lives become less meaningful.

Let's take a business example, where the owners of a business have been used to a high profit margin and, reluctant to reduce that margin, choose to cut salaries, informing employees that, in a down-turned economy, salaries must be reduced to keep the business alive and enable employees to keep their jobs. Where the truth lies becomes quite fuzzy, with an underlying reversal of cause and effect. Further, note that in this case employees are being given a chance to help keep the business functioning to ensure an income, albeit a reduced income. There is the allure of a *partnering* that is occurring, that management is doing everything they can to work through a difficult situation that directly impacts employees.

Layering can infer a continuous building of untruths, or the strategic weaving of untruth and truth. Although historically less used, in the current post-truth climate layering appears to be gaining more power. The continuous layering of untruths causes redundancy in the progression of thought. As lies continue to build, people actually forget prior lies. They also become comfortable with not hearing the truth. A side effect is development of a sense of belonging to something larger and, not wanting to stand out or be different—sometimes driven by fear of consequences (part of Phase 1 learning)—the loss of creativity and individuation. Global connectivity has allowed this to occur more rapidly and in a larger context.

<<<<<<<◇>>>>>>

INSIGHT: **As lies continue to build, people actually forget prior lies and become comfortable with not hearing the truth.**

<<<<<<<◇>>>>>>

A higher level of propaganda is to become creative in negative ways, that is, create a causal reality of intricately constructed lies that are hard to challenge (MacFlouer, 2004-16). Objects are created to convince people that what they last heard is connected to what you are telling them, even though these may be opposites. An example is the political blathering during the 2016 bid for the U.S. Presidency. A voice in a position of power can be destructive when connecting with people who do not have strong conceptually-developed minds, that is, still actively developing their Phase 1 skills. When a mind focused on cause and effect hears one recognizable truth, they can easily connect other things told to them as true, not recognizing the lack of consistency or the contradictions that are present. Responses may follow the path of false perceptions and logic such as: "If he told the truth in the past, then this must be true." Or, "If this was successful in the past, then it will be successful now." Or, "If he is wealthy and in a position of power, then it must be right."

A key factor in the weaving of truths and untruths is rhythm, which can lead to destruction of the mental faculties. If you can recognize the rhythm and disrupt it, the truth is easier to discern (MacFlouer, 2004-16).

****

TOOL 24-2: RHYTHM DISRUPTOR

This tool is based on concepts presented by MacFlouer (2004-16).

STEP 1: Identify any desire (feeling) you have that is related to what is being promised/said. These are not just mental ideas, but are also connected to emotions. Regardless of the level of truth, you are being offered something that you are told will be forthcoming in the future. *Tapping desire is the first beat to developing a rhythm and bringing others into that rhythm.*

NOTE: It is a good idea to understand your fixed desires, that is, those desires that come up over and over again in life. Do a periodic review of your desires. *Ask*: Do I really want this now, or is this a hangover from some emotionally-charged event from the past? Is this desire beneficial to me and/or others? Is this desire selfish? Is this desire worth spending my energy/thought/feelings pursuing?

STEP 2: Think about what has been promised/said in the past from this same source. Try to put this in a time sequence, that is, when was this promised/said? Create a timeline by drawing a straight line on a piece of paper, putting tick marks to indicate promises/statements with the date above the tick mark and a short description of the promise/statement below the tick mark.

HELPFUL HINT: When considered from the mental plane, when something is equally presented and balanced it connects to an event representing three parts of time (past, present, future). This means that it has a low degree of context sensitivity; it was true in the past, is true now and will be true in the future. In a lie, at least one part of time is imbalanced; thus, something SOUNDS or FEELS untrue. Listen to this feeling. You must recognize untruths before you can respond to them.

STEP 3: Look for a rhythm in what is being said. As MacFlouer (1999) warns, "Don't fall into the rhythm of the lie." The goal of propaganda is not to *convince* you of truthfulness, but to *confuse*, **drawing you into the rhythm of the lie so you cannot perceive the truth.**

STEP 4: Disrupt the rhythm by creating a discord. This can be done by engaging in a contemplative or reflective session where lies can be felt and recognized. Interacting and reflecting with trusted others who are open communicators can provide valuable input to this process.

****

Brainwashing

Brainwashing refers to mind control. It is the use of various techniques engaging the senses in an attempt to change the thoughts and beliefs of others against their will. In brainwashing, senses diminish such that the structure of thinking becomes discontinuous and there is a loss of sense-making ability. When the senses are not unified or balanced, there is a reduction in the ability to discern truth and untruth.

Thus, brainwashing most often includes some nature of sensory deprivation or overload.

While the virtual connectivity of today serves as an enabler for wider impact on the citizens of the world while simultaneously offering opportunities for growth and creativity, it makes people vulnerable to direction and control. For example, brainwashing occurs through the media. The young are programmed by specialized computer games that glorify violence, potentially leading to acceptance of the use of violence and a belief that the end justifies the means.

Further, media such as movies have the power to brainwash all ages, negatively and positively. Continuing with our example, the negative weakening effects of media violence alone can lead to subtle grades of depression, which "kill more people than all the other diseases of mankind combined" (Hawkins, 2002, p. 278). Let's lean on Hawkins' work to understand the full import of media violence on the physical body. Using Kinesiology testing, Hawkins was able to show that a typical television show produced weakening about 113 times in a single episode. As Hawkins explains,

> Each of these weakening events suppressed the observer's immune system and reflected an insult to the viewer's central as well as autonomic nervous system. Invariably accompanying each of these 113 disruptions of the acupuncture system were suppressions of the thymus gland; each insult also resulted in damage to the brain's delicate neurohormonal and neurotransmitter systems. Each negative input brought the watcher closer to eventual sickness and to imminent depression—which is now the world's most prevalent illness. (Hawkins, 2002, p. 278)

Thus, using Hawkins' levels of consciousness introduced in Chapter 5/Part I, any media event producing a state of consciousness that calibrates below 200 (the level of Courage), that is, those lower levels representing such states as Shame, Guilt, Apathy, Grief, Fear, Desire, Anger, and Pride, are destructive and unsupportive of life. From the body's response cited above, we can understand why.

Knowledge can be engaged as a force against propaganda when it is used to raise awareness, helping people discern a higher level of truth and become increasingly interactive with others, more conscious and therefore having greater freedom of thought. This facilitates movement toward intelligent activity.

Final Thoughts

While absolute truth may be a reality, it is beyond the capability of the human. When truth is linked with fact, it becomes as relative as knowledge, context sensitive and situation dependent. As described in *Urantia* (1955, p. 1297), "when truth becomes linked with fact, then both time and space condition its meanings and correlate its values. Such realities of truth wedded to fact become concepts and are accordingly relegated to the domain of relative cosmic realities." While truth is relative to the amount of information that has been garnered and, like knowledge, is situation dependent and context sensitive, higher order conceptual thinking has a higher level of truth.

"Being right" or "Not being wrong" is very much related to the ego and does not denote truth. In many situations, there is no right or wrong, just choice. By asserting that one is right, it assumes that other approaches are wrong, thus setting up forces. [See Chapters 3 and Chapter 4/Part I.]

As humans, we are reminded that while things are relative in time in the physical reality in which we live, we are all on the path searching for higher truth. "The more truth you know, the more truth you *are*, the more of the past you can understand and the more of the future you can comprehend" (*Urantia*, 1955, p. 1297). The search for truth is essential to co-creating the future. In the cycle of the individual change model introduced in Chapter 5/Part I, our search for truth begins with awareness, expands into understanding and believing, then feels good, coming with recognition of personal responsibility. It is then that the knowledge of how to act and the courage to act offer us choice. Happy journeying.

Questions for Reflection:

Would others say you focus more on seeking truth or defending current knowledge?

What are your truths and where did they come from?

When engaging stakeholders, do you focus on truth or do you share misinformation to achieve your own aims?

Am I able to recognize the rhythm of truths and untruths?

Chapter 25
Attention and Intention

We don't understand what it is until we work on it.

-Author Unknown

SUBTOPICS: EXPLORING ATTENTION ... EXPLORING INTENTION ... THE POWER OF INTENTION ... BRINGING THEM TOGETHER

FIGURES: **25-1**. ATTENTION AND INTENTION WEAVE OUR THOUGHTS AND FEELINGS INTO REALITY. **25-2**. THE CREATION PROCESS OF INTENTION AND EXPECTATION IS CONTINUOUS ... **25-3**. THE LIMITS OF THE MIND/BRAIN ARE THOSE WE SET UPON IT. INTENTION IS A TOOL FOR CREATION.

Directly related to consciousness, attention and intention are tools of the self, laying the web for interaction with the world in which we act. As we recognize, experience is the fundamental way people learn (see Chapter 9/Part II). This term covers much territory, from living in a certain environment to a direct interaction with another person, to a frightening event, to the internal experience of dreaming, meditation, reading or reflecting on action. All of these are ways that information can come to the attention of the mind and thereby interact and influence its thoughts and perceptions of the world.

For example, some 20 years ago in the U.S. Department of the Navy Acquisition System, change was afoot, with dozens of initiatives simultaneously pushed down from the Department of Defense that impacted every aspect of the acquisition process for multi-year, million-and-billion-dollar programs. While a myriad of resources from both the public and private sectors were available in support of this change, we were faced with how to quickly move the system from within (see Chapter 6/Part I on the Individual Change Model). The Inspector General teams served as a pivot point. The *inspection teams* were trained as knowledge brokers, with access in terms of availability and *understanding of* the change needed and support materials available, coupled with an understanding of future program office needs. These teams immediately scheduled pre-audits of every program office, with the checkpoints representing 100% implementation of each of the change initiatives. When the pre-audit was done, the team sat down with program office leaders, provided resources for every gap that was noted, and scheduled a full audit of completed implementation six months later. This process both gained the immediate *attention* of leadership and set the *intention* in terms of expected quality and timeliness for full implementation.

Attention can only occur in the NOW, and sustained attention is a series of NOWs. For example, the eyes work much like an old-time movie real, with a fixation occurring approximately three times a second as the eyes make a small, quick movement (a saccade) and then stop. However, we perceive it as a continuous flow of movement. Just as the eyes shift their focus from object to object, attention shifts driven by our thoughts and feelings. When these thoughts and feelings are focused and consistent accompanied by intelligent actions, we become the co-creators that we are. See Figure 25-1. Note that planning, introduced as a tool in Chapter 16/Part III, can help clarify and solidify intention. Planning uses patterns from the past to predict the future. Intention is all about the future. In this chapter we explore these tools of self in depth.

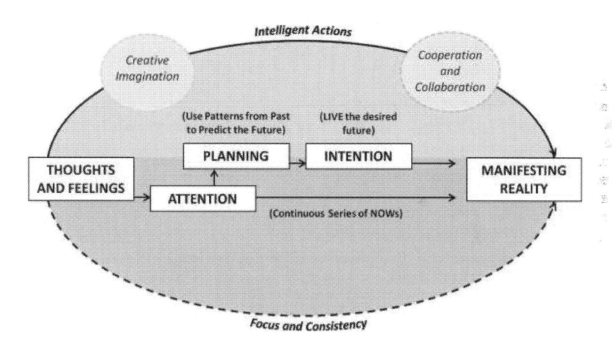

Figure 25-1. *Attention and Intention weave our thoughts and feelings into reality.*

Exploring Attention

Before the turn of the century, Portante and Tarro (1997) argued that attention had become the scarce resource of the information economy. They referenced Lanham (1993), a professor of rhetoric at UCLA, who was focused on the implications for information technology of human attention management. A primary point was that black-and-white text could never hold the attention of a generation stimulated by color and movement, brought up with the singing and dancing of numbers and letters on *Sesame Street*.

As the information age has exploded and the availability and accessibility of that information increased, the gap between the attention of individuals and organizations and the information that needs to be attended to has widened. Davenport and Beck (2001) describe attention as a slippery intangible asset, and begin their book *The Attention Economy* with a focus on the current attention deficit. For example, they describe an organization's attention deficit in terms of organizational ADD. The symptoms are the increased likelihood of missing key information needed for decisions; diminished time for reflection on anything but simple information transactions such as e-mail; difficulty holding others' attention; and a decreased ability to focus when necessary (Davenport & Beck, 2001, p. 7).

From a neuroscience perspective, spatial attention to a specific thing, person or event increases the intensity of the related neuronal firings, which in turn affects the conscious experience of focus, amplifying the contrast in the experience and making it less faint and more salient (Carrasco, 2004). This translates into increased memory and recall. Further, there are potential long-term impacts. As Jensen (2006, p. 10) says, "It is now established that contrasting, persistent, or traumatic environments can and do change the actions of genes." Similarly, focusing attention on a particular non-spatial stimulus feature such as color increases its representational precision resulting in more concrete conscious experiences (Maunsel and Treue, 2006; Asplund et al., 2014). Thus, attention directly impacts the breadth and depth of connections in the short and long-term.

Davenport & Beck (2001) introduce six basic units of currency for exchange in the attention market. We will use this model to further understand the elements of attention. Each unit emphasizes a facet of focused mental engagement, specifically: (1) aversive [conscious responses (example, "to death or defeat")], (2) captive [conscious and unconscious responses with choice when brought into awareness (example: advertising or bad weather)], (3) back-of-mind [unconscious automatic responses (example: driving to work)], (4) front-of-mind [conscious choices (example: choosing a spouse], (5) voluntary [conscious choices (example: engaging in a hobby], and (6) attractive [conscious and unconscious triggering through senses and feelings (example: a beautiful person or the thrill of victory)]. While Davenport & Beck categorize captive and voluntary as types of attention including choice, captive would include elements occurring in the unconscious which, until brought into the awareness of the individual (perhaps through feelings), would negate the element of choice. Their second category of attention, aversive versus attractive, is very much a push and pull or stick and carrot situation, that is, the push of the negative and the pull of positive rewards or beauty. (See Chapter 3e/Part V on The Harmony of Beauty.)

A fascinating finding in this work is the recognition that time management and attention management are not linked. (See Chapter 16/Part III for a discussion of the relationship between time and space.) This is consistent with the 21st century management focus on knowledge, that is, moving from a focus on efficiency to a focus on effectiveness. Knowledge worker accountability over the long-term is primarily for effectiveness (getting the desired results), and secondarily for efficiency (doing things at the least cost). When working in a complex environment, doing the right things often means losing some efficiency. For example, learning, networking, keeping the knowledge center up to date with what is learned, sharing knowledge with others, trying new ways of supporting customers, pursuing creative ideas for new innovations, and spending time thinking about complex situations could all be considered inefficient in a bureaucratic organization. Yet without these activities, today's organization would not be able to function, let alone excel, in a changing and uncertain world. Today's focus is on making and implementing *effective* decisions in the most efficient way possible.

<<<<<<<<<>>>>>>>

INSIGHT: **Time management and attention management are not linked.**

<<<<<<<<<>>>>>>>

Attention is organic; it is about people. Davenport & Beck (2001, p. 13) forward that "Since few of us have a good sense of how to process vast amounts of information effectively, we're bound to allocate attention ineffectively." We would argue otherwise. The human senses are exactly what *do* know how to process vast amounts of information effectively. Recall that knowledge is defined as the capacity (potential or actual) to take effective action. It is our senses—primarily focused at the unconscious level—that are the information processors providing the information for our decisions and actions. The effectiveness of those decisions and actions can be determined by a 0-1 probability of achieving an anticipated outcome (which determines the effectiveness of knowledge). Of course, in a complex decision-making environment, heading the right direction can be considered an effective outcome! (Bennet & Bennet, 2013)

Davenport himself can serve as an example of this process. His focus on attention had a personal impact on him. Recognizing that attention itself is an area of interest and significance in learning and the sharing of knowledge, Davenport explains, "In terms of attention, I did become much more conscious of the emails that

I send, the letters that I write, and the presentations that I give. I ask myself, am I getting the attention of the people this is targeted at? What can I do to make it more engaging for them, to get their attention? Am I allocating my own attention effectively?" This focus on attention changed his behavior, as has his passion around the work he is doing on personal information and Knowledge Management. He further explains, "It's how individuals manage their own personal information and knowledge environments, and that has changed my behavior, too. How could it not?" (Bennet et al., 2015c, p.196)

Attention is key to development of the self. Since consciousness is a part of self, then "it follows that what we pay attention to over time will shape that self" (Csikszentmihalyi, 1993, p. 217). Even the *objects and activities* that we pay attention to become part of our self. For example, when we are asked who we are, the response may be "a housewife" or "a dancer" or "a mechanical engineer", each a label that we have attached as a part of our self. In one context, the self could be thought of as a hierarchy of goals, because *it is the purpose and goals of the self that focus the largest amount of attention*. Not only *what* we pay attention to, but *how* we pay attention is important. For example, we might consider a person who continuously worries about getting hurt as neurotic, or a person who avoids eye contact and stays relatively quiet as shy.

<<<<<<<◇>>>>>>>

INSIGHT: **It is the purpose and goals of the self that focus the largest amount of attention.**

<<<<<<<◇>>>>>>>

This is consistent with the discussion in Chapter 5/Part I that at any given moment individuals and organizations function from a very definable band or region of thinking, talking and acting, reflecting areas of focus and different levels of consciousness. This is the threshold within which things make sense to us. Concurrently, we have discovered through neuroscience that in one situation our brain may keep individuals from paying attention (through monkey chatter or emotional distractions) and in another situation engage our full attention. Further, stress plays a large role in arousal and attention (see Chapter 13/Part III). Consider the amygdala, the part of the brain where incoming sensory input is continuously screened for potentially dangerous situations. If a threat is sensed, the amygdala immediately sends a signal that sets in motion a quick action such as the fight or flight response before the cortex is even aware of what has happened. As Zull (2002, p. 141) details, "our actions will not be controlled by our sensory cortex that breaks things down into details, but by our survival shortcut through the amygdala, which is fast but misses details." The negative impact of this is that excessive levels of cortisol (the substance the adrenal glands secrets during stress) can cause permanent damage to the locus ceruleus, which is important for selective attention (Byrnes, 2001). Begley (2007) also notes that attention, one of the parameters of successful learning, also *pumps up* neuronal activity. She says that, "Attention is real, in the sense that it takes a physical form capable of affecting the physical activity [and therefore the structure] of the brain" (p. 158).

We also now know that, in terms of mental development, it is the frontal lobes that help an individual pay attention and ask good questions. As Amen (2005, p. 115) describes, A more developed frontal lobe allows you to take better advantage of new knowledge, to know what to focus on, and to relate it to life experiences so that it has more useful value to you. The eighteen-year-old may be able to memorize facts more easily, but his frontal lobe isn't as good at selecting which facts to memorize.

As do other researchers in the field, Amen (2005) says that the best mental exercise is new learning, acquiring new knowledge, and doing things you've never done before. For example, the Nuns Study conducted by a research team from the Rush University Medical Center in Chicago, studied how often 801 older nuns, priests, and other clergy engaged in mentally stimulating activities such as reading a newspaper. The researchers discovered that,

> Those who increased their mental activity over the five years reduced their chance of developing Alzheimer's disease by one-third. These more mentally active individuals also reduced their age-related decline in overall mental abilities by 50 percent, **in concentration and attention span by 60 percent** [emphasis added], and in mental processing speed by 30 percent. (Amen, 2005, p. 114)

Let's briefly look at attention through a different lens. Throughout this book, we have referred to people as verbs, not nouns, designed to continuously experience and learn and expand. When people are alone with nothing to do, they have a tendency to be become listless and dissatisfied. As Csikszentmihalyi (1993, p. 33) reports,

> Paradoxically it is when we are ostensibly most free, when we can do anything we want to, that we are least able to act. In these situations the mind tends to drift, and sooner or later it hits on some painful thought or unfulfilled desire.

Csikszentmihalyi (1993) says there is an external approach and an internal approach to moving beyond anxiety or boredom and focusing the mind. Externally, order can be imposed on the mind by focusing attention. Examples would include doing a specific task, watching a movie, or engaging in a conversation. Internally, an individual can, over time, spend focused energy on purposeful activities, developing an inner discipline around accomplishing those activities. Examples would include training the body for a marathon, playing a musical instrument, or reading or mathematics.

As pointed out in Davenport and Beck's model for types of attention, there are both negative and positive attractors that draw attention. For example, a basic unit of currency is *aversive*, that is, paying attention to something to avoid negative experiences. However, focusing on the negative gives power to the negative, so there is a negative feedback loop that accompanies the focus on, for example, avoiding punishment or negative consequences.

Another basic unit of currency is *attractive*. While we used the earlier example of the thrill of victory, there is also a thrill provided by danger and the unknown. People are also attracted to negative outcomes. For example, remember the last time you passed an accident on the freeway, with your attention focused on the vehicles to see what happened. When we focus on something negative, we create a conflict in consciousness, or what is called *psychic entropy*. Whether experiencing depression, anger, fear or jealousy, what happens is that "attention turns to information that conflicts with goals; the discrepancy between what I desire and what is actually happening creates the inner tension" (Csikszentmihalyi, 1993, p. 36). These negative emotions take over consciousness, making it almost impossible to control our thoughts and actions.

Conversely, habits help us channel attention towards some goal. For example, in Western society there is Sunday morning church. Or, perhaps a habit you have embedded is the scanning or reading of books. If you are reading this text, then you have chosen to do so and set aside the time to do so. You are paying attention to—focusing upon—the content. Once you focus on a particular thought, a desire is triggered to turn this information into knowledge upon which to act (knowledge is the capacity, potential or actual, to take effective action). As an associative patterner, you are able to connect this thought to other thoughts important to you, and you will be able to use it in some particular way in the future, perhaps in service to a larger goal that would serve humanity.

In Buddhist meditation, the concept of *bare attention* is introduced to open up the mind. Bare attention is defined as "the clear and single-minded awareness of what actually happens *to* us and *in* us at the successive moments of perception" (Thera, 1962, p.30). The call is for us to pay attention to this very instant, the NOW, to what we are experiencing, separating our reactions from the actual events. This is the NOW reflected in Figure 25-1. Close your eyes for a moment and try this. It takes practice. As Epstein (1995, p. 110) describes, "just the *bare* facts, an *exact* registering, allowing things to speak for themselves as if seen for the first time ...." Note that while the "NOW" is a Phase 2 focus in our larger change model, it is also a prerequisite to achieving the creative leap.

When we focus our attention on something, actively experimenting and bringing to bear our mental faculties and feelings, thoughts emerge from within in terms of actions related to the focus of our attention. In other words, we are creating knowledge (the capacity to take effective action) in that area of focus. This leads us to the concept of intention.

Exploring Intention

As early as the hunter-gatherer, we see the beginnings of structure and dedicated efforts to meet objectives through intention, planned action, and individual roles (Bennet & Bennet, 2004). A choice of the self, intention relates to the world. Intention is the source with which we are doing something, the act or instance of mentally and emotionally setting a specific course of action or result, a determination to act in some specific way.

Searle (1983) believes that people have *mental states*, some conscious and some unconscious, which are intrinsically intentional. From his viewpoint, these are *subjective* states that are biologically based, that is, both caused by the operations of the brain and realized in the structure of the brain, with consciousness and intentionality "as much a part of human biology as digestion or the circulation of the blood" (Searle, 1983, p. ix). Intentionality is not a description of action, rather it is in the *structure of action*. We look to Searle's (1983, p. 1) theory of intentionality for a baseline definition: "Intentionality is the property of many mental states and events by which they are directed at or about or of objects and states of affairs in the world."

Thus, if you set an intention, it is an intention to *do something*. However, states such as those represented by beliefs, fears, hopes and desires insinuate intention, and they are *about something*. The relationship of intend and action has two schools of thought. The ideomotor model of human actions contends that human intentions are the starting point of the actions associated with those intentions (Prinz, 2005). Conversely, the sensory-motor model of human actions identifies sensory stimulation as the origination of actions.

Recall that the mind is an associative patterner that can be triggered by external events. While the direction of a belief would be from the mind to the world, the direction of a desire would be from the world to the mind, triggered by an external event. Does this insinuate a causal relationship between the external event and desire? Searle is careful with his response. He contends that causality is generally considered a natural relationship between world events, while *intentionality is not a natural phenomenon*, not part of the natural world, rather something transcendental, something that stands over or beyond (Searle, 1983). For purposes of this conversation, we defer to the concept of *deliberate intent*, that is, choice at the conscious level which, once direction is set, is supported at the unconscious level as we live out our day-to-day lives.

<<<<<<<<>>>>>>>

INSIGHT: **Deliberate intent occurs when choice is made and direction set at the conscious level, which is then supported at the unconscious level as we live out our day-to-day lives.**

<<<<<<<<>>>>>>>

Johnson (2007) agrees with the transcendental aspect of intent. She sees intent as residing in the depths of the soul, far beyond objectives, plans or strategies ... and even beyond hopes and expectations. We take pause with this comment to briefly look at the relationship between intention and expectation.

In the Law of Attraction writings, Abraham describes expectation in this fashion:

Expectation indicates the juncture between where you are and where you want to be. Where you want to be is your desire, and where you are is your Set-point or habit of thought. And, somewhere in there, is what we would call expectation. Expectation, whether it is wanted or unwanted, is a powerful point of attraction. Your expectation is always what you believe. But the word expectation does imply more what you are wanting than what you are not wanting. It is a more positive word than it is a negative word. But of course, you could expect negatively—and whatever you expect, you will get! (Abraham-Hicks, 2003)

As part of the Princeton Engineering Anomalies Research (PEAR) program active over a 25 plus year span, Jahn and Donne (2011) studied anomalous human/machine interactions, which focused on the effects of consciousness on physical systems and processes, and remote perception, the sending and receiving of information over distances. Consistent with Quantum biology proposed by Pribam (1998, 1993, 1991) and Popp (2002), they discovered that "the unconscious mind somehow had the capability of communicating with the subtangible physical world— the Quantum world of all possibility. This marriage of unformed mind and matter would assemble itself into something tangible in the manifest world" (McTaggart, 2002, p. 121). Thus, through the power of intent, of human wishing and will, we can create order. This touches the very essence of human creativity and "its capacity to create, to organize, even to heal" (McTaggart, 2002, p. 122).

While intention includes the *purpose and attitude* toward the *effect* of one's action, the outcome—with purpose implying having a goal in mind or the determination to achieve something, and attitude encompassing loyalty and dedication to achieving that goal—living (thinking and feeling) is not about the outcome. Rather, the focus is the continuous creation *process* of the relationship between intention and expectation. See Figure 25-2.

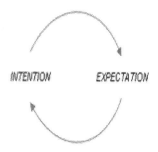

INTENTION   EXPECTATION

Figure 25-2. *The creation process of intention and expectation is continuous.*

In our discussion of emotions in Chapter 19/Part III, we quoted Willis (2012) as saying that in order to achieve balance to never expect more than events are going to be, thus learning to accept the way things are and eliminating disappointment. While certainly this approach will eliminate anything to be disappointed about, it also eliminates anything to be excited about, a direction to focus your attention and intention. We contend that it is better to have expectations equal to your vision of the future, that is, the way you want it to be. Thus, when your intention is set on this higher expectation, your energy will follow. A low expectation sets limits on what is being focused on. The limitation of **mundane expectations** causes a lack of development in both the self of the individual who sets the expectation and the selfs of those who experience the creation resulting from the expectation (MacFlouer, 2004-16). *Everyone lives the reality of what they expect.* (Abraham, May 7, 2003)

A large part of this book is focused on intentional or planned change, which is a personal and professional practice at every level of our society (Bennis et al., 1976). Intentional change arises from a conscious awareness, a focus, on a specific domain of knowledge and a vision of the current state and a desired future state. McWhinney (1997) says that conflict, the failure to manage differences in worldviews (multiple constructions of reality), is induced in all consciously chosen change. "Because conflict is present in every process of intentional change, all methods of change must deal with conflict, in some cases trivially, in others centrally." (p. 61) As such, this implies that as humans become conscious and through this consciousness act with intent on the world within which they live, they induce conflict. *This is part of the creative process, part of change, the conscious use of force(s) to create*. As Rollo May (1975, p. 100) writes in *The Courage to Create*:

Human freedom involves our capacity to pause between the stimulus and response and, in that pause, to choose the one response toward which we wish to throw our weight. The capacity to create ourselves, based upon this freedom, is inseparable from consciousness or self-awareness. (p. 100)

In developing his theory of intentional action and change, McWhinney (1997) discovered that in studying complex issues, the "more assiduously we pursue rational approaches the more deeply we will become mired in the anomalies obscured by our cultures" (p. 16). While our mental faculties are primary in the Western culture, they are not sufficient. As complex adaptive systems, hopefully by choice intelligent, the physical, emotional, mental and spiritual are entangled, and as they are brought into balance with an ever-expanding understanding of the past, present and future, provide us a platform for becoming co-creators of our reality.

The Power of Intention

Intent focuses energy and knowledge; knowledge is the "know how" and intent is *the power to focus the knowledge and maintain direction toward a sense of the anticipated future*. It may take the form of a declaration (often in the form of action), an assertion, a prayer, a cry for help, a wish, a visualization, a thought or an affirmation. (See the Addendum for an example in the life of the authors.) There is an outward movement of energy from the mind to the world and, as such, the motive of the intention is inextricably linked with the intent. This means *full involvement of the three planes through which we function*, with the mental and emotional taking the lead and physical actions—conscious and unconscious—following that lead.

Similarly, Abraham-Hicks (2005), who refers to setting intent as the power of attraction in terms of the vibrational energy beings that we are, says:

When you talk about what you want and why you want it, there's usually less resistance within you than when you talk about what you want and how you're going to get it. When you pose questions you don't have answers for, like how, where, when, who, it sets up a contradictory vibration that slows everything down.

In other words, the strength of intention can be reduced by the questioning of currently unanswerable issues brought into the mind by asking how, where, when, and who. The suggestion is to focus on the "what" and let the other aspects of the equation emerge.

According to Senge et al. (2004), *presencing,* or "letting come", which is consciously participating in a larger field for change, is a core capacity needed to access the field of the future. Intent is necessary for presencing. As Senge et al. (2004, p. 133) describe:

Genuine visions arise from crystallizing a larger intent, focusing the energy and sense of purposefulness that come from presencing ... Crystallizing intent requires being open to the larger intention and imaginatively translating the intuitions that arise into concrete images and visions that guide action.

For Senge, intent is based on purpose. Purpose is the reason for an organization to exist, that is, asking: *Why are we here?* (Senge, 1990) Thus, change is purposeful, and at the very core of change is learning, learning to do new things and learning to do things for a different reason (Bower, 2000). When this deep source of intention is tapped into, people experience synchronistic events. Synchronicity is a coincidence of events that seem related, yet with no obvious connection one to the other. (See the discussions on presencing and synchronicity in Chapter 22 as learning points along the way.)

Perhaps one of the most in-depth and focused experimentations on the effects of human intention on the properties of materials and what we describe as physical reality has been that pursued for the past 40 years by Dr. William Tiller of Stanford University. Tiller (2007) has demonstrated through repeated experimentation that it is possible to significantly change the properties of a physical substance by holding a clear intention to do so. Repeated both in the United States and Europe, Tiller's mind-shifting and potentially world-changing experiments began with using intent to change the acid/alkaline balance in purified water, which were followed by experiments with liver enzymes and the life cycle of the fruit fly. The ramifications of Tiller's experiments have the potential to impact every aspect of human life.[23-1]

What Tiller has discovered is that there are two unique levels of physical reality. The "normal level" of substance is the electric atom/molecule level, what most of us think of and perceive as the only physical reality, and consistent with what we have learned through Newtonian physics. However, a second level of substance exists that is a faster-than-light magnetic information wave level. While these two levels always interpenetrate each other, under "normal" conditions they do not interact; they are "uncoupled." Intention changes this condition, causing these two levels to interact, or move into a "coupled" state. Where humans are concerned, Tiller (2007) forwards that *what an individual intends for himself with a strong sustained desire is what that individual will eventually become.*

A fascinating finding by Tiller (2001) is that there is a threshold where conditioned state/space stabilizes. Tiller presents this in terms of a grid or lattice. Through intention space is conditioned, providing a *coherence* (consistency) in direction, which in turn creates an invisible structure in the environment akin to a scaffold that *holds the intention*. This invisible structure becomes part of a larger grid structure. This threshold is achieved through intention by the coupling of these two distinct fields.

While Tiller's descriptive language emerged from his own frame of reference, his results are not too different with what we are discovering about a Quantum Field. In Chapter 5/Part I we introduced the Observer Effect, recognition that the act of observing or measuring some parameter changes that parameter, that is, the observer affects the observed reality. This description emerged out of research by the Weizmann Institute of Science noting that, when observed, particles can also behave as waves (Buks et al., 1998). The import of this phenomenon shifts the focal point of the subject/object relationship back to the observer (as subject), which leads to the power of intent.

What can be learned from this work is that through science we are proving that *energy follows thought*. In a large sense, we've known this all along in terms of choosing sports in which we participate or when we choose to apply creative thought to produce innovation. More recently, from a neuroscience perspective, we have learned that the physical structure of the brain is changed by our thoughts, and, conversely, that the physical structure of our brain affects our thoughts. Thus, what we focus our attention on and the intent we set directly impacts *who we are and what we think*. Figure 25-3 is a graphic in support of "Conversations that Matter" focused on the power of intention.

<<<<<<<◇>>>>>>

INSIGHT: **Research on the power of intention reminds us that energy follows thought.**

<<<<<<<◇>>>>>>

McWhinney (1997) says that two or more realities play a distinct role in defining and directing change. He specifically calls out the *innate* reality and the *intended* reality, which are consistent with the concepts of the current state and intended future state. As he describes,

> Change takes place in the movement from a position in reality that is assumed to be the basic reality in the direction determined by the reality of *intention*. The *innate* arises within (is defined by) the reality that the person or organization takes as given; the *intended* uses the logic and constructs of the reality toward which one moves by choice. Thus the two (or more) realities that are present in effecting a change or solution play distinct roles—one defining, one directing. (p. 66)

In organizational and management literature, Bennet and Bennet (2004) identify intent as one of the four forces that directly influence an organization's success. These four forces are the force of direction, the force of intent, the force of knowledge and the force of knowing. These forces are aligned when:

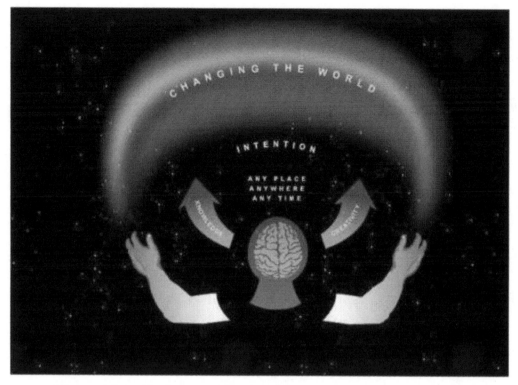

Figure 25-3. *The limits of the mind/brain are those we set upon it.*

Intention is a tool for creation.

* Direction is set and understood.

* Intent moves the organization or individual in the desired direction.

* Knowledge ensures effective actions follow intent and direction.

* Knowing improves knowledge, bolsters intent, and signals the organization or individual whether the actions and directions are on track.

(See the end of Chapter 2/Part I on the forces we act upon.) Indeed, these same four forces are at play in the self.

Bringing Them Together

In our normal everyday life, as we move in and out of familiar environments and situations, we are in a relatively low state of attention, and intention takes the form of anticipated outcome in response to our thoughts, words and actions. We are certainly taking in the sights, sounds and smells around us, at least unconsciously. Then, something occurs. It might be an unexpected incident, or maybe hearing a beautiful passage of music, or an unexpected election result, or watching a dramatic moment in the theatre or at a movie, or some thought triggering the excitement of possibilities. *You are at a point of peak intensity, fully attending to the instant.* And in that instant, a desire may emerge to do something with this; perhaps share that music with a loved one, or perhaps take that creative idea and act on it, or become an advocate to right some wrong. This is the birthing of intent.

It was in his search for a collective consciousness that Roger Nelson discovered that the intensity of attention and intention impacted the ability of consciousness to order or influence the external world. For example, he discovered **a positive correlation between the size and intensity of a crowd and the resulting effect**. As McTaggart (2002, p. 205) describes, "What appeared to be happening was that when attention focused the waves of individual minds on something similar, a type of group Quantum 'superradiance' occurred which had a physical effect." This *superradiance* clearly occurred **only** when there were *intense moments of like-mindedness*. Further, when Nelson explored sacred sites of Native American tribes, he discovered that there was a high degree of what he called *resonating consciousness*, whether or not a group was present. (Nelson, 1994, 1997) (Nelson et al., 1996, 1998) This is the conditioned space of Tiller, and consistent with enough thought flowing in the same direction in a Quantum Field for a shift to occur.

As we can see, attention and intention are interrelated, and both are necessary to balance current priorities with future opportunities and guide you in your personal Intelligent Social Change Journey toward intelligent activity. Your thoughts and actions gravitate toward what you pay attention to; and what you intend requires your attention. In the words of a popular Broadway song from some year ago, *you can't have one without the other.*

Questions for Reflection:

Is your attention focused on priorities and how often do you allow distractions to interfere with this focus?

Do you allow attention to become too focused and therefore miss opportunities?

How do your intentions influence the expectations of you and others?

Are your intentions and expectations appropriately aligned?

Chapter 26
The Mental Fabric

SUBTOPICS: Critical Thinking ... Thought ... Conceptual Thinking ... Connecting to Theory ... From Relativism to Heuristics

FIGURE: **26-1**. Changing our thoughts changes the structure of our brain, and the structure of the brain affects our thoughts ... **26-2**. The relationship among logic, concepts and heuristics.

TOOLS: **26-1**. Situational Backtalk ... **26-2**. Activating New Resources

The abilities to control our attention, remember, abstract, and reason are what sets the human apart from other animals. It is with these abilities that humans have built cultural systems such as language, religion, art and science. As individuals, organizations, countries or a global world, we require ordered systems of rules to engage in intelligent activity. At the highest levels, this is what we call civilization. As Csikszentmihalyi (1993, p. 41) says:

> It is good to have rational, logical structures by which to order thoughts and actions. Much of what we call civilization consists of attempts at rationalizing life, so that actions can be predictable and reasonable. But civilization is a fragile construction that needs constant protection and care. Without it, the mind will not behave logically.

However, it requires more than being logical. Is war logical? Is the economy of today logical? Csikszentmihalyi argues that rational behavior cannot happen by itself, that creating and preserving ordered systems of rules requires the investment of *psychic* energy, to which all people have access. This psychic energy takes the form of intuition, empathy, wisdom and creativity, a changing part of the human evolutionary process.

> We must foster **intuition to anticipate changes before they occur; empathy to understand that which cannot be clearly expressed; wisdom to see the connection between apparently unrelated events; and creativity to discover new ways of defining problems**, new rules that will make it possible to adapt to the unexpected [emphasis added]. (Csikszentmihalyi, 1993, p. 42)

While we agree, it is critical to recognize that *it takes the mind and development of our mental faculties to create knowledge*, that is, to use our intuition to *effectively act on and with the world.* We are mental beings. Neurons fire not only in our minds, but throughout our body, with connective tissue to all parts of our body. For example, we have an intelligent heart, which contains a large number of neurons. While often we are focused on the material world or our emotional projections and responses, we are mostly mentally focused. Everything about mental work can be applied to the physical world. *Life is more about how we think than how we feel,* developing our mental plane and improving our mental field, with our thought directly tied to our actions. It is only then that we are ready to tap into the higher energy of the intuitional field and, as co-creator, have the ability to bring those ideas into our current reality.

Developing our mental faculties and tapping into the intuitional field in support of the creative leap are part of our developmental Journey. Complex adaptive systems cannot stay in a state of stasis. They must move forward or fade away, and moving forward means changing. As James (1996, p. 23) says so eloquently, "Our brains must adapt to our changing environment. I believe that our current assignment is evolutionary, nothing less than the remaking of a man and woman into a more civilized form than our ancestors." We *can* change our minds, and we now know that changing our thoughts, in turn, changes the structure of our brain, and that affects our thoughts. Thus, the more we think, the more we can think. Our very thoughts are a powerful instrument of change!

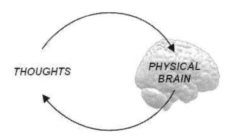

Figure 26-1. *Changing our thoughts changes the structure of our brain, and the structure of the brain affects our thoughts.*

Critical Thinking

Critical thinking, which includes the integrative competencies of systems thinking, complexity thinking and knowing, as well as Knowledge Capacities introduced in Chapter 21/Part III, provide ways for individuals to make sense of and evaluate the value of data and information, whether informational or opinion-based. In critical thinking, we are always searching for larger concepts, larger truths. Reconstruction, assessment, and evaluation are used to discern the information; to determine its status as deductive, inductive, or irrational; and to judge its accuracy and reliability. Deductive reasoning is a logical progression, with the conclusion based on multiple premises assumed to be true. Inductive reasoning starts with an observation or question, and then, by examining related issues, tries to figure out a theory. Both are involved with the search for truth.

<<<<<<<<>>>>>>>

INSIGHT: **The more we think, the more we can think. Our thought is a powerful instrument of change.**

<<<<<<<<>>>>>>>

The intent of critical thinking is to allow individuals to form their own opinions of information resources based on an open-minded evaluation of the features and components of those resources by using, for example, problem-solving skills. These skills would include listening, considering other points of view, negotiating, and evaluating one's own mental models. Critical thinkers consider not only the data and information, but the context of the resource, questioning the clarity and strength of reasoning behind the resource, identifying assumptions and values, recognizing points of view and attitudes, and evaluating conclusions and actions.

With the advent of the Internet, and the increase in the amount of data and information available, critical thinking becomes essential to functioning in the world. Halpern (1996) states:

> [Critical thinking] is used to describe thinking that is purposeful, reasoned and goal directed—the kind of thinking involved in solving problems, formulating inferences, calculating likelihoods, and making decisions when the thinker is using skills that are thoughtful and effective for the particular context and type of thinking task. (p. 117).

This includes meta-thinking, or thinking about our own thinking and decision processes in order to continually improve them.

Further, critical thinking includes, but is not limited to:

* Open-mindedness.

* Engagement in the constructive challenging of ideas and concepts to make balanced decisions and extract insights.

* An awareness that groups and other individuals can shape issues and may have their own agendas and interests in mind, and the ability to identify those agendas and interests.

* The ability to make detailed observations, question, analyze, make connections, and try to make sense of a situation, a set of behaviors, or a single piece of information out of context.

* Recognizing that there is no single right or wrong way to interpret information, but many different ways, and the ability to explore each interpretation in terms of its strengths and weaknesses.

****

TOOL 26-1: Situational Backtalk.

The knowing of a situation is a unique mental skill. Situational backtalk is a tool for perceiving or sensing surroundings to gain information. Recall that all knowledge is situation dependent and context sensitive. The back talk of the situation refers to both the situation *and* the context, that is, shifting your framework to look from the point of view of the situation, and taking into account the people, relationships, networks, events, culture and structure.

In systems language, you would identify the system in trouble and its subsystems, exploring the relationships among these systems and the state of boundary conditions, etc. In complexity language, you might look for and explore feedback loops, emergent properties, nonlinearities, time delays, trends and patterns, events and processes, sinks and sources, and so forth. (See Bennet & Bennet, 2013, for an in-depth treatment of decision-making in The New Reality.)

No matter what language best makes sense to you as the idea generator, the decision-maker, the bottom line is to look at (and listen to) the current situation at hand, not to rely on the way things have been done in the past. This is a rethinking of the way to look at the world emerging from the ability to *listen with humility*. (See the TOOL: Humility in Chapter 4/Part I.)

If you can't see the world from the perspective of others, you cannot understand others; if you can't see the world, it's very hard to know how to cope with it. (Source unknown.)

STEP (1): Be sure you have read all the reports and/or support papers on the situation or incident on which you choose to focus. Look at and understand the importance of any available pictures, memos, emails, etc.

STEP (2): Disconnect yourself from all distractions, surrounding yourself with any artifacts of the situation at hand. This may include situating yourself physically in the place where an event occurred, or having pictures, reports and/or support papers, etc. spread out in front of you.

STEP (3): Physically close your eyes and take several deep breaths, relaxing your body.

STEP (4): Starting at the very beginning, that is, *before* the situation or incident occurred, slowly re-create the situation or incident in your head. If you need to check the materials around you for details, open your eyes and do so, then start the process again from STEP (3), adding additional details as perceived.

STEP (5): When you are comfortable with your re-creation of the process, begin at STEP (3) again, only this time with your eyes open and taking notes as you re-create the process in your head. As you move through the process, every time there is a change of some nature briefly close your eyes and look at the details surrounding that change. Then open your eyes and record those details in your notes.

STEP (6): Review your notes, paying special attention to the details surrounding points of change. If clarification is needed, repeat STEP (5) with a focus on those details. *Ask:* What can be learned from the surroundings? Are there any items that may have had a strong impact on this situation?

STEP (7): Record the names and/or descriptions of other people involved in the situation or incident.

STEP (8): Focusing on one individual at a time, take a few minutes to think about—and write down in your notes—a general description of how each individual may see the world differently than you. Then move through your re-creation and try to see how that individual, *through the lens of their unique world view*, would perceive the situation. Make notes as insights emerge. Do this step for each individual involved in the situation or incident. *Then ask:* Which ones had a strong impact on this situation? What was that impact? What are the relationships among these individuals? Which ones are affected by this situation?

STEP (9): Step back and connect the dots, that is, bring all of this together. *Ask:* What new has been learned by this exercise? How can this benefit the situation? What are the necessary next steps that should be taken? And when you are ready, ACT.

****

Thought

Thought is a combination of choices, connecting a choice to other choices previously made, and affecting further choices by limiting or reducing those choices. Thought is heavily influenced by the unconscious. As Tallis (2002) forwards,

Virtually every aspect of mental life is connected in some way with mental events and processes that occur below the threshold of awareness…the profound importance of unconscious procedures, memories, beliefs, perceptions, knowledge, and emotions is recognized universally. (p. 182)

<<<<<<<◇>>>>>>>

INSIGHT: **Thought is a combination of choices, connecting a choice to other choices previously made, and affecting further choices by limiting or reducing those choices**.

<<<<<<<◇>>>>>>>

In the early days of evolution, humans did not think as well as they do today. As suggested by the structure of the brain, there would have been thought using narrow basic concepts and a small number of thought forms, although no doubt there were a few universal concepts about basic things like survival, food and the forms in the surrounding environment. (See the discussion of thought forms in Chapter 22.)

There are two levels of mental thought: logic, built on cause-and-effect (lower mental thought), and concepts that emerge from patterns (higher mental thought). Logic uses the past-present-future, in that order, with the primary focus on the past, and if you put everything together it supports itself, consistent with experience and with no conflicting information coming in through the senses. Lower mental thought begins with examples from experience, bringing examples together that result in new information. Through this knowledge from experience, the mind looks at how these examples are different and how they are similar.

But analysis alone cannot create concepts to challenge, and interact with, the environment. It is through grouping, joining and integrating these samples, the mind creates formulas (higher order patterns and their relationships, or concepts) for how things work together. These patterns now make it easier to recognize other examples, even when they occur at different places and times (bringing space and time closer together), and thus the search for ever-larger patterns (a higher level of truth) continues.

The other day one author was noting the high diversity of road signage, and how particular signs are designed in terms of logic and others are more conceptual in nature. Examples of street signs based on logic are: "Click it or ticket"; "Speed Limit 15 MPH When Flashing"; or "Slippery When Wet". These are very much cause-and-effect related; if this, then that. Examples of street signs that are more conceptual in nature are: "Curvy Road"; "Railroad Crossing"; "Construction Ahead"; or "Children at Play". Clearly, all four of these concepts mean to reduce speed, proceed with caution, and be prepared to stop. Thus, we acknowledge that, at least to some extent, both lower and higher mental thinking are necessary to navigate everyday life. Looking at these simple examples in terms of knowledge, the signage more conceptual in nature requires a higher level of context, an understanding of relationships among things. In this example that would most likely attain through experience in driving.

Conceptual Thinking

Let's explore conceptual thinking a bit deeper. In *The Tao of Personal Leadership*, Dreher (1995) writes:

> To succeed in any field, we must look to those skills that make us fully human: the ability to learn continuously throughout life, to communicate with others, to come up with creative new solutions, and to deepen our understanding, looking to the larger patterns within and around us. (Templeton, 2002, p. 256)

When we are able to discover those patterns in life, we have moved into the higher mental thought of conceptual thinking. (Conceptualizing was introduced as a modality of change in Chapter 9/Part II.) From the viewpoint of conceptual thinking, we are looking for logical examples that demonstrate the concepts and the relationship among concepts that are emerging in the mind. As we discover examples that lie outside of a concept, the concept is no longer true and must be shifted to include these new examples, ever asking *Why?* and expanding our level of truth. See Tool 24-1: Truth Searching.

As can be seen, upper mental thought (conceptual) builds on lower mental thought (logic). This is a shared process; the more examples that can be brought to bear, the greater the potential to find a higher level of truth. When these examples are shared in a cooperative and collaborative fashion, there is a balancing of thought and perceptions that occurs and an expansion of consciousness.

<<<<<<<<◇>>>>>>>

INSIGHT: **The more examples that can be brought to bear, the greater the potential to find a higher truth.**

<<<<<<<<◇>>>>>>>

It is more difficult to recognize our mental senses than our physical senses. For example, when you look at another individual what do you see? A first response might be descriptive characteristics of the individual and the backdrop against which you are seeing them. But we now know that we sense through three planes simultaneously, and that any emotional tags connected with that person or situation will be connected to that visual and "felt". Because the mental thoughts are not only past memories but very much connected to the NOW, and of an emergent quality, and because the conscious mind is of a linear nature, information being processed by our mental plane is harder to separate out. Yet, it is very much there.

Concepts as formulas facilitate rapid processing of large amounts of information coming in through all our senses on all three planes (physical, emotional and mental). Rather than addressing each sense separately, these formulas help build a predictive approach to accurately determine the outcome of various actions and interactions. Discernment and discrimination—representing the ability to identify and choose what is of value, and the equally difficult ability to toss aside that which is not of value— enable our thinking to challenge a concept and try to apply it to different situations. For example:

> *Within a specific domain of knowledge, when this action is taken within this situation and context, this is what is going to happen.*

OR, as a higher-order pattern,

> *Within a specific domain of knowledge, when this **type** of action is taken within this **type** of situation and context, this is the **type** of response that will occur.*

In the latter case, *type* refers to sameness in identity, although this may be a loose and popular identity (Butler, 1906), that is, similar. Each example would represent a token of this type. This sameness in identity may mean that two things are different parts of some wider unity that includes both, or they are both different members of the same class of things, or they are different parts of a resemblance structure, or they fall under the same predicate or concept (Armstrong, 1989). While we do not hold with the *Realist* belief that two things of the same type are strictly identical, simultaneously, we do not agree with the *Nominalist* belief that there are no strict identities reaching across different tokens of type. Further, we disagree with John Locke's (2016) description that all existing things are particulars. In other words, **there *are* universals, albeit these universals take the form of heuristics.**

Universals theory looks at resemblances of identity in terms of properties and relations. From these properties and their relationships, natural classes of things emerge. We add the term conditions to this description of universals, and defer to Armstrong's (1989) description that universals are the substance of the world, with substance something that is capable of independent existence. As a path to understanding the role of universals in the laws of nature, we look to *Natural Class* theory, which includes individuals, first-order tokens and classes of higher order (with definite truth conditions). The well-established discipline of *Set* theory supports the concepts of classes that have definite truth conditions. Further, Natural Class theory requires *relations among* individuals and classes of individuals, with the naturalness of the class a property of the class.

While there are certainly solid arguments against the acceptance of universals, we agree with Armstrong (1989) that (1) the less than exact resemblance of universals is analyzable in terms of an incomplete identity of universals, which themselves are universals, and (2) that there are irreducibly higher-order relationships holding *between* universals (Armstrong, 1989), both of which help substantiate the existence of universals.

While all this sounds a bit complex, as demonstrated in the paragraphs above, and by way of a quick summary, we are using our conceptual thought to create changes in our interactions in a continuous loop of discovery: creating formulas from the examples we perceive, applying those formulas, discovering more examples through searching out similarities and differences in those formulas, and continuously shifting and changing the formulas to find a higher truth, that is, discovering the nature of nature in terms of heuristics. **In this journey of discovery, we are using our mental faculties to co-evolve with—and co-create—the world within which we interact**, and we are inviting you along on the journey. The number of concepts that we create is directly related to the number and level of interactions that we have with our environment.

Hawkins (2002) says that for an individual to reach the stage of functioning primarily from reason requires a level of consciousness of 400 (the level of Reason) or above. As a comparative point, Hawkins examples Freud, Einstein and Descartes, who calibrate at 499 (the level of humanism). However, there are innate difficulties that reason brings with it. As Hawkins (2002, p. 281) describes: "But reason, so vulnerable to loss of perspective through self-absorption, has in the long run never provided man with any solid moral, or even intellectual, certainty. Again and again it has, to the contrary, led from the chaos of ignorance to an equally baffling cerebral maze." This has resulted in the arrogance ("I'm right, you're wrong, and I'm not listening) seen in individuals and organizations achieving high development of the mental faculties without a spiritual counterbalance.

Taking a consilience approach, we agree with Minsky when he suggests that the successful self has a *colossal collection* of different approaches to deal with different situations and contexts. As Minsky (2006, p. 6) describes:

If you "understand" something in only one way, then you scarcely understand it at all—because when you get stuck, you'll have nowhere to go. But if you represent something in several ways, then when you get frustrated enough, you can switch among different points of view, until you find one that works for you!

This "switching" can be done consciously (see Chapter 19/Part III on Knowledge Capacities), or it might originate from the unconscious. For example, Middlebrook (1974) says an individual is not a single self, but rather many selves, which shift and change as the individual moves from situation to situation. *We become what the situation demands*. We use the terminology "sub-personalities" to describe these sets of chunked knowledge that come to the fore when they are needed. This is addressed extensively in Bennet et al. (2015a). Brown (1979) offers that sub-personalities are "patterns of feelings, thoughts, behaviors, perceptions, postures and ways of moving which tend to coalesce in response to various recurring situations in life." The more an individual experiences similar situations, the stronger these sub-personalities become, eventually quite capable of driving actions, which, when recognized, we may be unable to change by a conscious decision or act of will. As Rowen describes, this experience of being *taken over* by a part of ourselves "lasts as long as the situation lasts—perhaps a few minutes, perhaps an hour, perhaps a few hours—and then changes by itself when we leave this situation and go into a different one" (Rowan, 1990, p. 7).

Minsky (2006, p. 24) says that "Each of our various Ways to Think results from turning certain resources on while turning certain others off—thus changing the way one's brain behaves." Resources refers to structures and processes ranging from perception to action. Ways to think include self-conscious emotions, self-reflective thinking, reflective thinking, deliberative thinking, learned reactions and instinctive reactions. Note that Minsky includes self-conscious emotions as a way of thinking. He argues that emotional states are not that different from what we call thinking, that they are certain *ways* of thinking, and that these different ways of thinking provide us resources that enable us to switch our thinking when necessary.

****

TOOL 26-2: ACTIVATING NEW RESOURCES

Next time you have a problem facing you, try one of these approaches to change your resources. The *Ways to Think* below are some of those suggested by Minsky (2008, pp. 226-228), with our explications.

Reasoning by Analogy. Connecting to a similar problem in the past, note the patterns of activity and relationships among activities, and apply those patterns to the new situation. Remember, knowledge is situation dependent and context sensitive. The learning is in understanding the patterns and relationships in one situation and being able to extrapolate those to another situation.

Dividing and Conquering. A larger problem may be made up of a number of smaller problems, which are easier to resolve. A corollary to this in complexity thinking is to simplify. A solution to part of the problem may serve as a stepping-stone for resolving the larger problem.

Reformulating. Look at the issue through different lenses. Minsky (2008) suggests looking for more relevant information. As he examples, "We often do this by making a verbal description—and then 'understanding' it in some different way!" (p. 227)

Planning. This is a goal setting and/or scenario planning approach and exploring how they affect each other. Working toward sub-goals and exploring scenarios helps build an understanding of what actions to take. See Tool 16-2: Scenario Building/Part III.

Elevating and Demoting. When there are too many details bogging you down, try thinking about the situation in more general terms. Move from specifics to generalities and look at the problem from that viewpoint. Conversely, if your problem is too vague, then try making it more concrete by adding detail.

Self-reflection. Address questions to your self. *Ask:* Why is this problem so hard? What might we be doing wrong? How might we make this easier? What can we do differently? Who might we ask to partner in solving this problem?

Logical contradiction. Take the opposite stance (this is a favorite, and is similar to the Knowledge Capacity of Reversal in Chapter 21/Part III). As Minsky (2008, p. 228) says, "Try to prove that your problem cannot be solved, and then look for a flaw in that argument." What fun! A related approach is to set up a debate. This is the inducing resonance approach to engaging tacit knowledge. (See Appendix D.)

External Representations. Writing ideas down—making notes and/or creating records, or building a PowerPoint presentation—helps organize and keep track of your thoughts. And the very act of creating diagrams and graphics helps in understanding the relationships among elements of a problem. Even if you don't find a solution, you will better understand the problem and be able to articulate it to others.

Imagining. Use your imagination to engage the problem. When we imagine we aren't taking any risks. And as you are imagining, *Ask:* How does it feel? Following are three specific ways to use your imagination (and feel free to imagine other ways that would be fun!)

(1) Wishful Thinking. Imagine all the resources (including time) that you want. What would you do? If you can't imagine it, reformulate the problem. Try simulating actions inside your mental models.

(2) Impersonation. Imagine you are someone else—a teacher, a scientist, a factory worker. *Ask:* What does this problem look like from this viewpoint? What actions would make sense?

(3) Storytelling. Imagine you are a storyteller in the future, telling the story about this problem and how it was solved. Take your time and enjoy the process. If you get stuck, imagine an adult or child asking a simple question, and then continue on until you get to the end, whatever you imagine that end to be. Above all, have fun!

****

Connecting to Theory

Fortunately, the mind, as a small piece of the self functioning within time and space, has been busy developing an internal mental structure to map and make sense of the external environment in which we interact. This hierarchal, nested structure, built by the cortex, is our perceived model of the real world (Hawkins, 2004), with this world view providing internal context to the situation at hand based on our life-long observations, experiences and reflection in terms of the strength of our personal meaning and essence. Thus, we are not limited by the observable context of the situation at hand, what we perceive as external reality. Through complexing (the learning and creation process) new possibilities can—and will if unbounded by limited paradigms—emerge. As this internal mapping of the external reality continues to shift and change, it provides the basis for our personal theory of how the world works.

As introduced in Chapter 7/Part II, a theory is considered a set of statements and/or principles that explain a group of facts or phenomena to guide action or assist in comprehension or judgment (American Heritage Dictionary, 2006; Bennet & Bennet, 2010a). Theories reflect higher-order patterns, that is, not the facts themselves, but rather the basic source of recognition and meaning of the broader patterns. While a written theory could be considered information, when understood such that it offers the potential to, or is used by, a decision-maker to create and guide effective action, it would be considered knowledge. Further, while in its incoming form it is Knowledge (Informing), when complexed with other information in the mind of the decision-maker to make decisions and guide action, it becomes part of the process that is Knowledge (Proceeding). As introduced above in the discussion about connecting conceptual thinking and examples, there is a symbiotic relationship between theory and practice that cannot be over-emphasized (Bennet & Bennet, 2014). This explains why examples excite theories, and why when we explore a theory we are always looking for examples.

<<<<<<<◇>>>>>>>

INSIGHT: **Examples excite theories, and when we explore a theory we are always looking for examples.**

<<<<<<<◇>>>>>>>

Recall that the mind is an associative patterner, an underlying assumption throughout this book. This bears review so that we can use it in the context of this chapter. Associative patterning is the process of the intermixing or complexing of external patterns (information from the perceived external environment) with internal patterns (memories) to create recognition, sense-making, meaning and, ultimately, knowledge. We learn by changing incoming signals (images, sounds, smells, sensations of the body) into patterns (of the mind and within the brain) that we identify with specific external concepts or objects. These incoming neuronal patterns have internal associations with other internal patterns that represent (to varying degrees of fidelity) the corresponding associations in the external world. The process of complexing creates new neural patterns that may represent understanding, meaning, and the anticipation of the consequences of actions, or, in other words, knowledge. Thus, the creation of knowledge is unique to each individual, with the interpretation and meaning of incoming patterns being very much a function of preexisting patterns in the brain. *This is the continuous process of creation.*

The associative patterning of the mind is supported by the way the mind stores past events or memories. The brain does not store exact replicas, but rather the meaning or essence of incoming information, that is, information meaningful to the individual mind/brain. This information is stored in invariant form as patterns of neuronal firings, their synaptic connections and the strengths between the synaptic spaces. By storing memories in invariant form, individuals are able to apply memories in situations that are similar but not identical to previous experiences.

When a new experience or situation is encountered, the brain tries to match it with past experiences and then identifies probable outcomes. A series of these similar experience-outcome events generates a belief, frame of reference, or mind-set that drives our decisions. When not limited by personal paradigms, the brain also puts past experiences together, coupled with new possibilities based on current data and the creation of new possibilities, to generate possible new scenarios for the future. The core pattern (a pattern of patterns) has the possibility of both hierarchical and associative relationships to other patterns.

While the associative patterning process is focused on the activity occurring within the mind/brain, it is incoming information picked up by the senses that is being associated. Changes occur in the brain through enriched environments, that is, when the surroundings contain many interesting and thought-provoking ideas, pictures, books, statues, plant life, etc. In response to these environments, thicker cortices are created, there are larger cell bodies, and dendritic branching in the brain is more extensive. The richer the environment, the more potential stimulation of your creative juices.

Further, as reiterated throughout this book, people are in continuous, two-way interaction with those around them and the brain is continuously changing in response. As Cozolino (2006, p. 3) says:

As a species, we are just waking up to the complexity of our own brains, to say nothing of how brains are linked together. We are just beginning to understand that we have evolved as social creatures and that all of our biologies are interwoven.

Significant social relationships stimulate learning and knowledge creation and shape the brain (Bennet et al., 2015b). The brain actually seeks out an affectively attuned "other" for learning. Continuous creativity means continuous exposure to a broad range of knowledge and experiences—*places and people and thoughts in resonance with who we choose to be.*

<<<<<<◇>>>>>>

INSIGHT: **The brain seeks out an affectively attuned "other" for learning and searches for places, people and thoughts in resonance with who we choose to be.**

<<<<<<◇>>>>>>

As we now recognize, we can "think" with a physical, emotional and/or mental focus, that is, from the physical, emotional and mental planes utilizing and combining information coming through our senses on each of those planes. However, the *nature of that thought* is quite different, dependent on the priority and combination of this focus. For example, if the thought is all about "me" (inward-focused having to do with enjoyment, control or wanting) then that thinking is primarily from the physical and emotional viewpoints and, most likely, being driven by the personality. Recall that the primary purpose of the personality is to ensure survival, avoid pain, and seek out pleasure (see Chapter 4/Part I). Along with the inward focus that occurs when we think too much of ourselves, comes an obstruction to further sense-making. This is because the senses nourish our interaction with the world. Their whole purpose for being is to process information to various degrees and in various forms to support our freedom and choices of action—our learning experiences. This is another reminder that we are a verb, not a noun, experiencing and learning, growing our self, and expanding our consciousness.

Thought, *something that we make up*, is focused from the mental plane. As Walsch (2009, p. 66) explains,

> [Thought] often bears no relationship to ultimate reality, it often bears no relationship to observed reality, yet it often does bear a relationship to distorted reality. In fact, it often *creates* it.

(See Figure 24-1 in Chapter 24) This is consistent with the power of thought and our role as co-creators of reality (see Chapter 23).

As introduced in Chapter 24, as we move from logic to conceptual thinking, thought has more truth and becomes more powerful. This is because when we focus from the mental plane we are closer to what is real versus unreal; we can perceive things and the relationships among them much more clearly than from the viewpoint of the physical plane, which is more focused on the past (memories) such that time and space are separated. Conversely, from the viewpoint of the mental plane, focusing thought in the now while using patterns from the past to extrapolate into the future, time and space are interchangeable; time has a full dimension and can be fully defined (MacFlouer, 2004-16).

While this is addressed more fully in Chapter 16/Part III, let's briefly explore this relationship of thinking with time. Our conscious thought is a linear, successive stream. We continuously chunk small bits of information together, bit after bit, seeking some coherence and order. This is time. As Wilber (1993, p. 84) says, "time is nothing more, nothing less, than thought's successive way of viewing the world." When we think with a mental focus, we both reach into the past and project into the future. The mind controls energies at a greater level. As introduced in the Introduction to Part II, the *causes* of things in the past reach into the future; the *effects* of things come from the past. The mind holds time in place and can flip from the past to the future at will, taking a pattern from the past and extrapolating it into the future almost instantaneously. Since these patterns form the basis of concepts, they are also expanding the level of truth as, in the course of living, additional working examples are identified and fit into—and/or expand—those concepts. (See Chapter 24 on the search for truth.)

From Relativism to Heuristics

In Chapter 2/Part I we first talked about the relativism of knowledge, that is, that knowledge was context-sensitive and situation-dependent. As a general definition, relativism is the belief that concepts such as right and wrong, goodness and badness, or truth and falsehood are not absolute, but change from culture to culture and situation to situation. In the human, relativism begins with emotional thinking, with something first felt and associated with some sort of imagery (MacFlouer, 2004-16), after which mental thought is created to rationalize or justify the thought and feeling, and/or the actions taken on the basis of that thought and feeling. Another part of relativism deals with comparison, comparing how we feel with how we think, which is relative in terms of the things about which we have strong desires.

Recall from the discussion above that mental thinking is *structured thinking with causal aspects*, that is, it deals with the past, present and future, giving us an understanding of time in relationship to activity. Without this element of time we can't understand logic or truth. Yet truth requires more than logic. Truth is discerned by *joining concepts with effects*, and discovering examples of the concepts so that one is supported by the other. The concept explains *why* the examples are doing what they are doing, and the examples *demonstrate application* of the concept. Further, when this understanding is shared with others, that is, when others, looking from their diverse frames of reference are able to recognize the truth of the concept through the examples, then truth is further validated. As introduced in Chapter 24, truth is the highest virtue of the mental plane.

When we move through the structured (and rigid) logic of lower mental thinking to conceptual thinking, and develop the ability to share the truth of that concept with others, we engage additional world views and frames of reference. No longer limited to one set of physical/emotional/mental plane viewpoints, we have collectively expanded our capacity and capability to effectively act in the world.

Relativistic thought interferes with truthful mental thinking (MacFlouer, 2004-16). This is because the focus is on the specific situation and context in order to make logical sense of what is happening, thus making it difficult to *look beyond* the situation at hand for a larger truth. Further, the framework from which we look is self-consistent and confined to the individual; rarely do we purposefully stop and try to sense from other people's perspectives, even if we have the capability to do so. Thus, there is a tendency to be *narrow-minded and prejudiced* in various ways, reacting with the belief that we are right and everyone else is wrong, and trying to force others to behave and feel the same way we do. See the discussion of egotism and arrogance in Chapter 4/Part I.

There are conditions that reflect vast differences in the way the Universe functions that are *not* relativistic in nature, yet *ecologically rational*, that is, "adapted to the structure of the information in the environment in which they are used to make decisions" (Gigerenzer et al., 1999, p. vii). These conditions are heuristics, rules of thumb used to guide actions. More specifically, they are criteria, methods or principles used to decide a course of action among various available alternatives in order to achieve a goal. As Gigerenzer et al. (1999, p. 22) explain, "The function of heuristics is not to be coherent. Rather, their function is to make reasonable, adaptive inferences about the real social and physical world given limited time and knowledge."

Figure 26-1 depicts the relationship among logic, concepts and heuristics. Note that understanding concepts builds on logical thinking, and that heuristics could not be understood without conceptual thinking. As we move through logic into concepts and heuristics there is increased clarity of mental sensing and an increased level of truth.

One author's first awareness of the power of heuristics came through the work of Dave Snowden, a compelling figure in the field of Knowledge Management, both brilliant and verbose, who uses the example of a flock of birds flying south. The reverse "V" formation reduces the wind factor; when the leading bird tires he falls back and another moves into that place and so forth, with a continuous rotation occurring. This example led the author to look for other examples in nature, of which there are many!

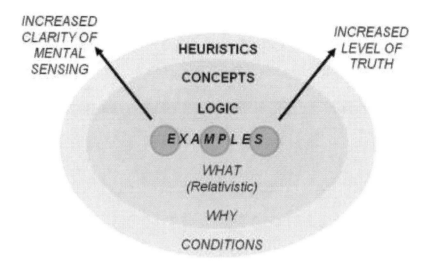

Figure 26-2. *The relationship among logic, concepts and heuristics.*

Heuristics represent a compromise between discriminating between good and bad choices, and the need for simple criteria to do so (Pearl, 1984). While based on learned experience, heuristics emerge from the natural order of things, and **may very well represent the Universals** introduced in the beginning of this chapter.

In the next chapter we take a closer look at wisdom.

Questions for Reflection:

How are you developing your mental fabric in order to operate at a Phase 3 level?

How well do you facilitate critical thinking conversations to refine priorities?

What heuristics do you apply as part of your decision-making?

Chapter 27
Moving into Wisdom

SUBTOPICS: INTELLIGENT ACTIVITY ... CONNECTING KNOWLEDGE AND WISDOM ... THE WISDOM OF MENTAL DISCIPLINE ... FINAL THOUGHTS

FIGURE: 27-1. THE INTEGRATION AND BALANCE OF DEVELOPMENT OF OUR MENTAL FACULTIES AND DEEPENING CONNECTIONS EMERGES AS WISDOM AND MANIFESTS AS INTELLIGENT ACTIVITY.

TOOL: 27-1. LEARNING FROM YOUR INNER SELF

The highest part of mental thought is wisdom. Representing *completeness and wholeness of thought*, wisdom is universally a lofty consideration, and too often we sense that it eludes us. The more we seek it, the more we understand that it comes through experiencing and learning, and brings with it the desire to learn more.

Wisdom occurs when activity matches the choices that are made and structured concepts are intelligently acted upon, thus **directly connecting wisdom to intelligent action**. As this relationship is described in *Urantia* (1955, p. 908):

> Knowledge can be had by education, but wisdom, which is indispensable to true culture, can be secured only through experience and by men and women who are innately intelligent. Such a people are able to learn from experience; they may become truly wise.

Intelligent Activity

Intelligent activities are continuously being created by people as, from one thought to the next, there is mental integrity, a consistency in the truth of thought. Recall that intelligent activity is described as *a state of interaction where intent, purpose, direction, values and expected outcomes are clearly understood and communicated among all parties, reflecting wisdom and achieving a higher truth*. Note that intelligence is not about who will benefit; it is what you do in interacting with others so they can do the same with others, building consciousness and freedom in those with whom we interact (MacFlouer, 2004-16).

Gardner (1993) originally identified seven different intelligences, then added two more, all of which impact intelligent action. Clearly there are overlaps, but identifying and naming differences enables us to deepen our understanding. The first two are (1) *linguistic intelligence* (language) and (2) *logical-mathematical intelligence* (including science), both of which are the primary focus of IQ and SAT testing, certainly necessary but not sufficient to navigate the life planes. (3) *Spatial intelligence* deals with the placement of objects in space and the relationships of these objects. Expanding from an active imagination, it includes the ability to form three-dimensional mental models and use those models to navigate through the world. (4) *Musical intelligence* includes the capacity to discern pitch, rhythm, timbre and tone. Recent findings in neuroscience suggest that the human brain may be hardwired for music. Wilson, a biologist, goes so far as to say "... all of us have a biologic guarantee of musicianship, the capacity to respond to and participate in the music of our environment [emphasis added]" (Wilson, as cited in Hodges, 2000, p. 18) (Bennet et al., 2015b). The sense of sound is primary, with thinking processes similar to logical-mathematical intelligence as well as an affective connection to the emotions. Music in terms of patterning was introduced in Chapter 17/Part III.

(5) *Bodily-kinesthetic intelligence* is embodied tacit knowledge (see Appendix D), also referred to as somatic knowledge. It is both kinesthetic and sensory. *Kinesthetic* is related to the movement of the body and, while important to every individual every single day of our lives, is a primary focus for athletes, artists, dancers, kids and assembly-line workers. It includes a sense of timing and rhythm, and good communication between the mind-body. A commonly used example is knowledge of riding a bicycle. *Sensory*, by definition and with a physical plane focus, is related to the five human senses of form through which information enters the body (sight, smell, hearing, touch and taste). An example is the smell of burning metal from your car brakes while driving or the smell of hay in a barn. These smells can convey knowledge of whether the car brakes need replacing (get them checked immediately), or whether the hay is mildewing (dangerous to feed horses, but fine for cows). These responses would be overt, bringing to conscious awareness the need to take effective action and enabling that action to occur. (See the model of tacit knowledges in Appendix D for more detail.)

(6) *Interpersonal intelligence* and (7) *intrapersonal intelligence* are both forms of personal intelligence, with the first directed outwards and the second directed inwards. "Interpersonal" infers the ability to interact cooperatively and collaboratively with others, with a sensitivity to their thinking and feeling (sympathy) that leads to understanding and, in its advanced forms, to empathy and compassion. It includes the honoring of diversity and the ability to view the world through multiple lenses. "Intrapersonal" is the realm of self knowledge, both of the individual self and of the human condition, and using this knowledge to effectively plan and direct one's actions.

Two additional intelligences, which were added later to the model, are (8) *naturalist intelligence* and (9) *existential intelligence* (Gardner, 2011). As an intelligence, "naturalist" infers the ability to discriminate among all living things. It includes a sensitivity to the connectivity of the natural world and the relationships and interactions that comprise our natural eco-system. "Existential" tackles the large questions around human existence: Where did we come from? How did we get here? Why do we die? What is the meaning of life? As can be seen, there are direct links between the development and balancing of these intelligences, *the development of self over a lifetime of experiences*, and the emergence of wisdom.

Sternberg (2003) notes that intelligence without wisdom has not served the world well, exampling cruel despots and greedy business tycoons who were quite intelligent and successful at the expense of others. This example points out that intelligence alone does not infer wisdom. Thus, Sternberg developed a balanced theory. As he describes:

> I view wisdom as the value-laden application of tacit knowledge not only for one's own benefit (as can be the case with successful intelligence) but **also for the benefit of others,** in order to **attain a common good**. The wise person realizes that what matters is not just knowledge, or the intellectual skills one applies to this knowledge, but **how the knowledge is used** [emphasis added]. (Sternberg, 2003, p. xviii)

This insinuates the spiritual counterbalance necessary when developing the mental faculties, and is consistent with the usage of wisdom in our definition of intelligent activity.

From another frame of reference, MacFlouer (1999) identifies seven energies, which he refers to as *rays*, that **develop the human in the journey toward intelligent activity**, wisdom and transcendence. These focused energies correlate to the planes of human focus introduced in Chapter 3/Part I, and several planes beyond those as the human evolves to higher levels of thought, becoming superhuman. The seven planes are: the physical, emotional, mental, intuitional, spiritual, monadic and divine. Each of the energies of the seven rays is focused on specific human actions from which *cosmic virtues* emerge. (Chapter 34/Part V focuses on virtues for living the future.)

Attempting to hold close to the author's intent while simultaneously taking a consilience approach, we communicate these energies consistent with the language forwarded in the current text. From the viewpoint of the physical plane (7th ray energy), this energy is focused on organization and synthesis, from which the *virtues of cooperation, collaboration and sharing* emerge. From the viewpoint of the emotional plane (6th ray energy) the focus is movement among energies, from which the *virtues of compassion and love* emerge. From the viewpoint of the mental plane (5th ray energy) the focus is on structure and formulating to both reduce forces and increase the replication of thought forms with other energies, from which the *virtue of truth* emerges. From the viewpoint of the intuitional plane (4th ray energy) the focus is on the balance and harmony of thought, from which the *virtue of beauty emerges*. From the viewpoint of the spiritual plane (3rd ray energy) the focus is on creating intelligent activity, "including perfect levels of changing itself and other energies in density in order to achieve intelligent activity through power and a growth in all life at once" (MacFlouer, 1999, p. 355), from which emerges more *intelligent life*. From the viewpoint of the monadic plane (2nd ray energy), the focus is on creating Oneness of all life, from which the virtue of *unlimited and unconditional love* and Oneness emerges. As this journey reaches its highest stage, the divine plane (1st ray energy), the focus is on creating new and more purpose for life, utilizing limits and increasing will through consistent choices, from which the virtue of *Universal Creation* emerges.

In this context, we use the concept of *limits* to denote a sacrifice, that is, a purposeful choice to limit a field of focus, thought or behavior in order to accelerate learning and expansion. As introduced in the U.S. Department of the Navy change agent's strategy presented in Chapter 12/Part 2 and briefly discussed in Chapter 23, limiting or bounding an idea or creation provides the opportunity to focus on that specific idea or creation and dig deeper into its value and potential. As we dig deeper into a specific domain of knowledge, we see more and more relationships and patterns, which precede the birth of new concepts, ideas and abilities in that area of focus. This is consistent with the discussion of attention and intention in Chapter 25.

<<<<<<<◇>>>>>>

INSIGHT: **As we dig deeper into a specific domain of knowledge, we see more and more relationships and patterns, which precede the birth of new concepts, ideas and abilities in that area of focus.**

<<<<<<<◇>>>>>>

From a systems perspective, setting a boundary helps identify a specific group of elements or objects, the relationships among them and their attributes. This perceived or assigned boundary, whether closed or with a degree of openness, separates the system in some way from the environment and other systems. While the region outside the boundary of a system is referred to as its environment, it is also a system, which is often referred to as the suprasystem. Every system has inputs (energy, information, people, or material) from the environment and provides outputs (energy, information, people or material) to its environment.

By setting limits (boundaries) it becomes easier to identify causal relationships within those limits, whether positive reinforcing feedback loops or negative balancing feedback loops. Positive feedback loops can help create new ideas, products and energy. Further, through setting limits there is a specific intent or purpose related to the identified system, with the system organized by the system designers to achieve that purpose. Principles from systems thinking such as the importance of structure and the tendency for systems to become more complex over time also apply. For example, consider the individuated human (complete with the emerging self and choice) as a system that is bounded in order to achieve a specific purpose. The structure would need to be supportive of that purpose in terms of physical, emotional and mental strengths and abilities. As the individual moves towards a specific goal in a shifting and changing environment, not only may that goal shift and change, but it also becomes necessary to expand options, increase variety and add flexibility (increased complexity) to achieve long-term survival of the system (in this case the individuated human). Thus limits—or sacrifice of the whole to focus on a specific part of the whole, a focus on subsystems of a larger system—can serve as a powerful tool for learning and expanding.

Connecting Knowledge and Wisdom

As Tom Stonier, a theoretical biologist, was developing a workable theory of information in the 90's, along the way he discovered new relationships between information and the physical Universe of matter and energy (Stonier, 1990; 1992; 1997). During this time frame, an intense interest in neuroscience research was unfolding as the creation and sophistication of brain measurement instrumentation became a reality. For the first time we could see what was happening *inside* the mind/brain as we process information and act on that information. In the mind/brain there is no clearly visible cause-and-effect relationship between information and knowledge; rather, knowledge is an emergent phenomenon. Considering the increasing focus on the workings of the mind/brain, it is not surprising that during this same timeframe the body of research focused on wisdom was rapidly expanding.

In the early years of Knowledge Management, a number of authors argued that wisdom was the end of a continuum made up of data→information→knowledge→ wisdom. One of the authors of this book was a part of that argument. Today we realize that while there certainly is a strong relationship, such a simple continuum could never be the case. As Peter Russell explains,

> Various people have pointed to the progression of data to information to knowledge ... continuing the progression suggests that something derived from knowledge leads to the emergence of a new level, what we call wisdom. But what is it that knowledge gives us that takes us beyond knowledge? Through knowledge we learn how to act in our own better interests. Will this decision lead to greater well-being, or greater suffering? What is the kindest way to respond in this situation? Wisdom reflects the values and criteria that we apply to our knowledge. Its essence is discernment. Discernment of right from wrong. Helpful from harmful. Truth from delusion. (Russell, 2007)

Wisdom is something more than knowledge. Let's explore this more. Csikszentmihalyi and Nakamura (2005) describe wisdom as referring to two distinct phenomena. The first is the *content* of wisdom (information and/or knowledge) and the second an individual's *capacity to think or act* wisely. Since the second part defines itself by itself, this invites a deeper exploration. Focusing on the content of wisdom, Clayton and Birren (1980) say that individuals perceive wisdom differently when socio-demographic variables are changed, that is, as we now recognize about knowledge, they consider wisdom as developed over time from a series of events both context sensitive and situation dependent in terms of culture and locality. Similarly, the works of Holliday and Changler (1986), Erikson (1988), Sternberg (1990), Jarvis (1992), Kramer and Bacelar (1994), Bennett-Woods (1997), and Merriam and Caffarella (1999) all take the position that wisdom is grounded in life's rich experiences,

> ... [wisdom] therefore is developed through the process of aging ... wisdom seems to consist of the ability to move away from absolute truths, to be reflective, to make sound judgments related to our daily existence, whatever our circumstances. (Merriam & Caffarella, 1999, p. 165)

There is an element of wisdom—both the content and the capacity—within each human. Recall a time in your life when a large issue or problem loomed in front of you. Things that used to work for you in the past didn't work, and there was a sense of confusion. An opportunity was there for you to shift your way of thinking and acting, and it was there because you were ready for it ... and the answer is there. It might stream from the unconscious, perhaps triggered by a passing unrelated conversation, or translated from an advertising sign along the road, or emerging as a picture in the mind. Somehow, you just *knew* the road ahead, and you *knew* that this was the direction you needed to head. This was inner wisdom emerging.

<<<<<<<<>>>>>>>

INSIGHT: **There is an element of wisdom—both the content and the capacity— within each human.**

<<<<<<>>>>>>>

Let's pause for a few minutes to explore your inner wisdom.

****

TOOL 27-1: Learning from Your Inner Self

Since wisdom requires experience, this exercise requires full engagement of your creative imagination.

STEP 1: As you read the newspaper, scan the Internet or listen to conversations regarding current news, choose one event or situation that bothers you, that attracts your attention. Then, look up more detail on the Internet and read a bit about it so that you increase your understanding of the circumstances of the event. *Do not* immerse yourself in this, nor do you want to deeply involve your emotions. Rather, note that you do not like the situation, read some of the details from a systems perspective, then let it go. This balance is important so that you don't fully engage previous mental models.

STEP 2: Later that evening, when you have a short period of time where you will not be interrupted, find a quiet place, make yourself comfortable, and close your eyes.

STEP 3: Engaging your creative imagination, picture yourself as the wise King Solomon. You are sitting on a high throne at the end of a large room, with your subjects grouped along each side of the room, quietly and reverently waiting.

STEP 4: Keeping your eyes closed, recall the event or situation that you identified earlier in the day. In the center of the room, all the subjects involved in that event or situation are standing expectantly in front of you. A quiet mumble arises from this group, acknowledging you as a person of wisdom, and agreeing that they will act as you direct them to act. They wait for your direction.

STEP 5: Imagine you, as King Solomon, closing your eyes (going within the within state you are already in) and reaching deep down inside for wisdom. Go deeper. You *know* the wisdom is there; it is just a matter of opening the door and receiving it. Take several deep breaths and recognize that thoughts are following your breath as you exhale. Now, as King Solomon, speak the words that come to your mind. Speak them out loud and listen to your Self.

While it may take several tries to successfully tap into the flow of thought that is emerging from within your depths, know that, in fact, it IS there. You are multidimensional, and you have been learning, expanding, connecting and discerning for the entire length of your life, whether or not you were aware of this learning. Repeat this exercise periodically until you are able to easily tap into the flow of knowledge and wisdom within you. Then act on it.

****

In the short discussion of wisdom above, recall that Csikszentmihalyi and Nakamura (1990) described wisdom as referring to two distinct phenomena: the *content* of wisdom and the *capacity* to think or act wisely. This parallels our understanding of knowledge as both Knowledge (Informing) and Knowledge (Proceeding), an information component and a process component. Knowledge and wisdom would then both deal with the *nature and structure of information*, with nature representing the quality or constitution of information, and structure representing the process of building new information, or learning. Wisdom represents *higher discernment* and the use of tacit knowledge, tapping into unconscious resources, to provide patterns that flow above the situation-dependent and context-sensitive knowledge—perhaps taking the form of intuition. The tacit knowledge driving what is surfaced would be both Knowledge (Informing) and Knowledge (Proceeding), although as noted by Goldberg (2005), primarily Knowledge (Proceeding).

Knowledge is still an important *part* of wisdom. Nussbaum (2000) forwards that all knowledge, and by extension learning, is in the service of wisdom. Nelson (2004) says that wisdom is the *knowledge of the essential nature of reality*. This could refer to the universals we explored through the idea of heuristics in Chapter 26, which reflects a higher truth emerging from conceptual thought. Further, Sternberg defines wisdom as "the application of tacit knowledge as mediated by values toward the goal of achieving a common good" (Sternberg, 1990, p. 353), thus suggesting that tacit knowledge is a prerequisite for developing wisdom and *defining wisdom in a social rather than individual context*. This is an important distinction, although in everyday language the term "wise" is often used in service to the individual. Note that over time, what is considered "wise" only from an individual perspective leads to separation, self-service, and learning limitations as the individual identifies with the knowledge they create. From the functional viewpoint of the mind/brain as an associative patterner, it would appear that information (as patterns of energy) is *intended to flow from person to person*, triggering experiential learning and expansion. This would indeed place learning (and the knowledge emerging from learning) in service to wisdom, and insinuate its connection to a greater social good. For a deeper treatment of wisdom see Bennet et al. (2015a and 2015b).

In summary, while not part of a linear continuum, the concept of wisdom is clearly related to knowledge—and, in particular, to tacit knowledge, a multi-dimensional resource—and can also be related to the phenomenon of consciousness. More importantly, wisdom is not in isolation; it appears to deal with the cognitive and emotional, personal and social, as well as the moral and religious aspects of life, **very much based on the interconnectedness of people.** And there we have it. The something more of wisdom.

In his book *Working Wisdom*, Costa (1995, p. 3) provides us with summary words that conceptually aid our understanding:

Wisdom is the combination of knowledge and experience, but it is more than just the sum of these parts. Wisdom involves the mind and the heart, logic and intuition, left brain and right brain, but it is more than either reason, or creativity, or both. Wisdom involves a sense of balance, an equilibrium derived from a strong, pervasive moral conviction ... *the conviction and guidance provided by the obligations that flow from a profound sense of interdependence* [emphasis added]. In essence, wisdom grows through the learning of more knowledge, and the practiced experience of day-to-day life—both filtered through a code of moral conviction.

Throughout this discussion we have presented knowledge in service to wisdom. That knowledge emerges from both the use of knowledge as effective action, and the use of information as ineffective action. In other words, we learn—and create knowledge—from both our successes and failures as we develop pattern thinking and move into the higher mental thought of conceptual thinking, which brings with it higher levels of truth. This development of our higher mental faculties enables recognition and understanding of patterns across domains of knowledge. This, however, does not produce wisdom. We've now discovered the more that is needed.

As we move through the Intelligent Social Change Journey, we *deepen our connections with others*, expanding from sympathy to empathy to compassion as we recognize the Oneness of all things. The "us" is part of the "I"; and the "I" becomes the "us". (See Chapter 35/Part V.) It is from this place of deep connection with others, which offers the potential for unconditional love, that virtue and morality guide our thoughts and actions. The balance of mental development and deepening connections to others emerges as wisdom and manifests as intelligent activity. See Figure 27-1.

The Wisdom of Mental Discipline

Development of wisdom can be escalated when an individual chooses to engage in mental discipline. What does this mean in practical terms? While during the course of life an intuitive flash can occur to pretty much anyone, disciplined preparation is required in order to interact with others and bring that idea into service, what could be defined in the business world as innovation.

Mental discipline is advantageous for *all* domains of knowledge. For example, an athlete requires disciplined preparation of the body accompanied by a harmonious consciousness (disciplined preparation of the mind) to perform well. Physical actions are repeated over and over again to embed them in the very fabric of our bodies such that they become an unconscious response to self (embodied tacit knowledge).

Mental is of, or having to do with, the mind; discipline as applied to the self is in terms of self-control, self-mastery, self-government, self-direction and self-reliance,

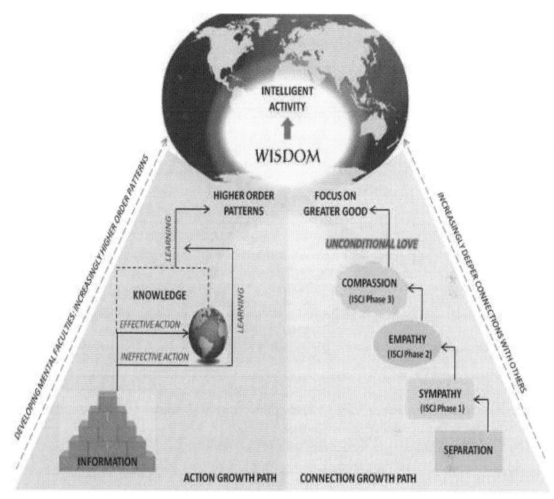

Figure 27-1. *The integration and balance of development of our mental faculties and deepening connections with others emerges as wisdom and manifests as intelligent activity.*

all connected with self-knowledge. For example, planning, discussed in Chapter 16/Part II, is a tool for preparation of the mind. It involves a higher level of truth, the ability to have more effectiveness and accuracy in our living, and increased intelligence in our actions. Then, there is the idea of consistency such that wisdom is intelligently applied wherever it can be useful, where it can be of service to others. These are good starting points. Now, as part of our developmental journey and deepening connections with others, we bring to this our understanding of the power of collaboration and cooperation and our role as co-creators.

The mental plane offers a continuous opportunity for growth, and there is great opportunity to do mental service in the world. As we develop mentally, our learning becomes part of our identity and our self changes and expands, resulting in more of us to interact with the world and a larger capacity to effectively act in and on the world. While Jung's theory of the collective unconscious lays a foundation for this interaction, Sheldrake's (1989) concept of formative causation makes this much more explicit. Through morphic resonance, **our thoughts have the capacity to influence other people, making it more likely for others to think in the same way we are thinking.** That our minds are much more permeable and porous to others than we have understood in the past has many implications. Our thoughts are not private, tucked away neatly in our brain. As Sheldrake (1995, p. 168-169) describes:

> From the point of view of formative causation, even our thoughts and attitudes influence other people, and we're in turn influenced by countless other people's thoughts and attitudes. So our minds are not insulated and separate in the way many modern people like to imagine, they're far more permeable to each other .... Formative causation makes us see societies and social groups as having a wholeness, a unity, and enables us to think more about the reality of the social forms in which we live.

This brings in Kant's (1993) categorical imperative as a basis of morality. Kant defined an imperative as a proposition that declares a certain action or inaction to be necessary. A categorical imperative is **an unconditional moral law**, a universal imperative for humanity (Pelegrinis, 1980). When we understand that our thoughts influence others, our thoughts become our responsibility as well as our actions and words, and this suggests the necessity for developing mental discipline

<<<<<<<◇>>>>>>>

INSIGHT: **When we understand that our thoughts influence others, our thoughts become our responsibility as well as our actions and words.**

<<<<<<<◇>>>>>>>

Because we are part of a larger eco-system and social beings in continuous two-way communication with those around us, we have the ability to develop mental sensing. As described by MacFlouer (1999, p. 630), there are three ways of mental sensing:

(1) Sensing what someone is thinking from thought that is relatively whole and truthful, in real time;

(2) Sensing one's own or another's egotistical thought that has been written or spoken—which causes pressure against one's own thought (many people are able to sense this kind of pressure); and

(3) Sensing another person's thought using all of the mental senses.

Strong thought is easier to sense. "Strong thought comes from the wholeness created from a well-focused concept that is connected to a complete series of thought forms [examples] that explain the concept" (MacFlouer, 1999, p. 630). MacFlouer goes on to provide a pragmatic approach to developing mental discipline. In an attempt to honor this thought while forwarding it in the context of this book, his seven methods will be loosely described below.

First, consistently (establishing a daily rhythm) reading material that increases truth in the mind (creating spiritual thought). It is suggested that this reading occur in the early morning upon waking when the mind is clearest, with the least amount of retained energy (see Chapter 20/Part III on stuck energy).

Second, practicing mental meditation, that is, using structured mental thought (logic and wisdom) to arrive at truth. This "includes planning new ways to think and then checking those new ways for validity by comparing the expected results with previous—known—outcomes [examples]" (MacFlouer, 1999, p. 632). (See the discussion of knowledge and the search for truth in Chapter 24.)

Third, reviewing and assessing the previous day's behaviors in comparison to what was planned to happen. The ability to control/influence the forces in our lives is a measure of our relative level of consciousness.

Fourth, releasing thought forms and ceasing logical thinking prior to relaxing and preparing for sleep.

Fifth, practicing mentally thinking for others. MacFlouer notes it is not necessary to communicate with others to develop this discipline.

Sixth, practicing humility, that is, when your thinking does not agree with others, assume you are wrong and the structured thought of others is right. (See Tool 4-1: Humility in Chapter 4/Part I.)

Seventh, and in the words of MacFlouer (1999, p. 633):

Write, speak, and teach truth to others when appropriate to do so for their mental benefit ... Each person who has created more wisdom in his or her own mental body needs to ***use that wisdom to create more truth in the mental bodies of others*** [emphasis added].

As we have seen consistently throughout this book, the highest virtue of the mental plane is truth, and the directing of energy outwards to others is key to the expansion of consciousness, that state of awareness and understanding of the connections and relationships among that of which we are aware (Bennet, 2001). As a higher-order pattern, wisdom moves across all domains of knowledge, manifesting in intelligent activity in service to the sharing of truth and the expansion of consciousness.

Final Thoughts

For those who grew up with biblical stories, there are many of these that convey the wisdom of King Solomon. One of them goes something like this. Two women came before the King with one live infant and one dead infant, each claiming the live infant as their own. After observing their behavior and noting neither was willing to back down, King Solomon ordered the live baby to be cut in half, with a part given to each mother. One woman immediately fell to her knees and begged the King to give the infant to the other woman so that the child could live. This, of course, was the mother. King Solomon was able to take understanding from one domain of knowledge and apply it to another.

We can think of wisdom as building on deep knowledge; in this example that is understanding the love and protective instincts of a mother, who would sacrifice herself for the welfare of the child. King Solomon had both the content (information and knowledge) and capacity to think and act wisely.

Just as the expert in a domain of knowledge can effectively extrapolate patterns from one situation to another, *a person who is wise can take learning lessons from one domain of knowledge and effectively apply them in another domain of knowledge for the greater good.* The "greater good" is that "something more" that emerged in our exploration of wisdom, that which emerges as we deepen our connections to others and recognize the Oneness of all.

Thus, we have now linked wisdom to higher mental thought developed through experience, mental discipline and deepening connections with others, all of which enable intelligent activity. And as Sternberg (2003, p. 188) reminds us, "Wisdom is not just a way of thinking about things; it is a way of doing things. If people wish to be wise, they have to act wisely, not just think wisely. We all can do this. Whether we do it is our choice."

Questions for Reflection:

What percentage of your time are you operating in intelligent activity as opposed to routine patterned activities?

How do I approach co-creating wisdom?

Chapter 28
Tapping into the Intuitional

SUBPARTS: Earned Intuition ... Revealed Intuition ... Controlled Intuition ... Mirror Neurons ... They all Work Together ... The Field of Ideas ... A Few Final Thoughts

FIGURES: 28-1. When the mental mind is used in a balanced way in service to others so that they may serve others (passing energy outwards), controlled intuition becomes available ... **28-2.** From a mental plane focus, we can access intuitive tacit knowledge embedded in the subconscious and that which is accessible through the larger field of the superconscious, which is spiritual in nature.

TOOL: 28-1. Redirecting the Mind; **28-2.** Sleep on It; **28-3.** Transmuting Negative Thought Forms

Intuition is the ability, without any time delay, to determine the causes of any and all effects regardless of the complexity of those effects. This intuition is a higher awareness, a deeper understanding, very much supported by our five senses of form and our two inner senses focused from the heart and crown energy centers. If we go to the dictionary, it says that intuition is the act or faculty of knowing or sensing without the use of rational processes; an immediate cognition (*American Heritage Dictionary*, 2006, p. 919). We agree with this definition as well.

From another perspective, Crandall sees insight as the result of searching for new relationships between concepts in one domain with those in another domain (Crandall et al., 2006). This creates a recognition and understanding of a problem within the situation, including the how and why of the past and current behavior of the situation. He says this is often the *result of intuition, competence, and the identification of patterns, themes and cue sets* (Crandall et al., 2006). Insight may also provide patterns and relationships that will anticipate the future behavior of the situation. Klein (2003) proposes that intuition is

> ... the way we translate our experiences into judgments and decisions. It is the ability to make decisions by using patterns to recognize what's going on in a situation and to recognize the typical action script with which to react. (p. 13)

Let's chew on those definitions and see if we can clarify these somewhat different perspectives. This requires looking at intuition through two different frames of reference, which, building on the concepts of earned knowledge and revelatory knowledge (Cooper, 2005), we will describe as *earned intuition* and *revealed intuition*.

Earned Intuition

Earned intuition would be that part of intuition emerging from the unconscious that is connected to our experiences and discoveries. When we are focused at the conscious mental level, we are always exploring cause and effect and working backwards, which uses up time. Fortunately, this is not the case with unconscious processing, from which indicators in the form of intuition can emerge in the blink of an eye. As Tallis (2002, p. 182) forwards, the activity underway in the unconscious is of profound importance since, "Virtually every aspect of mental life is connected in some way with mental events and processes that occur below the threshold of awareness." As we seek deeper understanding, the conundrum is that the cognitive processes that give rise to intuitive knowledge cannot be examined directly because they are not conscious, so we don't know exactly what they are (Carter, 2002). However, we are learning every day. [Note that although intuition is a subset of the unconscious, the unconscious does not imply intuition.]

Recall that learning is a modality of change. The unconscious can enhance learning effectiveness by developing understanding and insight over time, although it's processing power is relatively 700,000 times more powerful than the conscious mind, which assigns a new meaning to "over time." At a high level, we can say that information coming in from all of our senses is being associated. Thus, we can assume that when we take action based on our intuition, it often emerges from *associating previous experiences in our unconscious*. Recognizing the power of the unconscious, and understanding to some degree how it works, can help learners build and more fully engage their unconscious capability. There are a number of neuroscience findings from a ten-year learning experience of one of the authors which netted both a degree and a book (Bennet et al, 2015b), that may help us better understand intuition.

1. The unconscious brain is always processing. Because of this, all modes of learning are affected. Note that the brain uses 80 percent as much energy when sleeping as it does when awake (Schacter, 1996). This is consistent with the finding that the high rate of energy usage by the human brain is not changed much by mental activity (Laughlin, 2004). It is also known that when under deep anesthesia, 50 percent of the brain's energy consumption is used for maintenance. Specifically,

> Deep anesthesia abolishes electrical activity and reduces the metabolic rate of the whole brain by 50 percent, suggesting that, on average, energy consumption is equally divided between neural signaling and maintenance. (Laughlin, 2004, p. 188)

Building on these findings, it appears that our unconscious mind uses about 30 percent of the brain's energy for processing during sleep, that is, **If**, 50% of the brain's energy consumption is used for maintenance; **And**, 80% of the brain's energy is being used when we sleep; **Then**, 30% of the brain's energy is used by the unconscious mind during sleep. This would be much higher if the individual were awake. The unconscious would then be processing a great deal of information from the external environment.

2. The unconscious never lies. This concept taken from Kandel (2006) may seem odd, but when it is realized that the unconscious is a part of the overall living individual, "lying" to self would not make sense. This idea relates to the truth and how things work under the learning mode of reflective observation. Although the intuition coming from our unconscious may not be right, it is still what our unconscious *perceives as truth* based on what it has received from our experiences, thoughts and feelings.

3. The gaps are filled in (re-created) when a memory is recalled. This primarily relates to the sensing aspect of concrete experience. It makes the point that when we sense or feel our environment, not all of the incoming information goes into memory. In fact, at best only things that are meaningful to us are usually remembered. Memory storage, recall, and recognition all occur at the level of invariant forms, what Hawkins (2004) describes as "a form that captures the essence of relationships, not the details of the moment" (p. 82). This means that individuals cannot fully trust the details of their memory.

Further, an individual's reaction to an experience may be based on past misinterpreted information, that in turn may color the individual's immediate experience and therefore impact the quality or validity of an individual's intuition.

4. The unconscious produces flashes of insight. Christos (2003) notes that spurious memories can generate new ideas that combine in different ways to make new associations. This item affects intuition and meaning.

Revealed Intuition

In the opening paragraph we made the point that intuition is very much supported by our seven senses, and several times throughout this book we have forwarded that the mental is in service to the intuitive or, as we have referenced in the title of this chapter, the intuitional, referring to the intuitional plane.

As introduced in Chapter 3/Part I, we contend that for as far back as we can collectively remember, the human has been primarily focused on development of the mental faculties. In this rush (in evolutionary terms) for mental achievement, we have largely neglected our spiritual development, which facilitates entry into the higher energy realms. Recall that energy follows thought. When our thought is focused on the perceived objects of our physical reality that surround us, it is difficult to tap into the energy flows within, much less tap into that which is beyond our current understanding. This unbalanced mental growth is what has led to the arrogance often visible in the global business environment.

<<<<<<<◇>>>>>>

INSIGHT: **Spiritual development facilitates entry into the higher energy realms.**

<<<<<<<◇>>>>>>

While it may sound like a failing in current human history, that is not the intent. This rapid development of the mental offers considerable opportunity for the future of humanity, that is, *if* we are able to now bring the mental into balance on the physical and emotional planes, with the spiritual counterbalance woven throughout, which means bringing truth, compassion and unconditional love into our everyday lives as we cooperatively and collaboratively work together to achieve intelligent activity.

There are several reasons this is true. First, no one can argue the technological advancements over the past 10,000 years that have led us to today, nor the incredible shifts underway today in every area of human endeavor. If used for the benefit of all, these advances offer the potential to take humanity to the next level in terms of the growth of both individual and collective consciousness.

Second, even when an individual is able to access the higher energy fields and have brief flashes of intuition, without development of the mental faculties in a related domain of knowledge or the wisdom involved in translating a concept across domains of knowledge, it is difficult, if not impossible, to act on that intuitive flash. Further, these flashes happen sporadically, and the large amount of insight gleaned from the experience is difficult to grasp and quickly forgotten. A colleague and friend with whom one of the authors has had a number of conversations related to the importance of developing the mental faculties in support of the intuitive, called during the polishing of this chapter to say that at lunch in a Chinese restaurant she had just received a fortune that read, "Intuition and knowledge walk hand in hand." Well said!

At the simplest level of intuition, almost everyone has experienced the intuitive nudge. A nudge can be either earned or revealed intuition, or a combination of both!

For example, since the unconscious receives information from both the environment and higher energy fields of which the conscious mind may not be aware, an enhanced awareness of the unconscious may show itself through a sense that something is right or wrong (sensing), or a good or bad feeling about a situation (feeling). This sensing or feeling helps guide our reactions to future experiences. As Pert (1997) has noted, the emotional system works through the generation and transmission of chemicals throughout the body, which in turn impact neuronal activity. These chemical changes represent the emotional tag of the amygdala.

Revealed intuition from higher energy fields can take many other forms. In the book, *Thinking Fast and Slow*, Kahneman (2013) relates a story about firefighters in a kitchen on fire. The commander said let's get out of here without realizing why. The floor collapsed almost immediately after the firefighters escaped. Only after the fact did the commander realize that the fire had been unusually quiet and that his ears had been unusually hot. Together, those impressions prompted what he called a sixth sense of danger. He had no idea what was wrong. It turned out that the heart of the fire had not been in the kitchen, but in the basement beneath where the men had stood.

Another example is a tune playing over and over again in your head, with either the melody having personal significance or the words conveying a message. Another example is when a word or concept keeps coming into your reality through many different communications vehicles. When one of the authors was getting into a car on his way to lunch, he recalls feeling a warmth when his hand touched the door handle. and he had a knowing that there was going to be an accident. In *Blink*, Gladwell (2005) shares a story about Getty Museum art experts knowing that the *kouros* was a fake. The experts said that it was the feeling of thousands of humming birds popping in and out of their minds, accompanied by an immense rush of previous thoughts that led them to predict the statue's forgery. Synchronicities are another avenue of revealed intuition. Recall from Chapter 22 that a synchronicity can be thought of as a coincidence of events that seem related, yet with no obvious connection one to the other.

While intuition can certainly take the form of a day vision, a dream, or actually hearing a voice that conveys information you need or an idea for you to pursue, the information obtained through these more complete forms are more appropriately called revelatory knowledge. Note that revelatory knowledge, a form of knowing that has no traceable roots, can never be validated initially and must be self-authenticating. "It can only prove its worth over time based on the lasting quality and the integrity of its message" (Cooper, 2005, p. 22). As with experiential knowledge, it will evolve over time as an individual increases his understanding and expands his consciousness.

Controlled Intuition

The good news is that in the human journey of growth there are unending possibilities, and one of those possibilities is controlled intuition, the ability to tap at will into the intuitional plane. You can turn intuitive thought on and off, just as you do mental thought. Recall from Chapter 20/Part III the discussion on mental chatter, also known as the monkey mind, related to random energy sequences occurring throughout the day. Similar to the steps taken to eliminate mental chatter, the first step to turning on intuitional thought is to know that it can be done and recognizing that we are master of our thoughts. Second, is to set the intent, then quiet the mind and listen to our self. Quieting the mind can be in the form of meditation, brain wave entrainment and re-wiring, biofeedback, sensory perception exercises, conscious dreaming, reciting a mantra, paying more attention to synchronicities, or through deep breathing.

<<<<<<<<>>>>>>>

INSIGHT: **In the human journey of growth there are unending possibilities, and one of those possibilities is the ability to tap at will into the intuitional plane.**

<<<<<<<<>>>>>>>

One tool that is really easy to use, especially when it is difficult to quiet the mind with meditation, is to REDIRECT the mind with a mantra or song that is uplifting and shifts us into the vibration of love or reverence. There are two reasons this approach is so effective. First, recall from the discussion on "forgetting" and "letting go" in Chapter 20/Part III that the best process for "forgetting" is inattention by diverting the flow, and the very best way to avoid attending to some memory is to have a stronger, more significant memory replace it. Second, music and the human mind have a unique relationship, with neuroscience findings that show "all of us have a biologic guarantee of musicianship, the capacity to respond to and participate in the music of our environment" (Wilson, as cited in Hodges, 2000, p. 18).

****

TOOL 28-1: REDIRECTING THE MIND

This is a tool for stopping a negative thought pattern's neural firing in the moment and then redirecting it to a more positive one.

STEP (1): Identify a mantra or song that is uplifting and shifts you into the vibration of love or reverence. If you are a Christian, this could be the Lord's Prayer or a church hymn that lifts your spirit and is easily remembered. For example, one author discovered that he always whistled the tune to Amazing Grace in times of stress. The words that would run through his head are: "Amazing grace! how sweet the sound, that saved a wretch like me! I once was lost, but now am found, was blind, but now I see." Regardless of an individual's belief set, the concept of living in grace—with grace representing beauty, kindness and mercy—enables the perception of a positive learning experience (see Chapter 20/Part III). Eastern mantras such as the *Ohm Mani Padme Hum* serves this purpose, as does the heart sutra mantra of *Gate' Gate' Paragate Parasam Gate' Bodhi Svaha*. Just about every spiritual tradition has good options to draw from. And if an individual is more secular in nature, since we seem to be hard-wired for music, there are most likely favorite songs to be found in memory that catch hold of the mind and uplift.

STEP (2): Whenever you catch your thoughts or emotions spinning in a negative direction, make a ritual out of repeating the mantra, prayer or song to yourself over and over as many times and as often as needed until you feel your state of being shift into a more positive state.

NOTE: Even if you have not been aware of it, you may discover that you have unconsciously been using this tool throughout your life!

****

While the brain may have palpable limits, human consciousness is not bound by the body. The best way to start enhancement of the mind/brain is different for different people. For one author, it started with awareness of when she was automatically negating an intuitive thought that surfaced in her mind. Next, was the conscious decision to catch herself in such an act of negating "irrational thoughts" and suspending her doubt/disbelief in order to give them a try, so long as there was no harm in following the thought. This process helped her to start validating the intuitive thoughts and trusting them more. It also stopped the pattern she had of negating what seemed illogical. See also Appendix D, Engaging Tacit Knowledge.

Note that when we talk about controlled intuition, the "control" here refers to the ability to connect to the intuitional plane at will. Accessing the field at will is actually more of a surrender process, allowing the intuitive insights to rise up from the unconscious to the conscious, and this often takes relaxation and a loosening of focus. This is why people often have "Ah-ha!" moments when they are in the shower, or taking walk, or dreaming, or after a nap. Thus, controlled intuition does not insinuate controlling the content of thought. Most people assume that in order to create you have to control what you create. This need to control is an illusion, and *the need to create is not dependent upon the need to control*.

There are several pre-requisites for developing controlled intuition. How to begin has been the subject of the above paragraphs, that is, opening and becoming comfortable with the inner realms of consciousness, a Field of which you are a part. This is not always as easy as it sounds. We have programmed ourselves to focus on a perceived external physical reality; it is the world in which we are experiencing life—

interacting, learning and expanding. And in the process of living we are always anticipating the outcome of our decisions and actions. While intent certainly plays into controlled intuition, in order to tap into the intuitional plane at will there needs to be a degree of non-attachment to the answer or result. Attachments come from negative ego, which is the part of us that tried to control outcomes, and this counteracts the flow of intuition. The degree that we are attached to the answer or outcome is the degree to which we will skew the answers trying to emerge from the deeper self. While these inner realms have always been available to us, it is now in the midst of the Intelligent Social Change Journey that we are ready as a humanity to expand into Phase 3. So, a first step is rediscovering the fullness of who we are, and opening and strengthening our connections to the Field of consciousness.

<<<<<<<◇>>>>>>

INSIGHT: **A first step toward controlled intuition is rediscovering the fullness of who we are, and opening and strengthening our connections to the Field of consciousness.**

<<<<<<<◇>>>>>>

Second, you must have developed—and use—your lower mental mind in a balanced way. This balance refers to how your learning is acted upon in service to others, the larger ecosystem of humanity, and the world at large (see Chapter 32/Part V). Third, you must have developed your upper mental mind, that is, developed conceptual thinking and be ever seeking a higher level of truth in your thinking. Remember, the mental faculties are in service to the intuitional. Fourth, you must have deepened your connections with others. If these aspects sound familiar, note that they are the same conditions that move us toward wisdom, manifesting in intelligent activity! This is no coincidence.

Now, bring together the focus from your emotional plane, which tells you how you *feel* about a situation, and the mental plane, which tells you what you and others *think* about a situation, and helps you think in structured, causal logic and, as you expand your faculties, in concepts. Think of your mind as providing the gas for your thought, pulling information from the brain, a magnificent storage and information processing device (MacFlouer, 2004-16). The intent is to know the past, present and future, and determine the causes of things you are thinking about, that is, *why* something is happening.

When an individual can think through all three planes, making sure that they are in equal balance, that is, neither physical nor mental wants or emotions separately driving thought, that individual can develop controlled intuition.

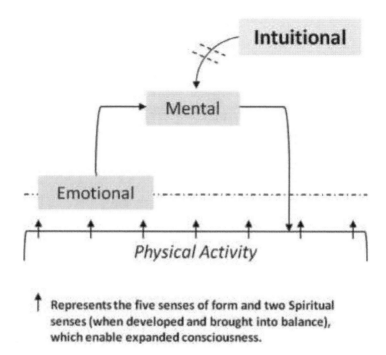

Figure 28-1. *When the mental mind is used in a balanced way in service to others so that they may serve others (sending energy outwards), controlled intuition becomes available.*

While the prerequisites are essential, there are other, more complex ways of tapping into the intuitional plane. Several of these were introduced in Chapter 22 in the discussion of divination. The *I Ching*, also called *The Book of Change* and considered a fundamental text of the Chinese culture, is arguably one of the oldest recorded works in existence. It represents "a way of knowing common to both magical or pre-technological cultures and to the world we contact each night in dreams" (Ritsema & Karcher, 1995, p. 11). While some historians date its origins back as far as 5,000 years, the most widely-accepted origin connects the *I Ching* with Fu His, a Chinese emperor circa 2582 BC. Fu His contemplated "the shapes of heaven, the patterns of the Earth, bird and animal markings and the movements of his body and soul" (p. 12). Through close association with and observation of the tortoise, he discovered a perfect mathematical model emerging from the broken and unbroken lines of the tortoise shell. These observations led to development of eight trigrams that he used to symbolize the eight natural elements: Heaven, Earth, Water, Fire, Thunder, Mountains, Wind and Lakes. Other teachers contributed their thought, with the trigrams eventually yielding 64 hexagrams. These symbols were passed from generation to generation as a tool for addressing difficult situations, especially those situations emotionally charged, where rational knowledge does not work and yet we must make decisions and act on those decisions.

The *I Ching* approach helps us create an imaginative space, an opening to tap into our unconscious. Coming to light through a particular situation with a specific context, the symbols help us experience the situation differently in order to understand the inner forces at play and how they are affecting us and shaping the situation. Note that the *I Ching* is built on an understanding that knowledge is situation dependent and context sensitive. Further, consistent with our understanding of knowledge, the *I Ching* does not advocate a passive approach to life, rather, it is about action and reaction, the essence of continual change (Legge, 1996). The *I Ching* supports the search for Truth (a larger truth), zooming in on the possible outcomes of decisions and actions. The world of *I Ching* is simultaneously an intellectual world with its own logic and boundaries and a mystical experience. While the system itself is based on mental development of mathematical formulas emerging from nature, the result of the *I Ching* process is an intuitive clarity called *shen ming* or *the light of the gods* (Ritsema & Karcher, 1995).

Interestingly, some of the greatest Western philosophers have honored the potential of the *I Ching*. For example, Confucius once said, "If some years were added to my life, I would give fifty to the study of the Yi (*I Ching*) and might then escape falling into great errors" (Legge, 1996, p. xi). And, as Carl Jung described, "The *I Ching* does not offer itself with proofs and results; it does not vault itself, nor is it easy to approach. Like a part of nature, it waits until it is discovered" (Legge, 1996, p. ix). For those interested in exploring this tool of change, a short but excellent treatment of application is provided by Karcher (1999). As Karcher begins his explanation, "The modern world thinks that change is objective and predictable. We use statistics and norms to describe it, and pretend it is the same for everyone. The old world saw things differently … This symbolic approach can help you deal with the changes in your life …." (Karcher, 1999, p. vii).

The *Tao Te Ching*, a book of around 5,000 words written over 2500 years ago, is perhaps the most translated classic next to the Bible. It has been explored and embraced by physicists, psychologists and business leaders for its potential to influence society. Lao Tzu is represented as a gifted scholar who lived in China during the Chou Dynasty and worked as the Custodian of the Imperial Archives. The Chou Dynasty was an era where hostile political actions and counter-actions spiraled out of control. It was Yin His, then Keeper of the Gate, later to become the Emperor of China, and, as noted above, today remembered as originator of the *I Ching*, who encouraged Lao Tzu to write down what he had learned for the enlightenment of others who were in a position to guide others, that is, princes, politicians, employers and educators (Wing, 1986).

Writing for these leaders, Lao Tzu urges them to discover themselves through fully sensing the world around them and reflecting deeply to develop our personal intuitive power. This personal power, or *Te*, is built up through an awareness and knowledge of the physical laws "as they operate both in the Universe and in the minds of others (*Tao*)" (Wing, 1986, p.11). Without using force, this power is then used to direct events *through attitude instead of action*, leading by guiding rather than ordering or directing, and managing people by letting them act on you instead of you acting on them. As can be seen, Lao Tzu believed in methods that did not create resistance (force) or lead to counter-reactions. Lao Tzu believed that through observing the laws of nature we could understand the way matter and energy function in the Universe. As Wing translates:

> [Lao Tzu] realized that excessive force in a particular direction tends to trigger the growth of an opposing force, and that therefore the use of force cannot be the basis for establishing a strong and lasting social foundation … He realized that the physical laws of the Universe directly affect the ways that individuals tend to behave and societies tend to evolve, and that to comprehend these laws could give a leader the power (*Te*) to bring harmony to the world. (Wing, 1986, p.11)

This is a reminder of what we discovered in Chapter 3/Part I, that excessive force exerted in a specific direction triggers opposing forces. This is a lesson we are still learning today.

Lao Tzu challenges us as leaders to develop an intellectual independence, that is, to trust our own perceptions and rely on our inspirations and instincts (our intuition), and to influence others using nature as our pattern. As Lao Tuz puts it:

> Evolved Individuals hold to the *Tao*,
> And regard the world as their Pattern.
>
> They do not display themselves;
> Therefore they are illuminated.
> They do not define themselves;
> Therefore they are distinguished.
> They do not make claims;
> Therefore they are credited.
> They do not boast;
> Therefore they advance. (Wing, 1986. p. 11)
> Since, indeed, they do not compete,
> The world cannot compete with them.
> (Wing, 1986, passage 22)

When individuals are focused on a conceptual thought, trying to determine the level of truth in that concept in service to a greater good, and interacting with others who are operating at a similar level of consciousness to do so, they are opening to the uncontrolled flooding of dozens to thousands or more concepts revolving around the area of focus. The process is both instantaneous and effortless. Note that several of the prerequisites for developing controlled intuition that were discussed above are present. As the group continues to work together, open to and sharing the new thoughts of each, the flooding of new ideas continues. When this occurs, lock in the feelings that accompany this experience. Given similar circumstances and intent, the memory of these feelings can help trigger a reoccurrence of this experience, moving you into the realm of controlled intuition.

As you participate repeatedly in this process, creating more whole thoughts (concepts with a higher level of truth) and sharing and using what is intuited to the benefit of others, the mental senses increase such that you have a greater capability to understand the concepts flooding in. As you reach the point of controlled intuition, tapping into the intuitional plane at will and choosing new thought instantly without effort, you are able to process incoming information at a rate of speed which helps unify your senses (MacFlouer, 2004-16). As this becomes part of your nature, you more easily identify truth, and your thinking aligns with higher and higher levels of truth.

Mirror Neurons

Another form of revealed intuition can be explained through our growing understanding of mirror neurons, a more recently discovered phenomenon in the brain relating to the ease and speed with which we understand simple actions. Research on experiments with Macaque monkeys that began in the early 1990s indicated that the activation of subsets of neurons in brain-motor areas appeared to represent actions. The initial experiments had one monkey grasp an object (an orange) while the experimenters monitored what went on inside an observer monkey's brain. Over the past 10 years many variations of this have verified that an observer's neurons fire (or mirror) the actor's neurons. Testing has moved from monkeys to great apes to humans. Non-invasive measurement techniques such as fMRI have enabled the experiments on humans to be greatly expanded.

These measurements have included mirror neurons in humans located in the frontal lobe and in the parietal lobe, which include Broca's area, a key area for human language (Iacoboni, 2008). Using fMRI, emotional mirrors have been discovered by,

> Feeling disgust activated in similar parts of the brain when human volunteers experienced the emotion while smelling a disgusting odor or when the same subjects watched a film clip of someone else disgusted. (Rizzolatti, 2006, p. 60)

As Rizzolatti (2006) described, "Subsets of neurons in human and monkey brains respond when an individual performs certain actions and also when the subject observes others performing the same movements" (p. 56). In other words, *the same neurons fire in the brain of an observer as fire in the individual performing an action.* These neurons provide an internal experience that replicates another's experience, thereby experiencing another individual's act, intentions, and/or emotions. These researchers also found that the mirror neuron system responded to the intentional component of an action as well as the action itself (Rizzolatti, 2006).

Carrying this idea further, Iacoboni proposes that mirror neurons facilitate the direct and immediate comprehension of another's behavior without going through complex cognitive processes. This makes the learning process more efficient because it can instantly transfer not only visuals but emotions and intentions as well. Mirror neurons also serve as a means of learning through imitation, which is "a very important means by which we learn and transmit skills, language and culture" (Rizzolatti, 2006, p. 61). Often, a significant part of learning requires good social communication, which includes parity and direct comprehension. Parity indicates that the meaning within the message is similar for both the sender and the receiver. Direct comprehension means that no previous agreement between individuals is needed for them to understand each other. From the neuroscience perspective, both of these aspects of communication seem to be inherent in the neural organization of individuals (Rizzolatti, 2006).

The question becomes how this phenomenon impacts revealed intuition. One answer is that it serves to explain how actionable tacit knowledge can be transferred between individuals and the potential of mimicry with no idea of where such knowledge was learned. The capacity to re-create feelings, perspectives, and empathy with people by reliving their experiences can greatly aid us in cooperative and collaborative endeavors.

Specific neuroscience findings related to mirror neurons that could potentially influence experiential learning as revealed knowledge include: (1) cognitive mimicry that transfers active behavior and other cultural norms; (2) rapid transfer of information that bypasses cognition; (3) neurons create the same patterns when we see something as when we do it; (4) what we see we become ready to do; and (5) mirror neurons facilitate neural resonance between observed actions and executing actions (Bennet et al., 2015b). Recognizing that no two people are, or ever will be, identical, it follows that levels of sensitivity to the energies of others and energies of the Field, as well as the processing of those energies through the senses, are different. This was reflected in the discussion of energy entanglement and electromagnetic sensitivity in Chapter 18/Part III.

They All Work Together

While for the sake of discussion and developing understanding we have addressed earned intuition and revealed intuition as separate things, since intuition is by its very nature primarily tacit, it is difficult to differentiate the two in terms of their source. Further, the two have the potential to work together.

Our intuitive tacit knowledge—along with our embodied, affective and spiritual tacit knowledge—is working for us 24/7, energetically on call when triggered by an internal or external stimulus, including needs, desires and what often appears as random bisociations. Note that in our model of tacit knowledges, intuitive tacit knowledge is described as a *sense* of knowing coming from inside an individual that may influence decisions and actions; yet the decision-maker or actor cannot explain how or why the action taken is the right one.

<<<<<<◇>>>>>>

INSIGHT: **Our intuitive tacit knowledge is working for us 24/7, energetically on call when triggered by an internal or external stimulus.**

<<<<<<◇>>>>>>

Damasio (1994, p. 188) calls intuition "the mysterious mechanism by which we arrive at the solution of a problem without *reasoning* toward it [emphasis added]." The unconscious works around the clock with a processing capability many times greater than the processing that occurs at the conscious level. But in order to use it, decision-makers must first be able to tap into their unconscious. Intuitive tacit knowledge is further explicated in Appendix D.

In the treatment of knowing provided in Appendix E, developed from the viewpoint of tacit knowledges, the concept of a superconscious is introduced. The superconscious is considered the Field that is described by Jung's collective consciousness and Chardin's Noosphere. The sense of knowing can occur not only by tapping into the tacit knowledges acquired and connected during the life experience, but also by tapping into this larger Field and, consistent with our earlier discussion, tapping into ideas with which we resonate. We expand on this below.

From the viewpoint of the human, we now bring into the conversation a fourth plane that is available to those humans who develop extraordinary creativity (see Chapter 29). While we will refer to this fourth plane as the intuitional plane, through connection to the superconscious it offers connectivity to higher intuitive thought, which includes expanded spiritual thought. See Figure 28-2, which was originally introduced in Chapter 4/Part I. Note that spiritual thought is available through all the planes regularly utilized by the human, that is, the physical, emotional and mental planes. As we navigate the challenges of the physical, emotional and mental planes, the spiritual is always available as a counterbalance so that we stay on track in our search for higher truths and expanded consciousness.

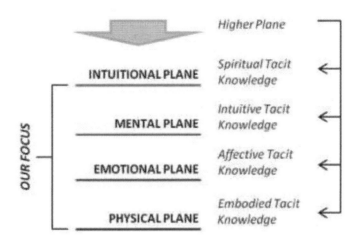

Figure 28-2. *From a mental plane focus we can access intuitive tacit knowledge embedded in the subconscious and that which is accessible through the larger Field of the superconscious, which is spiritual in nature.*

One of the ways to surface tacit knowledge is through inner tasking and lucid dreaming. One thought leader in the KMTL Study supported by the Mountain Quest Institute[28-1] touts this as his pathway to ideas. "It has been my experience from the beginning, as far back as I can remember, being able to state a problem in my head and then within a short period of time, definitely over night, having a variety of solutions available." See the tool below.

****

TOOL 28-2: SLEEP ON IT

Sleeping on a question or problem can yield an answer the next morning. This is a particularly powerful way to access tacit knowledge.

STEP (1) Prime your conscious mind. Early in the evening, prior to going to bed, take a focused period of time to "brainstorm" with yourself. *Ask* yourself a lot of questions *related* to the task at hand. Reflect carefully on the questions and be patient. This is the process of active reflection.

STEP (2) Before going to bed, ensure that you have a pen and paper available right beside the bed, accessible without you getting up. Write the specific problem or question you want to address on this pad of paper.

STEP (3) Tell yourself, as you fall asleep at night, to work on that specific problem or question.

STEP (4) When you wake up the next morning, but before you get up, lie in bed and ask the same question, listening patiently to your own quiet, passive thoughts. Frequently, but not always, the answer will appear.

STEP (5) Write the answer down quickly before it is lost from the conscious mind (as with dreams).

Another aspect of this approach is useful when a group or team is tackling a difficult problem. It has been found that the answers from the team can be improved if, rather than acting on the quick responses, *let the team sleep on the problem* and review the answers they come up with in the morning. What happens is that while you sleep your unconscious mind is processing the information taken in that day, keeping the valuable information and discarding that which doesn't make sense or is not important to you. It is also working on solutions to issues or problems that have come up that day. When the team gets back together the next day, there will be new ideas and thoughts, and a clearer vision of the best way ahead

****

The Field of Ideas

Systems knowledge, one of the knowledges needed in a changing, uncertain and complex world, leads to understanding connections, relationships, balances and tradeoffs. An intellectual aspect of leadership at all levels is considering the larger perspective, that is, the ability to conceptualize and strategize, to see the big picture and how everything fits together. But what does that big picture look like when we bring our expanded understanding to bear? How does an understanding of self and consciousness and the forces that we choose to engage fit into that picture? We may understand that we co-create our reality and that our thoughts, coupled with intent and expectations, lead us to thought forms, but where do those thoughts go when they are *not* acted upon? And do we have access to the thoughts of others that were not acted upon?

In the discussion of synchronicity in Chapter 22, we introduced Jung's collective unconscious and throughout the book refer to Pierre Theilhard de Chardin's Noosphere, "a human sphere, a sphere of reflection, of conscious invention, of conscious souls" (de Chardin, 1966, p. 63). Among other names, this Field has also been called the Akashic Field, the Zero Point Field, the Quantum Field and the God Field. To explore this Field further, let's think of this Field in terms of WiFi and the Internet. Thoughts, in the form of electromagnetic energy, are floating through the air, picked up by a grid that surrounds the world, float through the air again, and are brought to the screen for our consideration and potential use. Note that they are not brought to *any* screen, but to *the place* they are directed, a place where they will, at least most of the time, be welcomed. This analogy is similar to the idea of the Noosphere. Thoughts are energy patterns floating around the world waiting to be brought to the awareness of individuals who welcome them, those individuals who have expanded their threshold of focus and learning in a specific domain such that these thoughts are understandable and/or can be associated with other thoughts in their mind/brain.

Recall the discussion in Chapter 3/Part I regarding the amplitude, frequency and direction of forces. Thoughts can also be considered in terms of amplitude (strength), frequency (rate of occurrence over time) and direction. This promotes the idea that the thoughts are already there with specific characteristics, waiting to be discovered. ***When there is a resonance between the thought and the thinker, a connection occurs***. The higher the amplitude, the greater the frequency, the more thoughts heading the same direction, the quicker that thought moves into reality. This brings us back to the recognition that we have to take responsibility for our thoughts as well as our actions, for *who* we are as well as *who we are becoming*.

This discussion begs the question: What happens to those thoughts that are not so positive or well-intended and yet don't get acted upon, but are rather kicked out into the collective Field? Could it be that the individuals who tend towards more negative thoughts and emotions (whether consciously or unconsciously) welcome these in and act upon them? If so, what is the responsibility of a conscious individual to transmute those thoughts when they pass through our awareness, rather than to just reject them and kick them back out into the collective Field for someone else to pick up and act upon?

In Chapter 19/Part III, we discovered that emotions are intended as a guidance system, and that it takes only 17 seconds of focused feeling to shift from one emotional state to another. Once acknowledged, emotions are a choice. Since we are energetically in continuous interaction with others, it is quite difficult to not be impacted at some level by the thoughts and feelings flowing through our environment. We can all recall moments where negative thoughts and emotions touch us; our thoughts and feelings rise and dip, often at the behest of the situations we move through in our day-to-day life. Since the power of a thought force is related to how often it is repeated as well as the emotional charge behind it, this is especially relevant at this point in history with all the unrest, judgment and anger being generated and amplified by people around the world due to political polarization and opinion. As charged thoughts of judgment, separation, anger and fear are added to this Field, the situation energetically worsens, attracting partial thought forms resonating at this level, which strong emotions can thrust into reality.

The power of our thoughts and feelings, our attention and intention, can serve to transmute these thought forms as well as help bring balance to the Field. See the tool below on transmuting negative thought forms.

****

TOOL 28-3. TRANSMUTING NEGATIVE THOUGHT FORMS

STEP (1): Acknowledge the existence of the negative thought or emotion at the surface level without digging deeper into the thought or feeling. Identify where the thought or feeling resides in or around your body.

STEP (2): Using your creative imagination, see beautiful pink rays of light come down from above, stream through your body and swirl around the negative thought or feeling. See rich green streams of energy rise through your feet and join the pink light swirling around the negative thought or feeling.

STEP (3): Watch and feel as the swirls get faster and faster, with the negative thought or feeling dissipating into nothingness from the outside-in. Feel the power within you and, as the swirling light reaches the last center point of the negative energy, sense an explosion of color into white, filling you, surrounding you with joy.

STEP (4): In this state of joy, picture something or someone you love. Feel peace flow through your heart and send this peace and love into the larger Field to which we are all connected. Offer your appreciation for the experience and the opportunity to be of service to humanity.

****

Remember, emotions are a gift, a guidance system, to help us discover what we like and what we don't like. They are not intended to drive our actions—unless we choose to engage them to do so (see Chapter 3/Part I on forces and Chapter 19/Part III on emotions).

Just as all of us have creative potential, the *Field of Ideas* is available to all. In her ground-breaking work *The Field*, McTaggart (2002) says that both our waking thoughts and our dreams may be shared among all those who have ever lived. As she describes,

> We carry on an incessant dialogue with The Field, enriching as well as taking from it. Many of humankind's greatest achievements may result from an individual suddenly gaining access to a shared accumulation of information—a collective effort in the Zero Point Field—in what we consider a moment of inspiration. What we call 'genius' may simply be a greater ability to access the Zero Point Field. In that sense, our intelligence, creativity and imagination are not locked in our brains but exist as an interaction with The Field. (McTaggart, 2002, p. 139)

In 2005 we reached out to 34 Knowledge Management Thought Leaders located across four continents to explore the aspects of KM that contributed to the passion expressed by these thought leaders (what we refer to as the KMTL Study). By definition, thought leaders are part of a social network, part of a collective whole, with both formal and informal, visible and invisible, networks with whom they exchange viewpoints, engage in discussions and use as sounding boards. This network can be described as partners, co-authors, spouses, friends, mentors, colleagues, associates, thought partners, people we trust, and other people who work in the field. While we will delve into the results of this research in Chapter 36/Part V, a concept forwarded by many of these thought leaders was that the *ideas are already out there, just waiting to be recognized*, and we just need to be open to recognizing them and catching hold of them. For example, Etienne Wenger, the first to develop the community of practice idea for organizations, says that ideas are, "In the air … you know what I mean? It's not like you invented things, you just sit and they're in the air. And you say, oh yes, that's right, but it was already in the air, you know?"

Another thought leader referred to this Field of Ideas in terms of the Akashic Records. He says that along the way to becoming a thought leader he developed a holographic method to record interactions among people, and between people and computers in organizations, from spiritual models such as the Akashic Records. The Akashic Records represent the membrane of a higher frequency upon which every thought and every action is written such that the past and history can be read as a series of streams. The visioning of this capability birthed a new process.

A number of characteristics have been identified of people who can "repeatedly succeed, in the domain of ideas, in escaping from a basin of attraction into another, deeper one" (Gell-Mann, 1994, p. 369). These include focus/dedication to the task, awareness of being caught in an unsuitable basin, some level of comfort with teetering on the edge, and the capacity for formulating and solving problems. Formulation is critical in determining the boundaries of a problem.

Diving within to our sense of knowing becomes a critical ability to successfully living in a CUCA[28-2] environment. One thought leader shared that he listens to his inner voice. Knowledge and knowing are a source of this inner voice. Appendix D is the Knowledge Capacity of Engaging Tacit Knowledge. Tacit knowledge is within the storehouse of self, expanding and connecting within from the time each of us is in the womb. Appendix E is a treatment of Knowing developed for the U.S. Department of the Navy. Both of these appendices suggest ways of tapping into the Field.

A Few Final Thoughts

We would like to add a few random thoughts that are pertinent to the subject at hand. First, ideas are contagious. This is the concept of memes, which are ideas that become enculturated, thoughts that resonate and linger, attaching themselves to other thoughts in a continuing cycle of regeneration. As introduced earlier, memes evolve by natural selection in a process similar to that of genes in evolutionary biology. They are effective, potent ideas that out-propagate other ideas in a process of self-replication. Taking on a life of its own, a meme is a form of learning (an idea, instruction, behavior or piece of information) that is passed on by imitation. They spread themselves around indiscriminately without regard to whether they are useful, neutral, or positively harmful! And, over time, memes evolve as memes, building on memes, re-appearing and re-associating patterns of thought, taking on new meaning. An example is the growth path of new technologies or new management strategies.

Second, despite certain cognitive losses, we now know that the engaged, mature brain can make effective decisions at more intuitive levels. Goldberg (2005) points out that the aging brain can accomplish mental feats that are different than younger brains. He makes the point that although older people forget names, facts, and words, they have the capability of remembering high-level patterns and meaningful insights that we often consider as deep intuition and as wisdom. So, if we choose, the value of experience and individuation, and what each can contribute to the whole, continues to expand throughout our lives!

<<<<<<<>>>>>>>

INSIGHT: **The value of experience and individuation, and what each can contribute to the whole, continues to expand throughout our lives.**

<<<<<<<>>>>>>>

Finally, when confronted with a problem, the machinery of intuitive thought does the best it can. If the individual has relevant expertise, the situation will be recognized, and the intuitive solution that comes to mind is likely to be correct. This is what happens when a chess master looks at a complex position: the few moves that immediately occur to him are all strong. When the question is difficult and a skilled solution is not available, we often answer an easier one instead, usually without noticing the substitution.

Herbert Simon, a world class chess master coach, says that intuition is nothing more and nothing less than recognition (Ross, 2006b). Valid intuitions develop when experts have learned to recognize familiar elements in a new situation and to act in a manner that is appropriate to it. So, when is intuition really the use of judgment?

The typical definition of judgment is the act or process of judging the formation of an opinion after consideration or deliberation. (*American Heritage Dictionary*, 2011). In addition, it is *the mental ability to perceive and distinguish relationships* or the capacity to *form an opinion by distinguishing and evaluating*. Perhaps these two concepts are more intertwined then we previously perceived them to be. (Judgment is discussed in Chapter 35/Part V.)

Questions for Reflection:

How do you generate insights from patterns and relationships to anticipate future behavior?

How do I prepare to capture those flashes of insight?

Chapter 29
Exploring Creativity

SUBPARTS: FROM WHENCE DOES CREATIVITY COME? ... IS EVERYONE CREATIVE? ... KNOWLEDGE AS THE ACTION LEVER FOR CREATIVITY ... NEUROSCIENCE FINDINGS ... EXTRAORDINARY CREATIVITY ... FINAL THOUGHTS

FIGURES: 29-1. EXPLORING THE RELATIONSHIPS AMONG INFORMATION, KNOWLEDGE, CREATIVITY AND INNOVATION ... **29-2.** WHAT WE ARE LEARNING ABOUT CREATIVITY FROM THE MIND/BRAIN PERSPECTIVE.

TOOL: 29-1. QUIETING THE MIND

Creativity is the emergence of new or original patterns (ideas, concepts, or actions). Mihaly Csikszentmihalyi (1996), Professor of Psychology at the University of Chicago, notes that the term creativity originally meant to bring into existence something genuinely new that is valued enough to be added to the culture. Quantum physicist Amit Goswami (2014) offers his definition of creativity as the creation of something new in an entirely new context; *newness of the context* is the key.

Theoretical biologist Rupert Sheldrake (1989) says that creativity is a profound mystery precisely because it involves the appearance of patterns that never existed before. And Plato viewed creativity as both mysterious and divine:

> For the poet is an airy thing, a winged and a holy thing; and he cannot make poetry until he becomes inspired and goes out of his senses and no mind is left in him ... not by art, then, they make their poetry ... but by divine dispensation. (Warmington & Rouse, 1984, p. 18).

The romantic could substitute the word "exceptional" for "divine," glorifying creative people as gifted with talent (insight or intuition) that others lack.

For purposes of this book, we use the definition of creativity defined by Andreason (2005). Thus, we see creativity as emerging new or original ideas or seeing new patterns in some domain of knowledge. In other words, creativity can be considered as *the ability to perceive new relationships and new possibilities*, seeing things from a different frame of reference, realizing new ways of understanding, or having insight.

From Whence Does Creativity Come?

Arthur Koestler (1975) went beyond describing creativity as inspirational and romantic, and tried to understand how creativity happens. He felt that,

The moment of truth, the sudden emergence of a new insight, is an act of intuition. Such intuition gives the appearance of miraculous flashes, or short circuits of reasoning. In fact they may be likened to an immersed chain, of which only the beginning and the end are visible above the surface of consciousness. The diver vanishes at one end of the chain and comes up at the other end, guided by invisible links (p. 211).

While Koestler's words insinuate more, they do not *explain* the more.

Andreasen suggests there are five circumstances that create *cradles of creativity* (Andreasen, 2005). These are (1) an atmosphere of intellectual freedom and excitement; (2) a critical mass of creative minds; (3) free and fair competition; (4) mentors and patrons; and (5) at least some economic prosperity. Gell-Mann demonstrates a cradle of creativity by describing a shared experience in conceiving creative ideas. He was one of a small group of physicists, biologists, painters and poets that joined together in 1970 to talk about their experiences in getting creative ideas. As Gell-Mann (1994, p. 264) describes,

The accounts all agreed to a remarkable extent. We had each found a contradiction between the established way of doing things and something we needed to accomplish: in art, the expression of a feeling, a thought, an insight; in theoretical science, the explanation of some experimental facts in the face of an accepted 'paradigm' that did not permit such an explanation.

Each person had started with a focus on the problem and the difficulties they were trying to overcome. When further conscious thought was deemed useless, that stopped, although each continued to carry the problem around with them. Then, suddenly, while doing something quite different—shaving, cooking, or engaged in simple conversation—an idea just popped into thought.

Thus, the unconscious appears to play an essential role in creativity. Henri Poincaré (2001) suggests that creativity *tugs* on the unconscious. He builds on the four stages of creativity identified by Gram Wallas in his book, *The Art of Thought*, published in 1926. These are preparation, incubation, illumination, and verification. The initial phase, *preparation*, is the conscious probing of a problem or an idea. The second phase, *incubation*, occurs while the conscious mind is focused elsewhere, and may last for minutes, months, or years. During this time, the unconscious mind may well be contemplating the challenge and trying to make sense of the situation. Poincaré credited this phase with the novelties denied through waking, rational thought. The flash of insight, or tug, comes in the third phase, *illumination*, when creative thoughts burst through the unconscious stirring of incubation into the conscious, where it can be explored and tested in the fourth phase, *verification* or *validation*. Underlying all this, of course, is the openness to new ways of doing things.

<<<<<<<◇>>>>>>

INSIGHT: **The unconscious plays an essential role in creativity.**

<<<<<<<◇>>>>>>

Poincaré (1982) visualized the creative thought mechanism of the unconscious as similar to the workings of the atom.

> Figure the future elements of our combinations as something like the hooked atoms of Epicurus. During the complete repose of the mind, these atoms are motionless, they are, so to speak, hooked to the wall ...; On the other hand, during a period of apparent rest and unconscious work, certain of them are detached from the wall and put in motion. They flash in every direction ... [like] a swarm of gnats, or, if you prefer a more learned comparison, like the molecules of gas in the kinematic theory of gases. Then their mutual impacts may produce new combinations. (Poincaré, 1982, p. 389).

The role of this preliminary conscious work is to mobilize certain of these atoms,

> ... to unhook them from the wall and put them in swing ... After this shaking up imposed upon them by our will, these atoms do not return to their primitive rest. They freely continue their dance. Now, our will did not choose them at random; it pursued a perfectly determined aim. The mobilized atoms are therefore not any atoms whatsoever; they are those from which we might reasonably expect the desired solution (Poincare, 1982, p. 389).

Then, there is a bursting forth. As Tchaikovsky (2016) describes,

> Generally speaking, the germ of a future composition comes suddenly and unexpectedly...It takes root with extraordinary force and rapidity, shoots up through the Earth, puts forth branches and leaves, and finally blossoms. I cannot define the creative process in any way but this simile.

Jeffrey (2008) agrees that creativity is an aspect of consciousness, governed by impersonal attractor fields of varying strengths within the Universal Consciousness. Thus, creativity is the result of the assimilation and progressive organization of information, what could be described as evolutionary learning, which in turn produces the linear from the ever-present field of the nonlinear.

Is everyone creative?

Boden (1991) says yes, and we agree. Boden breaks creative thought (or creative people) into two types: P-creative (psychological or personal) and H-creative (historical). P-creative ideas are fundamentally novel with respect to the individual mind, the person who has them, and H-creative ideas are historically grounded, fundamentally novel with respect to the whole of recorded human history. Her point is that the H-creative ideas, which by definition are also P-creative, are the ones that are socially recognized as creative, but P-creative ideas are *possible in every human being*.

It would be difficult to cover the many approaches that have been taken to explore the subject of human creativity. Just to provide an idea of the massive amount of research, these include mystical approaches such as Rudyard Kipling's (1937/1985) Daemon; pragmatic approaches such as the lateral thinking of Edward DeBono (1992); the psychodynamic approach introduced by Freud (1908/1959); psychometric approaches, which involved laboratory testing as exampled by Guilford (1950) and Torrance (1974); cognitive approaches such as those forwarded by Finke, Ward and Smith (1992), which described a generative phase and exploratory phase to creativity; social-personality approaches focused on personality and motivational variables in combination with the sociocultural environment as exampled by Amabile (1983) and Eysenck (1993); evolutionary approaches instigated by Campbell (1960) and picked up by Perkins (1995) and Simonton (1999), saying there were two steps to creativity, blind variation and selective retention; and confluence approaches such as the work forwarded by Csikszentmihalyi (1988), Amabile (1996), and Gruber (1989).

<<<<<<<<◇>>>>>>>

INSIGHT: **Creativity is a choice; creativity can be developed.**

<<<<<<<<◇>>>>>>>

Ultimately, Sternberg, who takes a confluence approach, that is, integrating all the other approaches, says that *creativity is a choice*; in his words, it is a decision which has three parts: "The decision to be creative, the decision of how to be creative, and implementation of these decisions" (Sternberg, 2003, p. 125). Thus, he agrees that *creativity can be developed*. Sternberg (2003) forwards an investment theory of creativity, requiring a confluence of six interrelated resources: intellectual abilities, knowledge, styles of thinking, personality, motivation and environment. His bottom line is that creative intelligence is just a part of human creativity. More is needed. As he describes that "more",

> Creativity also involves aspects of knowledge, styles of thinking, personality, and motivation, as well as these psychological components in interaction and the environment. An individual with the intellectual skills for creativity but without the other personal attributes is unlikely to do creative work. (Sternberg, 2003, p. 188)

Let's briefly explore the relationships among information, knowledge, creativity and innovation.

Knowledge as the Action Lever for Creativity

Creativity comes exclusively from people, a capacity to see new ideas from associating internal and external information. Some experts believe that creativity should also have utility and lead to a new product or process, that is, innovation. Innovation means the creation of new ideas *and* the transformation of those ideas into useful applications; thus, the combination of creativity and contribution as operational values promote innovation. Values in this context have two dimensions: (1) that which is highly regarded, and (2) that which is perceived as worthy or desirable. As with all knowledge, values are relative, that is, context-sensitive and situation-dependent (Bennet & Bennet, 2007b; Avedisian & Bennet, 2010).

A creative environment is fueled by the values of integrity, empathy, transparency, collaboration, learning, and contribution that foster trust and a spirit of collaborative success (Avedisian & Bennet, 2010). These values are detailed in Appendix F. As an operational value, creativity is the ability to perceive new relationships and new possibilities, see things from a different frame of reference, or realize new ways of understanding/having insight or portraying something. Innovation represents the creation of new ideas and the transformation of those ideas into useful applications. Thus, as noted above, the combination of creativity and contribution as operational values brings about innovation.

<<<<<<<◇>>>>>>

INSIGHT: **A creative environment is fueled by the values of integrity, empathy, transparency, collaboration, learning, and contribution that foster trust and a spirit of collaborative success.**

<<<<<<<◇>>>>>>

As an idea generator, knowledge is the currency of creativity and innovation. As information flows freely and is generally available to all—and as people recognize the power of and creative potential in the mind/brain and learn to tap into that power and creativity to create change for the greater good—each individual has the ability to be a thought leader, taking effective action in their domain of focus. See Bennet et al. (2015c).

While knowledge comes from the past and creativity requires knowledge, both knowledge and creativity are capacities which can be applied in the present (actual) or engaged in the future (potential). Further, they both emerge from the associative patterning process of the brain, that is, the unique complexing of external and internal information (organized patterns). In Figure 29-1 we draw a dotted line between knowledge and creativity, which when combined lead to innovation. Note that innovation is not necessarily an immediate result. As Fritz Machlup said in the early 1960's in his seminal work on the knowledge economy, "We shall have to bring out clearly that this is not a simple unidirectional flow from one stage to the next, from inception to development, to eventual adoption, but there are usually cross-currents, eddies, and whirlpools." (Machlup, 1962, p. 179)

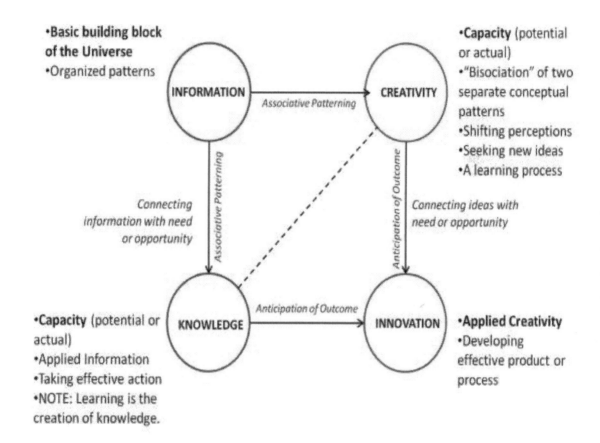

Figure 29-1. *Exploring the relationships among information, knowledge, creativity and innovation.*

Past experiences, feelings, knowledge, goals and the situation at hand all influence how creative an individual will, or can, be. It is the context of the activity or situation at hand (need, challenge, etc.) that triggers the putting things together (bisociation) in an unusual way to create (and recognize) something that may be new and potentially useful (innovation). Thus, knowledge—context sensitive and situation dependent—is the ***action lever for creativity***.

Neuroscience Findings

Neuroscience findings support that everyone is creative and creativity is a choice. Creativity is an inherent capability of every mind/brain (Hobson, 1999; Cristos, 2003). Learning consists of building new patterns within the mind that represent ideas, concepts, and capabilities, and processes that are internally imagined (creative imagination), or represent some interpretation of external reality. According to Stonier (1997), thinking involves *the association of different patterns* within the mind/brain. Since memory is distributed throughout the brain, these associative processes may contain random associations that can result in new ideas, concepts, or approaches. This is considered as ordinary creativity and can be very valuable as a form of self-learning.

These new patterns may represent insights or increased understanding of a situation, or perhaps a clarification of the meaning of a situation. They may come from the unconscious mind "playing with" ideas that are experienced during the night. This is most likely the source of the adage, "we need to sleep on it." (See TOOL 27-1 in Chapter 27.) Since much thinking is done by the unconscious during sleep, learning can be enhanced by making use of the mind's capability for creativity. Such practices as meditation, lucid dreaming and hemispheric synchronization can serve to improve creativity and problem solving. Other practices such as changing one's frame of reference and other Knowledge Capacities also create new ways of viewing problems.

Neuroscience findings related to creativity that we briefly address are: (1) an enriched environment can produce a personal internal reflective world of imagination and creativity; (2) conscious and unconscious patterns are involved with creativity; (3) the unconscious produces flashes of insight; (4) volleying between conscious and unconscious thinking increases creativity; (5) meditation quiets the mind; (6) extraordinary creativity can be developed; (7) free flow and randomness of mixing patterns can create new patterns; and (8) accidental associations.

(1) An enriched environment can produce a personal internal reflective world of imagination and creativity. This item is part of the environment, and as such may affect a number of the aspects of concrete experience and active experimentation. A rich environment entering the mind/brain/body through experiences increases the formation and survival of new neurons, stimulating the mind to associate patterns and create new possibilities. The literature suggests that an enriched environment contains many interesting and thought-provoking ideas, pictures, books, statues, etc. Byrnes

(2001) says that in an enriched environment there are physiological changes in the brain, specifically, thicker cortices are created, cell bodies are larger, and dendritic branching in the brain is more extensive. These changes have been directly connected to higher levels of intelligence (Begley, 2007, Jensen, 1998). Note that in today's world, the context of an enriched environment includes the augmentation of the brain/mind with technologies (Bennet et al., 2015b).

(2) Conscious and unconscious patterns are involved with creativity. Creative insight is the result of searching for new relationships between concepts in one domain with those in another domain (Crandall et al., 2006). It creates a recognition and understanding of a problem within the situation, including the how and why of the past and current behavior of the situation. It is often the result of intuition, competence, and the identification of patterns, themes and cue sets (Crandall et al., 2006). Insight may also provide patterns and relationships that will anticipate the future behavior of the situation.

(3) The unconscious produces flashes of insight. As was introduced in the previous chapter, spurious memories can generate new ideas that combine in different ways to make new associations (Christos, 2003). This relates to uncontrolled intuition.

(4) Volleying between the conscious and the unconscious increases creativity. "New ideas are generated through the process of shifting from conscious to unconscious as the mind contemplates and searches for solutions" (Christos, 2003, p. 90). The process of shifting between conscious and unconscious thinking makes use of the memories and knowledge in the unconscious and the goals and thinking of the conscious mind. This increases the chances of associating conscious ideas to create new ones. While this occurs in the transition from the waking state to the sleeping state (and vice versa), to do this while awake requires some level of control and discipline in implementation.

(5) Meditation quiets the mind. Again, meditation requires some level of control and discipline, and it can significantly enhance the ability to focus attention. In this context, quieting the mind means to reduce the noise that "bedevils the untrained mind, in which an individual's focus darts from one sight or sound or thought to another like a hyperactive dragonfly, and replace it with attentional stability and clarity" (Begley, 2007, p. 214). Quieting the mind allows the mind to focus attention on potential relationships that may create new ideas.

(6) Extraordinary creativity can be developed. A basic operation of the brain is that of associating patterns within the mind to create new patterns (thoughts, ideas, and concepts), what is referred to as ordinary creativity. As we have forwarded, everyone possesses ordinary creativity (Andreasen, 2005), the creation of new ways of doing things in their daily lives through discussing new ideas and developing insights and deeper understanding. In this sense *all learning is creating*. Recall that *extraordinary creativity* refers to highly creative people who often receive ideas through flashes of insights and moments of inspiration.

(7) Free-flow and randomly mixing patterns create new patterns. This relates directly to creativity and is one way to describe the interaction among neuronal networks and patterns to create new ideas. As described, this is a random emergent process stimulated by the continuous activity of the mind. While this activity is outside of conscious internal focusing or environmental external triggering, it is based on past exposure, experience and learning; thus future activity may be nurtured.

(8) Accidental associations can create new patterns. As an extension to (7) above, this makes the point that creativity can happen by accident *within an active mind that plays with ideas, connections, and their relationships*.

Figure 29-2 is a summary graphic of these findings.

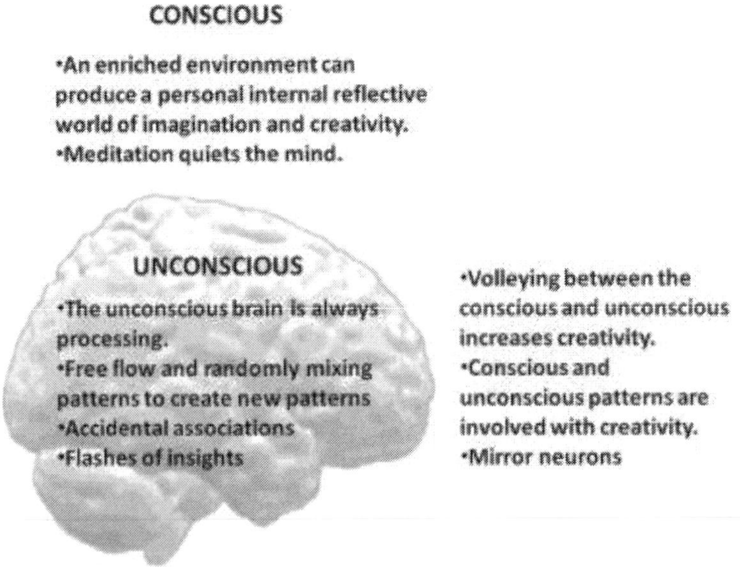

CONSCIOUS

•An enriched environment can produce a personal internal reflective world of imagination and creativity.
•Meditation quiets the mind.

UNCONSCIOUS

•The unconscious brain is always processing.
•Free flow and randomly mixing patterns to create new patterns
•Accidental associations
•Flashes of insights

•Volleying between the conscious and unconscious increases creativity.
•Conscious and unconscious patterns are involved with creativity.
•Mirror neurons

Figure 29-2. *What we are learning about creativity from the mind/brain perspective.*

Here's what we have learned from these findings. Since both conscious and unconscious patterns are involved in creativity, it just makes sense that *volleying between the conscious and unconscious increases creativity*. Further, it makes sense that the environment in which you are conscious is enriched, while, simultaneously, meditation is used to quiet the mind, that is, *moving from an outer enriched state to an inner enriched state*.

Recognizing that we are multidimensional and that the unconscious brain is always processing, randomly mixing patterns to create new patterns, it can be seen that the experiences to which we expose ourselves and the people with whom we interact directly impact our creativity. Even when we are consciously unaware of our surroundings and the activities underway, information is being received and processed. The flow of our everyday lives really counts!

****

TOOL 29-1: QUIETING THE MIND

STEP (1): *Location*. Find a quiet and comfortable place to sit or lie for a half hour (or more), keeping a pen and pad of paper nearby for emerging thoughts. This may be inside or outside, depending on your comfort level.

STEP (2): *Clearing your mind*. Close your eyes and use your imagination to create a mental exercise that will allow you to empty your mind of past and present worries and concerns. As an example, here is an exercise adapted from The Monroe Institute[29-1]. Imagine a large box with a heavy lead top, which is open.

(a) In your hands is a checklist. On that checklist are all the incidents in your life that have troubled or bothered you in any way, the names of any people with whom you have had an altercation, all the worries that are currently in your mind, and any future commitments that are prominent in your mind. You do not have to bring these things into conscious thought. Just acknowledge that the list is complete, fold it up and put it in your box.

(b) Now, do a quick scan of your body for any aches and pains. Focus on the place where the ache or pain is manifesting, imagine it as clay, and reach in and pull out all the clay, rolling it into a ball and bouncing it into your box. Do this for each area where an ache or pain is manifesting.

(c) Next, do a quick scan for fear, all fears, large or small, wherever fear resides in your body. Focus on each place and, imagining the fear as a stream of yellow, orange or red light, stream it into the box.

(d) Next, focus inside your brain and imagine all the monkey chatter underway as old-fashioned tickertape, the stuff you've seen in the movie *Miracle on 24th Street* being thrown out of windows during the Macy's holiday parade. Grab two or three big handfuls of this tickertape to clear out the monkey chatter, putting each handful in your box.

(e) Finally, reach inside your chest, pull out your ego, and put it inside the box. Don't worry, you can always retrieve it later (or the part of it you choose to retrieve).

(f) Now, close that heavy lead top and push the box around behind you. Imagine a vacuum cleaner hose coming from that box to your left shoulder. Should any negative image, ache, fear or monkey chatter come up during your quiet time, just send it up that vacuum cleaner hose to your box.

STEP (3): *Float*. For those who regularly meditate, clearing your mind may have already taken you into a place of floating, a quiet mind state. One way to achieve this is to focus on the Fontanelle, the soft spot at the top (center) of your head that served you as an infant. This focus is not accomplished by thought, but rather a feeling of the inner eyes looking upward. This becomes easier with practice.

STEP (4): Once you have achieved this quiet place, relax and enjoy it, letting free-flowing thoughts and visuals play in this space, opening your eyes and briefly jotting down notes when something of meaning to you emerges, then continuing your float. A common visual during this event is the opening and dissolving of colorful energy bubbles. Enjoy the energy and allow your body to relax.

STEP (5): When you feel complete bring your awareness back to your outer enriched environment, knowing that you can return to this quiet place whenever you choose.

****

Extraordinary Creativity

Let's explore this idea of extraordinary creativity a bit further. *Extraordinary creativity* relates to certain individuals who have the capacity to repeatedly create novel ideas or processes that push the limits of understanding or application. These are the truly creative people who keep an open mind, maintain a high curiosity, and investigate many paths toward new possibilities. They have a particular mental capability and capacity for challenging the status quo and seeing things from unique perspectives (Andreasen, 2005).

Ideas are often received through flashes of insights and moments of inspiration (see Chapter 28). Inspiration has historically been described as a transfusion of soul or breath of divinity from the gods received by a fortunate individual. Today, inspiration is described as an insight that cuts across categories or leaps over normal steps of reasoning. In this experience there is a psycho-logical element that we are abandoning our thought to another force, a powerful flow of ideas.

This experience does not appear to be designed or purposed; in fact, to labor or work toward it can move us in the opposite direction. However, English Professor Robert Grudin (1984) thinks that we can practice *deserving it* through embedding habits in our daily lives. Describing these habits as a demanding and integral code, Grudin collectively calls these habits the ethics of inspiration. This utopian code includes: love of one's work, fidelity, concentration, love of problems, a sense of the openness of thought, boldness, innocence, an uncensored mind, civility, gentleness, and liberty. This is a good set. As Grudin describes, "It is a garden of mind, recalling Eden, Rousseau's vision of philosophy as a recapturing of nature, and Milton's idea that the purpose of education was to rebuild the ruins of the Fall." (Grudin, 1984, p.15.)

Extraordinarily creative people "go into a state *at the edge of chaos*, where ideas float, soar, collide and collect" (Andreasen, 2005, p.159) While this state may result in something of value becoming a reality, all too often the flash is there and then gone, disappearing into a Field of Ideas to which we may or may not again connect (see Chapter 28). This is what can be referred to as uncontrolled intuition. What we are searching for is how the individual can, at will, take the creative leap and purposefully tap into the Field of Ideas. This is the capacity for controlled intuition.

The really interesting news is that ordinary people can become extraordinarily creative! Further, ordinary people can become an inspiration to others. As Green (2016, p. 1) writes,

> When we think about inspiration, what inspires us most are ordinary people who have done extraordinary things. We appreciate when someone has the ability and willingness to be selfless, creative, innovative, or just dares to be different .... The beautiful thing about inspiration of this kind is that "ordinary" part .... [E]ach of them came from backgrounds of great poverty and difficulty. Each of them faced giant mountains to climb. They managed to reach the summit of those mountains not simply because they were great leaders, but because they were not afraid to be who they were. They were authentic.

There are many techniques, both individual and group processes, that serve to open the mind to new possibilities and stimulate creative thinking. Such processes use all forms of learning with some being from concrete experience, dialogue, or social interaction; others from internal reflection and comprehension. In either case, if learners understand the dangers of assuming they already "know" the answer, they may deliberately keep an open mind and improve both the efficiency and the effectiveness of their learning and creativity. *Becoming aware that every healthy mind is capable of creativity, and that the rules and practices of creative thinking are available to anyone*, opens the door to enhanced individual and organizational creativity and learning capacity.

Final Thoughts

We now recognize that everyone has the capacity for creativity and that creativity is a choice. Through exploring findings from neuroscience, we begin to understand potential ways of tapping into our creativity. The two summary paragraphs introduced above bear repeating here:

First, since both conscious and unconscious patterns are involved in creativity, it just makes sense that *volleying between the conscious and unconscious increases creativity*. It also makes sense that the environment in which you are conscious is enriched, while, simultaneously, meditation is used to quiet the mind, that is, *moving from an outer enriched state to an inner enriched state*.

Recognizing that we are multidimensional and that the unconscious brain is always processing, randomly mixing patterns to create new patterns, it can be seen that the experiences to which we expose ourselves and the people with whom we interact directly impact our creativity. Even when we are consciously unaware of our surroundings and the activities underway, information is being received and processed.

We reiterate: *The flow of our everyday lives really counts!*

Questions for Reflection:

What am I doing to expand my creative capacity?

How and how often do I interact with others to create and develop new ideas?

How might I create an enriched environment, both inner and outer?

Chapter 30
The Creative Leap

SUBPARTS: EXPANDING OUR CREATIVE CAPACITY ... BEYOND CONTEXT AND SITUATION ... FROM THE QUANTUM PERSPECTIVE ...AN IN-DEPTH LOOK ... ARE YOU READY TO LEAP? ... IN SUMMARY

FIGURES: 30-1. THERE IS A MULTIPLIER EFFECT OF IDEAS AS THEY ARE SHARED, WITH ALL BENEFITING ... **30-2.** FACILITATING THE CREATIVE LEAP (A QUICK REVIEW).

TOOL: 30-1. HONORING MISTAKES

Understanding and applying the concepts of the previous 29 chapters has begun the process in our Intelligent Social Change Journey of preparing us to make a creative leap, which changes our direction and the frequency of our energy flows. This includes the prerequisites of self: (1) rediscovering the fullness of who we are, and opening and strengthening our connections to the Field of consciousness (Chapter 28); (2) achieving balanced lower mental thought, focused on service to others (Chapter 26); (3) development of higher mental thought, conceptual thinking and the search for truth (Chapter 24); and (4) deepening our connections with others (Chapter 27). With this preparation, there is the opportunity to expand our creative capacity, and that is the first topic of this chapter.

Expanding Our Creative Capacity

It should be clear by now that experience and learning (the creation of knowledge) provide the fodder for human creativity. Nonetheless, there are a number of specific ways to expand our creative capacity. We will introduce and briefly discuss four of these: freedom of thought and self-expression; embracing the mythic worldview; bringing the past and future together to illuminate the present; and knowledge sharing, streaming our thoughts outward.

Freedom of thought and self-expression.

Freedom and choice are synonymous. In Chapter 19/Part III we referenced the emergent concept of neo-management control, which posits that management through individual freedom is a defining element of the 21st century workforce (Walker, 2011). This is because of the growing recognition of *the value of innovation, which emerges from creativity and self-expression*. We specifically focus here on freedom of thought, which enables the diversity necessary for continuously expanding our world.

When discussing this concept among ourselves, the authors asked: How do you know your thinking is free? Even with the awareness that we have mental models, and even if we periodically engage in self-reflection, self knowledge is difficult to achieve. We all have limits in terms of mental models and personal paradigms. Perhaps the greatest tool we have in this regard is openness to learning. In Chapter 4/Part I we introduced the tool of humility. *The simple and profound conscious choice of humility provides an opportunity to ensure freedom of thought.* In taking this approach, you assume the ideas of the "other" are right and reflect on these ideas from that perspective, seeking truth. When contrasted with ego ("I am right") and arrogance ("I am right; you are wrong; and I don't care what others think"), it is clear that utilizing the tool of humility moves the individual beyond embedded mindsets, providing an opening for learning from others. This also benefits others. Openness to the thoughts of others allows them to be freer in their thinking, thus increasing their contribution to the diversity of thought and increasing the potential for bisociation.

<<<<<<<◇>>>>>>

INSIGHT: **The simple and profound conscious choice of humility provides an opportunity to ensure freedom of thought.**

<<<<<<<◇>>>>>>

Embracing the mythic worldview.

The mythic worldview of reality introduced in Chapter 13/Part III supports the creative leap as we co-create our reality. We look to some representative authors quoted in this text, specifically, McWhinney, Bradley and Carse, for their descriptions of this worldview.

> If I were to speak from the mythic view, I would say (to myself): "All the world is my creation; you, my readers, are my creation; I people the world, I create its phenomena, and I assign it in time and locate it in space—which themselves are given meaning by my thought." McWhinney, 1997, p. 43

> I cannot transcend experience and experience is my experience. From this it follows that nothing beyond myself exists; for what is experienced is the [self's] state. (Bradley, 1966, p. 218)

> The mythic reality is a world of story in which we assign and play a role, both created and to be created. Part factual and part fiction, "Whole civilizations arise from stories—and can rise from nothing else … Myths, told for their own sake, are not stories that have meanings, **but stories that give meanings**" [emphasis added]. (Carse, 1986, p. 168)

Thus, the mythic reality is the realm of free-will, without limitation, while embracing that we are all part of a larger Quantum Field, that is, *Oneness with individuated volition*. The power of myth in the planning process has long been acknowledged. As introduced in Chapter 16/Part III, planning is a learning process with two parts: the creation of myths about social realities and the process of emergence (Michael, 1977).

Bringing the past and future together to illuminate the present.

As McWhinney notes, in the mythic world view the phenomena that is created is assigned in time and located in space. There is a direct relationship between maturity, and the unit of time consciousness in any given intellect. Whether the time unit being considered is a day, a year, or a longer period, inevitably it becomes the criterion by which the conscious self evaluates the circumstances of life, and by which the conceiving intellect measures and evaluates its temporal existence (MacFlouer, 2004-16). To become mature is to live more intensely in the present while at the same time *escaping the limitations of the present*. Founded on past experience, the plans of maturity are coming into being in the present in such a manner as to enhance the value of the future.

<<<<<<<◇>>>>>>>

INSIGHT: **Time is the criterion by which the conscious self evaluates the circumstances of life and by which the conceiving intellect measures and evaluates its temporal existence.**

<<<<<<<◇>>>>>>>

We look to *Urantia* (1954) to help us better understand this concept: *The maturity of the developing self brings the past and future together to illuminate the true meaning of the present.* For example, an entrepreneur combines the knowledge and capabilities he has gained from the past with the vision he has of the future to make meaningful decisions in the present. *As the self matures, it reaches further and further back into the past for experience, while its wisdom seeks to penetrate deeper and deeper into the unknown future.* As the conceiving self extends this reach ever further into both the past and the future, so does judgment become less and less dependent on the momentary present. In this way, the decision-action loop begins to escape the fetters of the moving present—perceived roadblocks in the present—and takes on aspects of past-future significance. One way of perceiving this is to focus on the "what" and "why" (which represent a future desired state and experience from the past) and let go of the "how" (which represents movement in the present) such that your decisions are not impacted by perceived limitations of the present.

<<<<<<<◇>>>>>>

INSIGHT: **As the conceiving self extends its reach ever further into both the past and future, so does judgment become less and less dependent on the momentary present**.

<<<<<<<◇>>>>>>

This process enables the individual to see the wholeness of events spanning time. For example, when the time unit of immaturity concentrates meaning-value into the present moment, it divorces the present of its true relationship to that which is not-present, that is, the past-future. When the time unit of maturity is proportioned, it reveals the co-ordinate relationship of past-present-future such that the self begins to gain insight into the wholeness of events, even to the point that the individual "begins to view the landscape of time from the panoramic perspective of broadened horizons, begins perhaps to suspect the non-beginning, non-ending eternal continuum, the fragments of which are called time" (*Urantia*, 1954, p. 1295-1296).

Knowledge sharing, streaming our thoughts outward.

Streaming our thoughts outward can be described in terms of knowledge sharing, cooperation and collaboration, or social knowledge, and, as a result, our own learning and expanding. As we interact with others, we develop a deeper understanding of others and ourselves and an appreciation for diversity. This understanding helps us create without force, embracing a collaborative advantage rather than a competitive advantage. (See Chapter 14/Part III for an in-depth discussion of collaborative and competitive advantage.) Collaborative advantage is a "win-win" in a global world. We are able to gain the advantage of other's thinking at or above our personal level of thinking, while simultaneously creating in a way that is uniquely ours. We are concurrently individuated and one.

We now understand from neuroscience findings that the mind is an associative patterner, recreating knowledge for the moment at hand. Simultaneously, we understand that creativity is the bisociation of two or more ideas to create a new idea or apply an idea in a new context. Thus, *there is a multiplier effect of ideas as they are shared*. The more we share and participate in cooperative and collaborative experiences, the more opportunity for the bisociation of ideas. See Figure 30-1.

As a humanity, we are action-oriented and knowledge-driven. Just as a winding stream in the bowels of the mountains curves and dips through ravines and high valleys, so, too, with knowledge. In a continuous journey towards intelligent activity, context-sensitive and situation-dependent knowledge, imperfect and incomplete, experientially engages a changing landscape in a continuous cycle of learning and expanding. It is the context of the activity or situation at hand (need, challenge, etc.) that triggers the putting things together in an unusual way to create (and recognize) something that may be new and potentially useful (innovation). *We as a humanity are in a continuous cycle of knowledge creation such that every moment offers the opportunity for the emergence of new and exciting ideas, all waiting to be put in service to an interconnected world.*

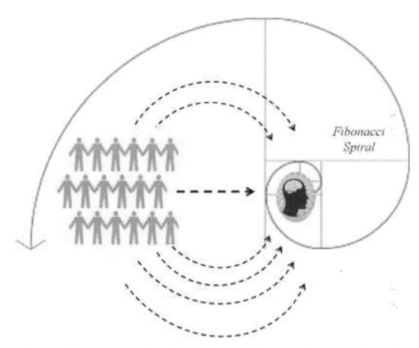

Figure 30-1. *There is a multiplier effect of ideas as they are shared, with all benefiting.*

Recall that all knowledge is incomplete. When knowledge is focused inward, that is, *not* shared, it has diminishing value as others continue to connect with the ever-changing and expanding reservoir of knowledge. An individual with bounded knowledge has ceased learning, over time losing any value it may have had in terms of taking effective action and thus reverting to information. Further, there is a diminishing of consciousness and meaning. MacFlouer (2004-16) emphasizes that **we can't stand on the sidelines, that the greatest meaning of life comes with co-creating**. When we cease co-creating, when we cease learning, we enter a downward spiral that is characterized by the loss of consciousness, the loss of meaning, and, eventually, the loss of life.

Beyond Context and Situation

The creative leap is the result of creative imagination grounded in the bisociation of multiple points (ideas/concepts) of knowledge and knowing comprising more than half the field of thought. Now, that is a mouthful! Let's explore this concept a bit more. The creative leap is a combination of conscious choice (self), with connected thoughts heading the same direction, and unconscious participation, with the leap occurring in the NOW state yet not constrained by, nor necessarily even connected to, a perceived current reality (Bennet et al., 2015b; Bennet et al., 2015a). This disconnection means that the creative leap is potentially beyond current context-sensitivity and situation-dependence, that is, the new condition may produce an entirely new context and situation, or be something entirely new in a similar context and situation.

While the creative leap occurs through connections with the intuitional plane, and therefore *may* be an outcome of controlled intuition, it is not controlled intuition. Recall that we defined intuition as the ability to determine the causes of any and all effects, a higher awareness, a deeper understanding, an immediate cognition. Controlled intuition was described as the ability to tap into the intuitional plane at will. In terms of relationship, the creative leap is that which *may* occur when you tap into the intuitional plane.

However, development of the mental faculties is in service to both controlled intuition and the creative leap. This is not a new idea. Tim Brown, the CEO and President of IDEO, ranked independently as one of the ten most innovative companies and designer of such innovations as the first mouse for Apple and Palm V, understands that intuitive leaps follow along the path of mental development. As he says in the opening description of his book, we don't simply realize solutions; we design them:

> **The myth of innovation is that brilliant ideas leap fully formed from the minds of geniuses.** [Emphasis added] In reality, most innovations are borne from rigor and discipline. Breakthrough ideas—whether for a new bicycle, an advertising campaign, a treatment plan for diabetes, or a program aimed at tackling the national obesity epidemic—emerge not by chance, but by studying and embracing the immediate challenges we encounter every day in our offices and homes, laboratories and hospitals, classrooms and conference rooms, and in all the spaces in between. (Brown, 2009, front flap)

The visual depiction of design thinking printed on the inside cover of Brown's book, *Change by Design*, is worth purchasing the book. Embracing a human-centered approach, it graphically connects the new social contract, converting need into demand, inspiration, observation and empathy; deep-diving and surfacing; thinking with our hands; building an experience culture, and so much more. The bottom line of his message is that design thinking combines the creation of elegant objects and beautifying the world around us with necessity and utility, constraint, and possibility and demand (see Chapter 33/Part V on the harmony of beauty). Design thinkers combine rigorous observations of the use of spaces and objects and the services that use them, discover patterns within complexity and chaos, synthesize ideas from diverse fragments, and convert issues and problems into opportunities (Brown, 2009).

Brown links design thinking to intuition. As he describes, "It is not only human-centered; it is deeply human in and of itself. Design thinking relies on our ability to be intuitive, to recognize patterns, to construct ideas that have emotional meaning as well as functionality, to express ourselves in media other than words or symbols" (Brown, 2009, p. 4) We would also link it to the ability to synthesize and the development of pattern thinking (see Chapter 17/Part III), and would suggest: It is time to become a design thinker.

From the Quantum Perspective

The creative leap occurs as expanding consciousness achieves a consistency of focus with energies in the Quantum Field flowing in the same direction. Thus, the creative leap "might simply be a sudden coalescence of coherence in The Field" (McTaggart, 2002, p. 95), that is, *increased* thought heading the same direction. Recall that consciousness is defined as a process—a sequential set of ideas, thoughts, images, feelings and perceptions and an understanding of the connections and relationships among them that represent the sum total of who we are, what we believe, how we act and the things we do, thus fully engaging all the senses. The Quantum Field is a probability field; the greater the focus in a specific direction, that is, the more energy moving in a consistent direction, the greater the probability of what is in that direction occurring, yet until the instant of that leap all that is possible exists.

<<<<<<<◇>>>>>>>

INSIGHT: **The Quantum Field is a probability field where all that is possible exists. The more energy moving in a consistent direction, the greater the probability of what is in that direction occurring.**

<<<<<<<◇>>>>>>>

When we explore the past and future in the co-evolving NOW, Phase 2 of the Intelligent Social Change Journey, an important aspect of our creative imagination which emerges from patterns of the past is our *assumption of continuity*. The developing mental mind is pulled into this assumption because it is consistent with mathematics, objective and logical. But,, this is thinking that is superseded, because "Quantum physics, from its very inception, has beaten the doctrine of continuity to a pulp" (Goswami, 2000, p. 30).

Quite different than the concept of continuity, a fascinating characteristic of the Quantum Field is the capacity for instant change from one state to another. From the Quantum viewpoint, something can go from point A to point B at the subatomic level *without ever having been anywhere in between*. This is the concept of the Quantum leap—where an electron orbiting one atom jumps to another atom—that was introduced by Nobel Prize-winning physicist Niels Bohr, and the basis for what we call the creative leap. Since the Quantum Field is a probability field, this instantaneous shift or change is unpredictable. Thus, much like intuition, the starting point of the creative leap can be described and known but the ending point of the creative leap is unknown, although it will be *in the direction of thought and energy in the Field*. The example of "Conversations That Matter" introduced in Chapter 11/Part II is aimed at preparing the way for the unknown to occur.

The Planck (1920) constant, or Quantum constant, is a measure of the degree to which energy is indefinite within time or space, that is, a measure of the effect that thought has on energy. The greater the thought, the less controlled by gravity and the greater the potential for a creative leap to occur in the Field. As soon as a field becomes greater than it is not, it is automatically re-invented. We now can begin to understand how development of the mental faculties serves the potential for a creative leap, both in terms of direction and strength.

An In-Depth Look

The creative leap occurs in concert with a continuous loop of creative thought moving through Wallas's (1926) four stages of creativity: preparation, incubation, illumination and verification. Because we live in a changing, uncertain and complex environment, it is often difficult to trace back the triggers or ideas that spur our creative thought, nor is it necessary to do so as we share our ideas, and the next idea comes to mind.

You as a human have been participating in and preparing yourself for creativity since your inception. *Creation is an element of your natural state of being*. When creating for the benefit of others, you are sharing a part of yourself, willing to give to and serve others so they can do the same. In this mode of creation, there are no forces pushing against you. Thus, everything becomes effortless and you, and others, become more creative.

If something is forceful it is lacking in creativity. A forced field is missing the element of interactive choices, the ability within a field to produce a consistency of choices (or "will") that allows co-creation. When two or more people are working together and sharing thoughts in service to the other, or others, forces are diminished. We now have identified an important step in the Preparation phase, that is, *the reduction of forces.* This is consistent with the deepening of connections with others.

One way to reduce forces in the midst of the creative process is through honoring mistakes. We briefly present this as a tool.

****

TOOL 30-1: HONORING MISTAKES

Use mistakes as learning experiences. Pushing ourselves beyond our limitations opens us up to making mistakes. While few people choose to make mistakes, these mistakes nonetheless provide learning experiences, and are a way to develop humility. Here's a three-step approach to success:

STEP (1) Be as creative as possible, creating in the most effective, efficient and practical way while remaining humble. Be aware that the more you create, the greater the potential that mistakes will be made.

STEP (2) Be the first to admit/acknowledge your mistakes, and show gratitude to those who show you your mistakes.

STEP (3) After acknowledging the mistakes, try to learn from them and improve on them. And, SIMULTANEOUSLY:

STEP (4) Do the best you can to help others to be as creative as possible. Try to help them see more creative ways.

STEP (5) When others make a mistake, help them improve without being critical of them.

STEP (6) Show gratitude to everyone who displays the behaviors described in STEPS (4) and (5) above.

****

It is assumed that the mental work has been done in terms of learning in, and focusing on, the knowledge domain of interest. Remember, the mental faculties are in service to the intuitive. We can use our minds to create the conditions for creativity. When intuition occurs in your domain of experience and knowledge, it is to a large extent earned intuition. Creative juices follow the earned intuitional track for several reasons. First, because this is our area of interest it is where we focus our attention and set our intention (see Chapter 25). Second, this is the viewpoint from which we discover patterns and have developed a higher level of conceptual thinking and discernment of truth. Similarly, a major finding of Sternberg (2003) was that creativity has a tendency to be domain-specific. This does not mean that creative thought is limited to a specific domain. Quite to the contrary. Recall the discussion of wisdom in Chapter 27. As you develop expertise in a domain of knowledge, you are able to recognize patterns and extrapolate those across from one situation to another. As you shift frames of reference, you begin to see similar patterns in other domains of knowledge. When this is coupled with intent for the greater good, you have moved into the state of wisdom.

There is a diversity of opinion regarding the relationship of wisdom and creativity. For example, Sternberg (2003) says that they are two entirely different ways of thinking, with creativity requiring a brashness and wisdom requiring balance. Conversely, Galenson (2013)[30-1] says that wisdom can be the source of creativity. He goes on to explain that creativity can be viewed in two ways: as *conceptual creativity*, which can be brash, and *experimental creativity*, which is balanced, noting that the latter is directly related to both age and wisdom. Archetypal examples of Old Masters who exhibited the latter include Darwin, Cezanne and Hitchcock. As Robert Frost, who wrote his famous poem "Stopping by the Woods on a Snowy Evening" at the age of 48, forwarded: Young people can have insight and a flash here and there, but older poets can provide a clarification of life that "begins in delight and ends in wisdom" (Galenson, 2013).

Sternberg (2009) used a WICS model in teaching at Yale. WICS represents Wisdom, Intelligence, and Creativity Synthesized. Creativity helps to form a vision of where to go and cope with change along the way, intelligence is needed to discern good ideas and convince others of their value, and wisdom is required to ensure the common and greater good over the short and long term. This is consistent with the definitions and usage of these terms in this book.

In the past, people would try to separate from their emotions in order to fully engage their creative imagination, then try to tap into their intuition to create an imaginative picture. Once an idea emerged, the individual might meditate to help fill in the pieces, often engaging various types of yoga to build a unified mental structure that would lead to something different (MacFlouer, 2004-16). Today, recognizing the value of bisociation, we prepare our minds by looking at the world through multiple frames of reference, interacting intelligently with others, and accessing that place where creative ideas emerge.

<<<<<<<◇>>>>>>>

INSIGHT: **To fully engage our creative imagination, we prepare our minds by looking at the world through multiple frames of reference, interacting intelligently with others, and accessing that place where creative ideas emerge.**

<<<<<<<◇>>>>>>>

One secret is balance, that is, bringing the physical, mental and emotional planes into balance, looking for *whole thought* that triggers the intuitional mind. In this context, whole thought is inclusive, thinking through the physical, mental and emotional planes; considering the past, present and future; and taking into account short and long-term outcomes for the common and greater good. This requires full consciousness, interacting at a full level of sensing while simultaneously balancing the senses (see Chapter 32/Part V on Balancing and Sensing).

While meditation is a practice that can facilitate this state, all too often the thought that emerges is selfish, focused on the individual, thus not capable of moving beyond self to tap into the larger Field of Ideas. More recently, organizations have recognized the power of mindfulness in support of creativity. For example, Google, Target, Aetna, Intel and General Mills offer mindfulness programs for employees. Google Thailand has designed a space for mindfulness meditation and provides a daily break for this practice. Mindfulness improves focus and clarity, while helping people be fully present in the NOW moment.

This capability becomes stronger when collaboratively working with others, becoming a unified one, creating together while not losing individual consciousness. As stated above, when a group is intelligently working together there are no forces hindering creativity and the application of that creativity, or innovation. This requires humility, opening ourselves to others' thoughts and ideas, and, for the moment, not locked into our own thought, and open to the possibility that others' thoughts are right. Humility as a tool was introduced in Chapter 4/Part I. Taking this approach provides the opportunity for listening, reflecting, learning and expanding. Through this approach, the group is working together in a search for truth, which is the hallmark of scientific thinking. (See Chapter 24.)

Note that **all thought is not equal.** Thought carries motive. MacFlouer (2004-16) says that minds have the ability to affect the speed and direction of energy through *emotive energy*, that is, energy that has motive to it. Motive is the substance within living things. For us to live, energy must flow through us (see Chapter 16/Part III). As Keeran (1997-2004, p. 3) says, "The basic goal of humans, as well as of any living organism, is to achieve and maintain a balanced internal energy flow despite environmental disruptions." All of our thoughts have an energy strength. Recalling our earlier discussion, in order to thrive creativity requires outward focused thought through knowledge sharing, cooperation and collaboration. The motive behind thought, which can be focused inward or outward, is embedded in the thought. If the motive is based on personal desires that are only self-serving, that thought will be met with forces. Thus, motive is very much an element in the ability to tap into the intuitional plane. Thinking about self does not expand self and, as forces are created, causes you to stay in the same place.

Negative emotions can also create barriers. For example, fear closes off the ability to learn and moves an individual into a lower level of thinking, and consciousness is reduced. Further, while an individual who carries fear *may* tap into the intuitional plane, what is received or perceived would be distorted through the lens of fear.

Figure 30-2 provides a visual review of elements in preparation for the creative leap, including prerequisites of self, expanding our creative capacity, and developing controlled intuition (introduced in Chapter 28). When the field is prepared, a Phase change occurs in the Intelligent Social Change Journey, that is, the movement from Phase 2 toward Phase 3, expanding from the co-evolving model to embrace the creative leap. The creative leap, then, is instantaneous and not constrained by a perceived current reality. It is the result of creative imagination grounded in the bisociation of multiple points (ideas/concepts) of knowledge and knowing comprising more than half the field of thought.

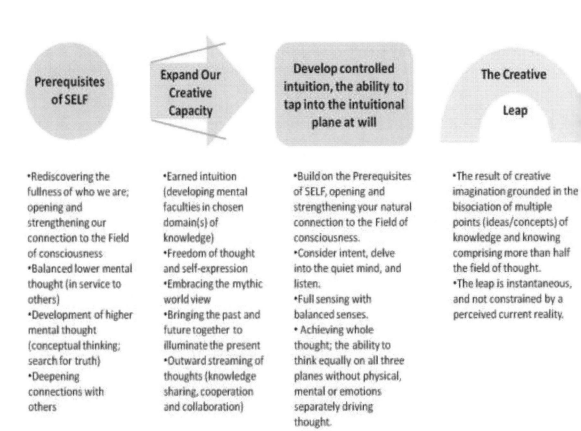

Figure 30-2. *Facilitating the Creative Leap (a quick review).*

Are You Ready to Leap?

While Quantum awareness seeped into human consciousness well over a hundred years ago, the last 20 years have ushered in an explosion of Quantum research and literature, with much creative imagination at play. Despite this flood, most people still think along the lines of evolution, that is, that things are gradually developed and that big changes require big efforts. Understanding Quantum allows us to dismiss this learned, often culturally implanted, belief and lifestyle.

Almost everyone living today has started to "jump", if not "leap", and these jumps are moving us in unexpected directions. The creative leap is a part of the human experience. For example, reflect on the nexus of the pre-adolescent years and the hormonal rush introducing the physical and psychological transition into puberty. It happened in the instant; you were one thing, then another; all of a sudden you were different. And this amazing change is what is happening today to the human race.

In her book *Jump Time*, Jean Houston, scholar, teacher and co-director of the Foundation for Mind Research, introduces the concept *jump time* as the precursor to an upcoming Quantum leap for each citizen of the Earth. As she describes, we live in an amazing time "that demands that we 'Jump!' to a new dispensation of humanity" (Houston, 2000). This will be expanded on further in Chapter 38/Part V.

A jump, or leap, is not gradual; you are sensing two different ways of being in the instant, the past and future, and then there is one and the future becomes the present. Thinking takes a jump, from nothing to everything suddenly, and then things are different. Surprises that completely change your lives are hovering probabilities right around the corner. For example, one of the authors, who is adopted, has lived a full life and for many years been at the top of the hierarchy of her family, that is, with no living parents or siblings or known extended family. Then, with 2016 in full swing, a full sister 15 months younger was discovered! The siblings have rapidly integrated into each other's lives, forever changing the past, present and future, and the journey of discovery continues.

<<<<<<<◇>>>>>>

INSIGHT: **A leap is not gradual; you are sensing two different ways of being in the instant, the past and future, and then there is one and the future becomes the present.**

<<<<<<<◇>>>>>>

If truth be told, the content of this book flows through the creative stages of preparation, incubation, illumination and verification, with the growth and expansion of the Intelligent Social Change Journey supported by cognitive theory, social theory, systems and complexity theory, leadership theory, and learnings from neuroscience, psychology, cell biology and spirituality, among other fields. The preparation phase was consciously begun three years ago, although no doubt the seeds of change were planted far earlier within each of the authors. The incubation phase went on for several years while other projects were focused on and created. When illumination finally came, it came quickly as a creative leap and an unexpected, entangled message, with all 36 of the original chapters writing themselves simultaneously! And then we entered the verification phase, where through conversation and dialogue and focused attention, the authors ensured, aided by several committed readers, a consistency of the message. And then, this book is delivered to you.

In Summary

The creative leap can only occur when thought is focused outward and in service to others. As you tap into the larger flow of ideas, you become extraordinarily creative, and, balancing your senses, are able to move beyond the mental world into intuitional thought, the stream of creativity, when you choose to do so.

Through thought we create ourselves and the abilities we have. Energy following thought is becoming more intelligent. As we tap into the intuitional plane, we enter a new way of thinking and being, and creating leads to creating, which when shared becomes knowledge for others, who in turn create and share, with all returned "tenfold." And the world becomes a better place as we learn to navigate these inner realms—creating harmony through beauty, expanding good character, developing conscious compassion, engaging knowledge in new ways, and expanding our consciousness. (See Part V.)

This is the growth of beauty of thought, with ever-increasing levels of truth unfolding, connecting thought to thought and field to field. In this process, creation is an ever-expanding spiral, allowing life to become more conscious and creative in new ways. The creation of thought is the creative force of the Universe.

Questions for Reflection:

How can you ensure that your knowledge base keeps expanding?

Can you recall times in your life when a creative leap has occurred? What were the circumstances leading up to that creative leap?

How might a field become "greater" than it "is not" in an organizational setting? How could the organization be reinvented when this occurs?

Can you imagine operating at high levels of creativity that lead to conscious compassion?

How would you estimate the risk of a creative leap as compared to the learning acquired from an ineffective leap?

A Preview of Part V: Living in the Future

[Excerpt from Chapter 31/Part V]

As we make the creative leap into this new reality, we go through an alchemical process of purifying and raising our existence to a new, higher level of being. Alchemy is an ancient tradition that holds some of the keys to what the transformational process involves. The concept of participating in our own evolution, in order to accelerate its progress, is central to the tradition of alchemy. Real Alchemy is the art and science of how to consciously and intentionally speed up evolution. Alchemy is the epitome of integrating science, spirit and consciousness together. For purposes of this discussion, Alchemy is considered *the art and science of transformation and transmutation; of changing something into something even better* (Hauck, 1999, p. 4-5).

While many people think of Alchemy as some archaic fringe science focused on turning lead into gold, historically some of the most innovative scientists bringing the greatest inventions and discoveries to humanity were Alchemists. For example, scientific giants such as Isaac Newton, Roger Bacon, Robert Fludd, Leonardo DaVinci, Robert Boyle, Paracelsus, Tycho Brahe, Nicola Tesla and Wolfgang Pauli all studied and were inspired by Alchemy (Linden, 2003). Modern sciences such as physics, chemistry, astronomy, biology, allopathic medicine, pharmacology, psychology, as well as oriental medicine and other holistic health remedies developed out of the ancient traditions of Alchemy. However, where modern sciences have taken a purely materialistic and reductionist approach, Alchemy is intimately connected with the philosophies and practices of Hermeticism, mythology and spirituality. Because of this, Alchemy not only holds the secretes to understanding and harnessing the process of transformation at many different levels, it also holds a key to bridging the fields of science, spirit and consciousness.

Part of why Alchemy became so misunderstood is that symbolism and metaphor have been used to communicate the teachings of alchemy in a language of images and symbols rather than a language of words. Some such symbols are still in use today. For example, one to the most prominent Alchemical symbols is the Caduceus, used by today's medical industry. The Caduceus is the staff with wings, knob on top, and either one or two serpents intertwining up the staff. The former (one serpent) is the Staff of Asclepius, while the latter (two serpents) is the Staff of Hermes. Asclepius was the Greek god of medicine; Hermes, son of Zeus, was the god of commerce. While today's medical industry seems to have forgotten the roots of this symbol, it is waiting there to reveal its secrets again when people are ready to start looking and remembering that there is a deeper meaning behind it.

\# \# \#

Appendix A: The Overarching ISCJ Model

The Intelligent Social Change Journey (ISCJ)

NOTE: Each model builds on the understanding gained from experiencing the previous phase

Phase 1: LEARNING FROM THE PAST

CHARACTERISTICS: Linear and Sequential; Repeatable; Engaging past learning; Starting from current state; Cause and effect relationships.

Phase 2: LEARNING IN THE PRESENT

CHARACTERISTICS: Recognition of patterns; Social interaction; Co-evolving with environment through continuous learning, quick response, robustness, flexibility, adaptability, alignment.

Phase 3: CO-CREATING OUR FUTURE

CHARACTERISTICS: Creative imagination; Recognition of global Oneness; Mental in service to the intuitive; Balancing senses; Bringing together past, present and future; Knowing; Beauty; Wisdom.

SOCIAL STATE (Depth of Connection)

SYMPATHY → EMPATHY → COMPASSION

MOVEMENT

EXPANDED CONSCIOUSNESS → (Open to the Spiritual)

REDUCTION OF FORCES → (Engage forces by choice)

INCREASED INTELLIGENT ACTIVITY → (Growth of wisdom)

FORCES occur when one type of energy affects another type of energy in a way where they are moving in different directions. Bounded (inward focused) and/or limited knowledge creates forces.

CONSCIOUSNESS is considered a state of awareness and a private, selective and continuously changing process, a sequential set of ideas, thoughts, images, feelings and perceptions and an understanding of the connections and relationships among them and our self.

INTELLIGENT ACTIVITY represents a perfect state of interaction where intent, purpose, direction, values and expected outcomes are clearly understood and communicated among all parties, reflecting wisdom and achieving a higher truth.

KNOWLEDGE (The capacity (potential or actual) to take effective action)

NATURE
- Product of the past
- Context sensitive, situation dependent
- Partial, incomplete

- Expanded knowledge sharing, social learning, cooperation, collaboration
- Questioning of why?
- Pursuit of truth

- Recognition that with knowledge comes responsibility.
- Conscious pursuit of larger truth
- Knowledge selectively used as a measure of effectiveness

REFLECTION
- Review of interactions, feedback
- Determination of cause and effect (logic)
- (Inward focus) Questioning decisions and actions: Why did I intend? What really happened? Why were there differences? What would I do the same? What would I do different?

- Deeper development of conceptual thinking (higher mental thought)
- Connecting power of diversity and individuation to whole
- (Moving toward outward focus)
- Recognition of different world views; the exploration of information from different perspectives
- Expanded knowledge capacities.

- Valuing of creative ideas. Asking larger questions: How does this idea serve humanity? Are there any negative consequence?
- (Outward focus). Openness to other's ideas with humility: What if this idea is right? Are my beliefs or other mental models limiting my thought? Are hidden assumptions or feelings interfering with intelligent activity?

COGNITIVE SHIFTS:
- Recognition of importance of feedback; impact of external forces
- Ability to recognize systems; impact of
- Recognition and location of "me" in the larger picture (conscious awareness)
- Early pattern recognition and concept development

- Ability to recognize and apply patterns at all levels within a domain of knowledge to predict outcomes
- Growing understanding of complexity.
- Increased connectedness of choices; recognition of direction you are heading; expanded meaning-making
- Expanded ability to bisociate ideas; increased creativity

- Sense and knowing of Oneness
- Development of both lower (logic) and upper (conceptual) mental faculties, which work in concert with the emotional guidance system
- Application of patterns across knowledge domains for greater good
- Recognition of self as a co-creator of reality
- Ability to engage in intelligent activity.
- Developing the ability to tap into the intuitional plane at will

Taken from: Bennet, et al (2017). The Profundity and Bifurcation of Change, Parts I through V, Frost, WV: MQIPress.

Developed by Mountain Quest Institute. Contact alex@mountainquestinstitute.com for permission.

Appendix B: Five-Book Table of Contents

The Profundity and Bifurcation of Change
The Intelligent Social Change Journey

For Each:
Cover
Title Page
Quote from *The Kybalion* .
Table of Contents
Tables and Figures
Appreciation

Preface

Introduction to the Intelligent Social Change Journey

Part I: LAYING THE GROUNDWORK

Part I Introduction

Chapter 1: Change is Natural
    CHANGE AS A VERB...OUR CHANGING THOUGHTS...FINAL THOUGHT
Chapter 2: Knowledge to Action
    KNOWLEDGE (INFORMING) AND KNOWLEDGE (PROCEEDING)...LEVELS OF KNOWLEDGE...FROM
    KNOWLEDGE TO ACTION...THE NATURE OF KNOWLEDGE...LEVELS OF COMPREHENSION...FINAL
    THOUGHTS
Chapter 3: Forces We Act Upon
    AMPLITUDE, FREQUENCY AND DURATION...FROM THE VIEWPOINT OF THE INDIVIDUAL...CONTROL
    AS FORCE...REDUCING FORCES...THE SELF AND FORCES...FROM THE SPIRITUAL
    VIEWPOINT...STRATEGIC FORCES IN ORGANIZATIONS...THE CORRELATION OF FORCES...FINAL
    THOUGHTS
Chapter 4: The Ever-Expanding Self
    THE SUBJECT/OBJECT RELATIONSHIP...THE PERSONALITY...CHARACTERISTICS OF
    PERSONALITY...DEVELOPMENT OF SELF...THE HEALTHY SELF...THE CONNECTED SELF...
    INDIVIDUATION...THE POWER OF HUMILITY...FINAL THOUGHTS
Chapter 5: The Window of Consciousness
    PROPERTIES OF CONSCIOUSNESS...THE THRESHOLD OF CONSCIOUSNESS...LEVELS OF
    CONSCIOUSNESS...MEANING AND PURPOSE...CONSCIOUSNESS AS A QUANTUM FIELD...FLOW AS
    THE OPTIMAL EXPERIENCE...CONSCIOUSLY ACCESSING THE UNCONSCIOUS...FINAL THOUGHTS

APPENDICES:
Appendix A: The Overarching ISCJ Model
Appendix B: The Table of Contents for All Parts
Appendix C: *An Infinite Story*
Appendix D: Engaging Tacit Knowledge
Appendix E: Knowing
Appendix F: Values for Creativity

ENDNOTES

REFERENCES

About Mountain Quest
About the Authors

TOOLS

Part I: Introduction
3-1. Force Field Analysis
4-1. Self Belief Assessment
4-2. Humility
5-1. Engaging Tacit Knowledge (See Appendix D.)

Part II: Learning From the Past
7-1. Personal Plane-ing Process
7-2. The Five Whys
9-1. Engaging Outside Worldviews
9-2. Practicing Mental Imagining
10-1. Grounding through Nature
10-2. Relationship Network Management
11-1. Co-Creating Conversations that Matter

Part III: Learning in the Present
13-1. Trust Mapping
14-1. Building Mental Sustainability
16-1. Integrating Time into the Self Experience
16-2. Scenario Building
17-1. Thinking Patterns
17-2. Storying: Capture (see Appendix G)
17-3. Storying: Sculpt (see Appendix G)
17-4. Storying: Tell (see Appendix G)

Appendix D
Engaging Tacit Knowledge

[Detail for the Tool "Engaging Tacit Knowledge" introduced in chapter 5. Skip to the subtitle "Accessing Tacit Knowledge" below if you already understand the concepts of "knowledge", "tacit" and the four types of tacit knowledge: embodied, intuitive, affective and spiritual.]

SUBTOPICS: BACKGROUND ... THE TYPES OF TACIT KNOWLEDGE ... ACCESSING TACIT KNOWLEDGE ... SURFACING ... EMBEDDING ... SHARING ... INDUCING RESONANCE

FIGURE: D-1. CONTINUUM OF AWARENESS OF KNOWLEDGE SOURCE/CONTENT ... D-2. ACCESSING TACIT KNOWLEDGE

Background

Knowledge—the capacity (potential or actual) to take effective action—was introduced in Chapter 3. Our focus in this Part Is on that knowledge residing in the unconscious, that is, tacit knowledge (Item 1-E). Tacit knowledge is the descriptive term for those connections among thoughts that cannot be pulled up in words, a knowing of what decision to make or how to do something that cannot be clearly voiced in a manner such that another person could extract and re-create that knowledge (understanding, meaning, etc.). An individual may or may not know they have tacit knowledge in relationship to something or someone; but even when it is known, the individual is unable to put it into words or visuals that can convey that knowledge. We all know things, or know what to do, yet may be unable to articulate why we know them, why they are true, or even exactly what they are. To "convey" is to cause something to be known or understood or, in this usage, to transfer information from which the receiver is able to create knowledge.

As a point of contrast, explicit knowledge is information (patterns) and processes (patterns in time) that can be called up from memory and described accurately in words and/or visuals (representations) such that another person can comprehend the knowledge that is expressed through this exchange of information. This has historically been called declarative knowledge (Anderson, 1983). Implicit knowledge is a more complicated concept, and a term not unanimously agreed-upon in the literature. This is understandable since even simple dictionary definitions—which are generally unbiased and powerful indicators of collective preference and understanding—show a considerable overlap between the terms "implicit" and "tacit," making it difficult to differentiate the two. We propose that a useful interpretation of implicit knowledge is knowledge stored in memory of which the individual is not immediately aware which, while not readily accessible, may be pulled up when triggered (associated). Triggering can occur through questions, dialogue or reflective thought, or happen as a result of an external event. In other words, implicit knowledge is knowledge that the individual does not know they have, but is self-discoverable! However, once this knowledge is surfaced, the individual may or may not have the ability to adequately describe it such that another individual could create the same knowledge; and the "why and how" may remain tacit.

A number of published psychologists have used the term implicit interchangeably with our usage of tacit, that is, with implicit representing knowledge that once acquired can be shown to effect behavior but is not available for conscious retrieval (Reber, 1993; Kirsner et al, 1998). As described in the above discussion of implicit knowledge, what is forwarded here is that the concept of implicit knowledge serves as a middle ground between that which can be made explicit and that which cannot easily, if at all, be made explicit. By moving beyond the dualistic approach of explicit and tacit—that which can be declared versus that which can't be declared, and that which can be remembered versus that which can't be remembered—we posit implicit as representing the knowledge spectrum between explicit and tacit. While explicit refers to easily available, some knowledge requires a higher stimulus for association to occur but is not buried so deeply as to prevent access. This understanding opens the domain of implicit knowledge.

Tacit and explicit knowledge can be thought of as residing in "places," specifically, the unconscious and the conscious, respectively, although both are differentiated patterns spread throughout the neuronal system, that is, the volume of the brain and other parts of the central nervous system. On the other hand, implicit knowledge may reside in either the unconscious (prior to triggering, or tacit) or the conscious (when triggered, or explicit). Note there is no clean break between these three types of knowledge (tacit, implicit and explicit); rather, this is a continuum.

Calling them interactive components of cooperative processes, Reber agrees that there is no clear boundary between that which is explicit and that which is implicit (our tacit): "There is ... no reason for presuming that there exists a clean boundary between conscious and unconscious processes or a sharp division between implicit and explicit epistemic systems ..." (Reber, 1993, p. 23). Reber describes the urge to treat explicit and implicit (our tacit) as altogether different processes the "polarity fallacy" (Reber, 1993). Similarly, Matthews says that the unconscious and conscious processes are engaged in what he likes to call a "synergistic" relationship (Matthews, 1991). What this means is that the boundary between the conscious and the unconscious is somewhat porous and flexible.

Knowledge starts as tacit knowledge, that is, the initial movement of knowledge is from its origins within the Self (in the unconscious) to an outward expression (albeit driving effective action). What does that mean? Michael Polanyi, a professor of chemistry and the social sciences, wrote in The Tacit Dimension that, "We start from the fact that we can know more than we can tell" (Polanyi, 1967, p 108). He called this pre-logical phase of knowing tacit knowledge, that is, knowledge that cannot be articulated (Polanyi, 1958).

The Types of Tacit Knowledge

Tacit knowledge can be thought of in terms of four aspects: embodied, intuitive, affective and spiritual (Bennet & Bennet, 2008c). While all of these aspects are part of Self, each represents different sources of tacit knowledge whose applicability, reliability and efficacy may vary greatly depending on the individual, the situation and the knowledge needed to take effective action. They are represented in Figure D-1 along with explicit and implicit knowledge on the continuum of awareness.

Embodied tacit knowledge is also referred to as somatic knowledge. Both kinesthetic and sensory, it can be represented in neuronal patterns stored within the body. Kinesthetic is related to the movement of the body and, while important to every individual every day of our lives, it is a primary focus for athletes, artists, dancers, kids and assembly-line workers. A commonly used example of tacit knowledge is knowledge of riding a bicycle. Sensory, by definition, is related to the five human senses of form through which information enters the body (sight, smell, hearing, touch and taste). An example is the smell of burning rubber from your car brakes while driving or the smell of hay in a barn. These odors can convey knowledge of whether the car brakes may need replacing (get them checked immediately), or whether the hay is mildewing (dangerous to feed horses, but fine for cows). These responses would be overt, bringing to conscious awareness the need to take effective action and driving that action to occur.

	TACIT Kn			IMPLICIT Kn	EXPLICIT Kn
SPIRITUAL	**INTUITIVE**	**AFFECTIVE**	**EMBODIED**	•Stored in memory but not in conscious awareness	•Information stored in brain that can be recalled at will
•Based on matters of the soul	•Sense of knowing coming from within	•Feelings	•Expressed in bodily/material form	•Not readily accessible but capable of being recalled when triggered	•In conscious awareness
•Represents animating principles of human life	•Linked to FOR	•Generally attached to other types or aspects of knowledge	•Stored within the body (riding bike)	•Don't know you know, but self-discoverable	•Can be shared through social communication
•Focused on moral aspects, human nature, higher development of mental faculties	•Knowing that may be without explanation (outside expertise or past experience)	•Why (evasive or unknown)	•Can be kinesthetic or sensory	•Ability may or may not be present to facilitate social communication.	•Can be captured in terms of information (given context)
•Transcendent power	•24/7 personal servant of human being		•Learned by mimicry and behavioral skill training	•Why (questionable)	•Expressed emotions (visible changes in body state)
•Moves knowledge to wisdom	•Why (unknown)		•Why (evasive)		•Why (understood)
•Higher guidance with unknown origin					

IMPLICIT Kn

UNCONSCIOUS AWARENESS — *Level of Awareness of Origins /Content of Knowledge* → **CONSCIOUS AWARENESS**

Figure D-1. *Continuum of awareness of knowledge source/content.*

Intuitive tacit knowledge is the sense of knowing coming from inside an individual that may influence decisions and actions; yet the decision-maker or actor cannot explain how or why the action taken is the right one. The unconscious works around the clock with a processing capability many times greater than that at the conscious level. This is why as the world grows more complex, decision-makers will depend more and more on their intuitive tacit knowledge, a combination of life lessons. But in order to use it, decision-makers must first be able to tap into their unconscious.

Affective tacit knowledge is connected to emotions and feelings, with emotions representing the external expression of some feelings. Feelings expressed as emotions become explicit (Damasio, 1994). Feelings that are not expressed—perhaps not even recognized—are those that fall into the area of affective tacit knowledge. Feelings as a form of knowledge have different characteristics than language or ideas, but they may lead to effective action because they can influence actions by their existence and connections with consciousness. When feelings come into conscious awareness, they can play an informing role in decision-making, providing insights in a non-linguistic manner and thereby influencing decisions and actions. For example, a feeling (such as fear or an upset stomach) may occur every time a particular action is started which could prevent the decision-maker from taking that action.

Spiritual tacit knowledge can be described in terms of knowledge based on matters of the soul. The soul represents the animating principles of human life in terms of thought and action, specifically focused on its moral aspects, the emotional part of human nature, and higher development of the mental faculties (Bennet & Bennet, 2007c). While there is a "knowing" related to spiritual knowledge similar to intuition, this knowing does not include the experiential base of intuition, and it may or may not have emotional tags. The current state of the evolution of our understanding of spiritual knowledge is such that there are insufficient words to relate its transcendent power, or to define the role it plays in relationship to other tacit knowledge. Nonetheless, this area represents a form of higher guidance with unknown origin. Spiritual knowledge may be the guiding purpose, vision and values behind the creation and application of tacit knowledge. It may also be the road to moving information to knowledge and knowledge to wisdom (Bennet & Bennet, 2008d). In the context of this book, spiritual tacit knowledge represents the source of higher learning, helping decision-makers create and implement knowledge that has greater meaning and value for the common good.

Whether embodied, affective, intuitive or spiritual, *tacit knowledge represents the bank account of the Self.* The larger our deposits, the greater the interest, and the more we are prepared for co-evolving in a changing, uncertain and complex environment.

Accessing Tacit Knowledge

There are many ways to bring our tacit resources into our consciousness. For example, we propose a four-fold action model with nominal curves for building what we call extraordinary consciousness, that is, expanding our consciousness through accessing tacit resources. The four approaches to accessing include surfacing, embedding, sharing and inducing resonance. (See Figure D-2 below.)

Surfacing Tacit Knowledge.

As individuals observe, experience, study and learn throughout life they generate a huge amount of information and knowledge that becomes stored in their unconscious mind. Surfacing tacit knowledge is focused on accessing the benefit of that which is tacit by moving knowledge from the unconscious to conscious awareness. Three ways that tacit knowledge can be surfaced are through external triggering, self-collaboration and nurturing.

The process of triggering is primarily externally driven with internal participation. For example, conversation, dialogue, questions, or an external situation with specific incoming information may trigger the surfacing of tacit knowledge needed to respond. Triggering is often the phenomenon that occurs in "sink or swim" situations, where an immediate decision must be made that will have significant consequences.

Although collaboration is generally thought about as interactions among individuals and/or groups, a type of collaboration that is less understood is the process of *individuals consciously collaborating with themselves*. What this means is the conscious mind learning to communicate with, listen to, and trust its own unconscious based on a relationship built over time between the self and the personality. With the self in charge, the selection process and semantic complexing of all the experiences, learning, thoughts and feelings throughout life is consistent with the focus and purpose of the self. One way to collaborate with your self is through creating an internal dialogue.

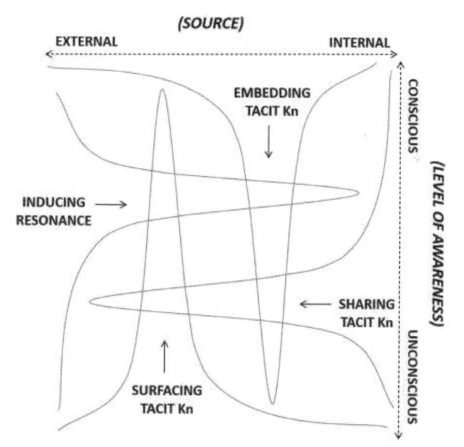

Figure D-2. *Accessing Tacit Knowledge.*

For example, accepting the authenticity of, and listening deeply to, a continuous stream of conscious thought while following the tenets of dialogue. Those tenets would include: withholding quick judgment, not demanding quick answers, and exploring underlying assumptions (Ellinor & Gerard, 1998, p. 26), *then* looking for collaborative meaning between what you consciously think and what you feel. A second approach is to ask yourself a lot of questions related to the task at hand. Even if you don't think you know the answers, reflect carefully on the questions, and be patient. Sleeping on a question will often yield an answer the following morning. Your unconscious mind processes information 24/7; it is not a figment of your imagination, or your enemy. To paraphrase the Nobel Laureate Neuroscientist Dr. Eric Kandel, your unconscious is a part of you. It works 24 hours a day processing incoming information on your behalf. So, when it tells you something via intuition, lucid dreaming, etc., you should listen carefully (but it may not always be right) (Kandel, 2006).

Although requiring time, openness and commitment, there are a number of approaches readily available for those who choose to nurture their sensitivity to tacit knowledge. These include (among others) meditation, inner tasking, lucid dreaming, and hemispheric synchronization. Meditation practices have the ability to quiet the conscious mind, thus allowing greater access to the unconscious (Rock, 2004). Inner tasking is a wide-spread and often used approach to engaging your unconscious. Tell yourself, as you fall asleep at night, to work on a problem or question. The next morning when you wake up, but before you get up, lie in bed and listen to your own, quiet, passive thoughts. Frequently, but not always, the answer will appear, although it must be written down quickly before it is lost from the conscious mind. Like meditation, the efficacy of this approach takes time and practice to develop (Bennet and Bennet, 2008e).

Lucid dreaming is a particularly powerful way to access tacit knowledge. The psychotherapist Kenneth Kelzer wrote of one of his lucid dreams:

> In this dream I experienced a lucidity that was so vastly different and beyond the range of anything I had previously encountered. At this point I prefer to apply the concept of the spectrum of consciousness to the lucid dream and assert that within the lucid state a person may have access to a spectrum or range of psychic energy that is so vast, so broad and so unique as to defy classification. (Kelzer, 1987)

Another way to achieve sensitivity to the unconscious is *through the use of sound*. For example, listening to a special song in your life can draw out deep feelings and memories buried in your unconscious. Sound and its relationship to humans has been studied by philosophers throughout recorded history; extensive treatments appear in the work of Plato, Kant and Nietzsche. Through the last century scientists have delved into studies focused on acoustics (the science of sound), psychoacoustics (the study of how our minds perceive sound) and musical psychoacoustics (the discipline that involves every aspect of musical perception and performance). As do all patterns in the mind, sound has the ability to change and shape the physiological structure of the brain.

For example, hemispheric synchronization (bringing both hemispheres of the brain into coherence) can be accomplished through the use of sound coupled with a binaural beat. (See Bullard and Bennet, 2013 or Bennet et al., 2015b for in-depth treatment of hemispheric synchronization.) Inter-hemispheric communication is the setting for brain-wave coherence which facilitates whole-brain cognition, assuming an elevated status in subjective experience (Ritchey, 2003). What can occur during hemispheric synchronization is a physiologically reduced state of arousal, quieting the body *while maintaining conscious awareness* (Mavromatis, 1991; Atwater, 2004; Fischer, 1971; West, 1980; Delmonte, 1984; Goleman, 1988; Jevning et al., 1992), thus providing a doorway into the unconscious. It is difficult to imagine the amount of learning and insights that might reside therein—and the expanded mental capabilities such access may provide—much less the depth and breadth of experience and emotion that has been hidden there, perhaps making such access a mixed blessing

Embedding Tacit Knowledge.

Every experience and conversation are *embedding* potential knowledge (information) in the unconscious as it is associated with previously stored information to create new patterns. Thinking about embedding as a process for improving our tacit knowledge can lead to new approaches to learning. Embedding is both externally and internally driven, with knowledge moving from the conscious to the unconscious through exposure or immersion, by accident or by choice. Examples include travel, regularly attending church on Sunday, or listening to opera and imitating what you've heard in the shower every day. Practice moves beyond exposure to include repeated participation in some skill or process, thus strengthening the patterns in the mind. For example, after many years of imitation (practice) look at what Paul Potts, an opera singer and winner of the *Britain's Got Talent* competition in 2007, accomplished!

Creating tacit knowledge occurs naturally through diverse experiences in the course of life as individuals become more proficient at some activity (such as public speaking) or cognitive competency (such as problem solving). When the scope of experience widens, the number of relevant neuronal patterns increases. As an individual becomes more proficient in a specific focus area through effortful practice, the pattern gradually becomes embedded in the unconscious, ergo it becomes tacit knowledge. When this happens, the reasons and context within which the knowledge was created often lose their connections with consciousness.

Embodied tacit knowledge requires new pattern embedding for change to occur. This might take the form of repetition in physical training or in mental thinking. For example, embodied tacit knowledge might be embedded through mimicry, practice, competence development or visual imagery coupled with practice. An example of this would be when an athlete training to become a pole vaulter reviews a video of his perfect pole vault to increase his athletic capability. This is a result of the fact that when the pole vaulter performs his perfect vault, the patterns going through his brain while he is doing it are the same patterns that go through his brain when he is watching himself do it. When he is watching the video, he is repeating the desired brain patterns and this repetition strengthens these patterns in unconscious memory. When "doing" the pole vault, he cannot think about his actions, nor try to control them. Doing so would degrade his performance because his conscious thoughts would interfere with his tacit ability.

In the late 1990's, neuroscience research identified what are referred to as mirror neurons. As Dobb's explains,

> These neurons are scattered throughout key parts of the brain—the premotor cortex and centers for language, empathy and pain—and fire not only as we perform a certain action, but also when we watch someone else perform that action. (Dobbs, 2007, p. 22)

Watching a video is a cognitive form of mimicry that transfers actions, behaviors and most likely other cultural norms. Thus, when we *see* something being enacted, our mind creates the same patterns that we would use to enact that "something" ourselves. As these patterns fade into long-term memory, they would represent tacit knowledge—both Knowledge (Informing) and Knowledge (Proceeding). While mirror neurons are a subject of current research, it would appear that they represent a mechanism for the transfer of tacit knowledge between individuals or throughout a culture. For more information on mirror neurons, see Gazzaniga, 2004.

Intuitive tacit knowledge can be nurtured and developed through exposure, learning, and practice. Knowledge (Informing) might be embedded through experience, contemplation, developing a case history for learning purposes, developing a sensitivity to your own intuition, and effortful practice. Effortful study moves beyond practice to include identifying challenges just beyond an individual's competence and focusing on meeting those challenges one at a time (Ericsson, 2006). The way people become experts involves the chunking of ideas and concepts and creating understanding through the development of significant patterns useful for solving problems and anticipating future behavior within their area of focus. In the study of chess players introduced earlier, it was concluded that "effortful practice" was the difference between people who played chess for many years while maintaining an average skill and those who became master players in shorter periods of time. The master players, or experts, examined the chessboard patterns over and over again, studying them, looking at nuances, trying small changes to perturb the outcome (sense and response), generally "playing with" and studying these *patterns* (Ross, 2006). In other words, they use *long-term working memory, pattern recognition and chunking* rather than logic as a means of understanding and decision-making. This indicates that by exerting mental effort and emotion while exploring complex situations, knowledge—often problem-solving expertise and what some call wisdom—becomes embedded in the unconscious mind. For additional information on the development of expertise see Ericsson (2006). An important insight from this discussion is the recognition that when facing complex problems which do not allow reasoning or cause and effect analysis because of their complexity, the solution will most likely lie in studying patterns and chunking those patterns to enable a tacit capacity to anticipate and develop solutions. For more on the reference to wisdom see Goldberg (2005).

Affective tacit knowledge requires nurturing and the development of emotional intelligence. Affective tacit knowledge might be embedded through digging deeply into a situation—building self-awareness and developing a sensitivity to your own emotions—and having intense emotional experiences. How much of an experience is kept as tacit knowledge depends upon the mode of incoming information and the emotional tag we (unconsciously) put on it. The stronger the emotion attached to the experience, the longer it will be remembered and the easier it will be to recall. Subtle patterns that occur during any experience may slip quietly into our unconscious and become affective tacit knowledge. For a good explanation of emotional intelligence see Goleman (1998).

Spiritual tacit knowledge can be facilitated by encouraging holistic representation of the individual and respect for a higher purpose. Spiritual tacit knowledge might be embedded through dialogue, learning from practice and reflection, and developing a sensitivity to your own spirit, living with it over time and exploring your feelings regarding the larger aspects of values, purpose and meaning. Any individual who, or organization which, demonstrates—and acts upon—their deep concerns for humanity and the planet is embedding spiritual tacit knowledge.

Sharing Tacit Knowledge

In our discussion above on surfacing tacit knowledge, it became clear that surfaced knowledge is new knowledge, a different shading of that which was in the unconscious. If knowledge can be described in words and visuals, then this would be by definition explicit; understanding can only be symbolized and to some extent conveyed through words. Yet the subject of this paragraph is sharing tacit knowledge. The key is that **it is not necessary to make knowledge explicit in order to share it**.

Sharing tacit knowledge occurs both consciously and unconsciously, although the knowledge shared remains tacit in nature. *There is no substitute for experience.* The power of this process has been recognized in organizations for years, and tapped into through the use of mentoring and shadowing programs to facilitate imitation and mimicry. More recently, it has become the focus of group learning, where communities and teams engage in dialogue focused on specific issues and experiences mentally and, over time, develop a common frame of reference, language and understanding that can create solutions to complex problems. The words that are exchanged serve as a tool of creative expression rather than limiting the scope of exchange.

The solution set agreed upon may retain "tacitness" in terms of understanding the complexity of the issues (where it is impossible to identify all the contributing factors much less a cause and effect relationship among them). Hence these solutions in terms of understanding would not be explainable in words and visuals to individuals outside the team or community. When this occurs, the team (having arrived at the "tacit" decision) will often create a rational, but limited, explanation for purposes of communication of why the decision makes sense.

Inducing Resonance.

Through exposure to diverse, and specifically opposing, concepts that are well-grounded, it is possible to create a resonance within the receiver's mind that amplifies the meaning of the incoming information, increasing its emotional content and receptivity. Inducing resonance is a result of external stimuli resonating with internal information to bring into conscious awareness. While it is words that trigger this resonance, it is the current of truth flowing under that linguistically centered thought that brings about connections. When this resonance occurs, the incoming information is consistent with the frame of reference and belief systems within the receiving individual. This resonance amplifies feelings connected to the incoming information, bringing about the emergence of deeper perceptions and validating the re-creation of externally-triggered knowledge in the receiver.

Further, this process results in the amplification and transformation of internal affective, embodied, intuitive or spiritual knowledge from tacit to implicit (or explicit). Since deep knowledge is now accessible at the conscious level, this process also creates a sense of ownership within the listener. The speakers are not telling the listener what to believe; rather, when the tacit knowledge of the receiver resonates with what the speaker is saying (and how it is said), a natural reinforcement and expansion of understanding occurs within the listener. This accelerates the creation of deeper tacit knowledge and a stronger affection associated with this area of focus.

An example of inducing resonance can be seen in the movie, *The Debaters*. We would even go so far as to say that the purpose of a debate is to transfer tacit knowledge. Well-researched and well-grounded external information is communicated (explicit knowledge) tied to emotional tags (explicitly expressed). The beauty of this process is that this occurs on *both sides* of a question such that the active listener who has an interest in the area of the debate is pulled into one side or another. An eloquent speaker will try to speak from the audience's frame of reference to tap into their intuition. Such a speaker will come across as confident, likeable and positive to transfer embodied tacit knowledge, and may well refer to higher order purpose, etc. to connect with the listener's spiritual tacit knowledge. An example can be seen in litigation, particularly in the closing arguments, where for opposing sides of an issue emotional tags are tied to a specific frame of reference regarding what has been presented.

[Excerpted from Bennet et al. (2015)]

Appendix E
The Art of Knowing

[We explore knowing from a more pragmatic viewpoint inclusive of brief exercises to expand our external sensing capabilities. To this end, a Knowing Framework developed for the U.S. Department of the Navy is utilized. For purposes of this discussion, Knowing is poetically defined as **seeing beyond images, hearing beyond words, sensing beyond appearances, and feeling beyond emotions.** *In this treatment, it is considered a sense that emerges from our collective tacit knowledge.]*

SUBTOPICS: CRITICAL AREAS OF KNOWING ... PRINCIPLES OF KNOWING ... THE COGNITIVE CAPABILITIES ... THE COGNITIVE PROCESSES ... THE SELF AS AN AGENT OF CHANGE

FIGURE: THE ETERNAL LOOP OF KNOWLEDGE AND KNOWING

Every decision, and the actions that decision drives, is a learning experience that builds on its predecessors by broadening the sources of knowledge creation and the capacity to create knowledge in different ways. For example, as an individual engages in more and more conversations across the Internet in search of meaning, thought connections occur that cause an expansion of shallow knowledge. As we are aware, *knowledge begets knowledge*. In a global interactive environment, the more that is understood, the more that can be created and understood. This is how our personal learning system works. As we tap into our internal resources, *knowledge enables knowing, and knowing inspires the creation of knowledge.*

The concept of "knowing" is not easy to define, since the word and concept are used in so many different ways. We consider Knowing as a *sense* that is supported by our tacit knowledge. In this appendix, we provide a Knowing Framework (published as a chapter in Bennet & Bennet, 2013) that focuses on methods to increase individual sensory capabilities. This Framework specifically refers to our five external senses and to the increase of the ability to consciously integrate these sensory inputs *with our tacit knowledge*, that knowledge created by past learning experiences that is *entangled with* the flow of spiritual tacit knowledge continuously available to each of us. In other words, knowing—**driven by the unconscious as an integrated unit**—is the *sense* gained from experience that resides in the *subconscious* part of the mind, *and* the energetic connection our mind enjoys with the *superconscious*.

The subconscious and superconscious are both part of our unconscious resources, with the subconscious directly supporting the embodied mind/brain and the superconscious focused on tacit resources involving larger moral aspects, the emotional part of human nature and the higher development of our mental faculties. When engaged by an intelligent mind which has moved beyond logic into conscious processing based on trust and recognition of the connectedness and interdependence of humanity, these resources are immeasurable.

In Figure E-1 below, the superconscious is described with the terms spiritual learning, higher guidance, values and morality, and love. It is also characterized as "pre-personality" to emphasize that there are no personal translators such as beliefs and mental models attached to this form of knowing. In Chapter 26/Part IV, the flow of information from the superconscious is very much focused on the moment at hand and does not bring with it any awareness patterns that could cloud the decision-makers full field of perception.

In contrast, the memories stored in the subconscious are very much a part of the personality of the decision-maker, and may be heavily influenced by an individual's perceptions and feelings at the time they were formed. Embodied tacit knowledge would be based on the physical preferences of personality expression while affective tacit knowledge would be based on the feelings connected with the personality of the decision-maker. For example, if there was a traumatic event that occurred in childhood that produced a feeling of "helplessness," later in life there might be neuronal patterns that are triggered that reproduce this feeling when the adult encounters a similar situation. While these feelings may have been appropriate for the child, they would rarely be of service to a seasoned, intelligent decision-maker.

Descriptive terms for the subconscious include life learning, memory, associative patterning, and material intellect. The subconscious in an autonomic system serving a life-support function (see the discussion of personality in Chapter 4). We all must realize that **the human *subconscious* is in service to the conscious mind**. It is not intended to dominate decision-making. The subconscious expands as it integrates and connects (complexes) all that we put into it through our five external-connected senses. *It is at the conscious mind level that we develop our intellect and make choices that serve as the framework for our subconscious processing.*

Figure E-1 is a nominal graphic showing the continuous feedback loops between knowledge and knowing. Thinking about (potential) and experiencing (actual) effective action (knowledge) supports development of embodied, intuitive and affective tacit knowledges. When we recognize and use our sense of knowing—regardless of its origin—we are tapping into our tacit knowledge to inform our decisions and actions. These decisions and actions, and the feedback from taking

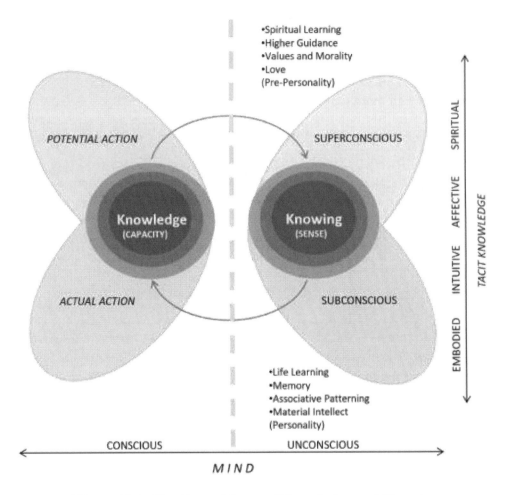

Figure E-1. *The Eternal Loop of Knowledge and Knowing*

those actions, in turn expand our knowledge base, much of which over time will become future tacit resources. Since our internal sense of knowing draws collectively from all areas of our tacit knowledge, the more we open to this inner sense, respond accordingly, and observe and reflect on feedback, the more our inner resources move beyond limited perceptions which may be connected to embedded childhood memories.

Critical Areas of Knowing

The Knowing Framework encompasses three critical areas. The first is "knowing our self," learning to love and trust ourselves. This includes deep reflection on our self in terms of beliefs, values, dreams and purpose for being, and appreciation for the unique beings that we are. It includes understanding of our goals, objectives, strengths and weaknesses in thought and action, and internal defenses and limitations. By knowing ourselves we learn to work within and around our limitations and to support our strengths, thus ensuring that the data, information, and knowledge informing our system is properly identified and interpreted. Further, knowing our self means recognizing that we are social beings, part of the large ecosystem we call Gaia and inextricably connected to other social beings around the world, which brings us to the second critical element: knowing others.

We live in a connected world, spending most of our waking life with other people, and often continuing that interaction in our dreams! There is amazing diversity in the world, so much to learn and share with others. Whether in love or at war, people are always in relationships and must grapple with the sense of "other" in accordance with their beliefs, values and dreams.

The third critical area is that of "knowing" the situation in as objective and realistic a manner as possible, understanding the situation, problem, or challenge in context. In the military this is called situational awareness and includes areas such as culture, goals and objectives, thinking patterns, internal inconsistencies, capabilities, strategies and tactics, and political motivations. The current dynamics of our environment, the multiple forces involved, the complexity of relationships, the many aspects of events that are governed by human emotion, and the unprecedented amount of available data and information make situational awareness a challenging but essential phenomenon in many aspects of our daily lives.

As we move away from predictable patterns susceptible to logic, decision-makers must become increasingly reliant on our "gut" instinct, an internal sense of knowing combined with high situational awareness. Knowing then becomes key to decision-making. The mental skills honed in knowing help decision-makers identify, interpret, make decisions, and take appropriate action in response to current situational assessments.

This construct of knowing can be elevated to the organizational level by using and combining the insights and experiences of individuals through dialogue and collaboration within teams, groups, and communities, both face-to-face and virtual. Such efforts significantly improve the quality of understanding and responsiveness of actions of the organization. They also greatly expand the scope of complex situations that can be handled through knowing because of the greater resources brought to bear—all of this significantly supported by technological interoperability.

Organizational knowing is an aspect of *organizational intelligence*, the capacity of an organization as a whole to gather information, generate knowledge, innovate, and to take effective action. This capacity is the foundation for effective response in a fast-changing and complex world. Increasing our sensory and mental processes contributes to the "positioning" understood by the great strategist Sun Tzu in the year 500 B.C. when he wrote his famous dictum for victory: *Position yourself so there is no battle* (Clavell, 1983). Today in our world of organizations and complex challenges we could say "Position ourselves so there is no confusion."

By exploring our sense of knowing we expand our understanding of ourselves, improve our awareness of the external world, learn how to tap into internal resources, and increase our skills to affect internal and external change. The Knowing Framework provides ideas for developing deep knowledge within the self and sharing that knowledge with others to create new perceptions and levels of understanding. Since each situation and each individual is unique, this Framework does not provide specific answers. Rather, it suggests questions and paths to follow to find those answers.

Principles of Knowing

In response to a changing environment, the Knowing Framework presented below in its expanded form was first developed at the turn of the century for the U.S. Department of the Navy. There are a number of recognized basic truths that drove its development. These truths became the principles upon which the Knowing Framework is based.

(1) Making decisions in an increasingly complex environment requires new ways of thinking.

(2) All the information in the world is useless if the decision-maker who needs it cannot process it and connect it to their own internal values, knowledge, and wisdom.

(3) We don't know all that we know.

(4) Each of us has knowledge far beyond that which is in our conscious mind. Put another way, we know more than we know we know. (Much of our experience and knowledge resides in the unconscious mind.)

(5) By exercising our mental and sensory capabilities we can increase those capabilities.

(6) Support capabilities of organizational knowing include organizational learning, knowledge centricity, common values and language, coherent vision, whole-brain learning, openness of communications, effective collaboration, and the free flow of ideas.

The concept of knowing focuses on the cognitive capabilities of observing and perceiving a situation; the cognitive processing that must occur to understand the external world and make maximum use of our internal cognitive capabilities; and the mechanism for creating deep knowledge and acting on that knowledge via the self as an agent of change. Each of these core areas will be discussed below in more detail.

The Cognitive Capabilities

The cognitive capabilities include observing, collecting and interpreting data and information, and building knowledge relative to the situation. The six areas we will address are: listening, noticing, scanning, sensing, patterning, and integrating. These areas represent means by which we perceive the external world and begin to make sense of it.

Listening

The first area, listening, sets the stage for the other five cognitive capabilities. Listening involves more than hearing; it is a sensing greater than sound. It is a neurological cognitive process involving stimuli received by the auditory system. The linguist Roland Barthes distinguished the difference between hearing and listening when he says: "Hearing is a physiological phenomenon; listening is a psychological act." What this means is that there is a choice involved in listening in terms of the listener choosing to interpret sound waves to potentially create understanding and meaning (Barthes, 1985).There are three levels of listening: alerting, deciphering and understanding. Alerting is picking up on environmental sound cues. Deciphering is relating the sound cues to meaning. Understanding is focused on the impact of the sound on another person. Active listening is intentionally focusing on who is speaking in order to take full advantage of verbal and non-verbal cues.

In developing active listening, imagine how you can use all your senses to focus on what is being said. One way to do this is to role-play, imagining you are in their shoes and feeling the words. Active listening means fully participating, acknowledging the thoughts you are hearing with your body, encouraging the train of thought, actively asking questions when the timing is appropriate. The childhood game of pass the word is an example of a fun way to improve listening skills. A group sits in a circle and whispers a message one to the next until it comes back to the originator. A variation on this theme is Chinese Whispers where a group makes a line and starts a different message from each end, crossing somewhere in the middle and making it to the opposite end before sharing the messages back with the originators. Another good group exercise is a "your turn" exercise, where one individual begins speaking, and another person picks up the topic, and so forth. Not knowing whether you are next in line to speak develops some good listening skills.

The bottom line is that what we don't hear cannot trigger our knowing. Awareness of our environment is not enough. We must listen to the flow of sound and search out meaning, understanding and implications.

Noticing

The second area, noticing, represents the ability to observe around us and recognize, i.e., identify those things that are relevant to our immediate or future needs. We are all familiar with the phenomenon of buying a new car and for the next six months recognizing the large number of similar cars that are on the streets. This is an example of a cognitive process of which we are frequently unaware. We notice those things that are recently in our memory or of emotional or intellectual importance to us. We miss many aspects of our environment if we are not focusing directly on them. Thus, the art of noticing can be considered the art of "knowing" which areas of the environment are important and relevant to us at the moment, and focusing in on those elements and the relationships among those elements. It is also embedding a recall capability of those things not necessarily of immediate importance but representing closely related context factors. *This noticing is a first step in building deep knowledge, developing a thorough understanding and a systems context awareness of those areas of anticipated interest.* This is the start of becoming an expert in a given field of endeavor, or situation.

A classic example of mental exercises aimed at developing latent noticing skills is repetitive observation and recall. For example, think about a room that you are often in, perhaps a colleague's office or a friend's living room. Try to write down everything you can remember about this room. You will discover that despite the fact you've been in this room often, you can't remember exactly where furniture is located, or what's in the corners or on the walls. When you've completed this exercise, visit the room and write down everything you see, everything you've missed. What pictures are on the walls? Do you like them? What personal things in the room tell you something about your colleague or friend? How does the layout of furniture help define the room? (These kinds of questions build relationships with feelings and other thinking patterns.) Write a detailed map and remember it. A few days later repeat this exercise from the beginning. If you make any mistakes, go back to the room again, and as many times as it takes to get it right. Don't let yourself off the hook. You're telling yourself that when details are important you know how to bring them into your memory. As your ability to recall improves, repeat this exercise focusing on a street, a building, or a city you visit often.

Scanning

The third area, scanning, represents the ability to review and survey a large amount of data and information and selectively identify those areas that may be relevant. Because of the exponential increase in data and information, this ability becomes more and more important as time progresses. In a very real sense, scanning represents the ability to reduce the complexity of a situation or environment by objectively filtering out the irrelevant aspects, or environmental noise. By developing your own system of environmental "speed reading," scanning can provide early indicators of change.

Scanning exercises push the mind to pick up details and, more importantly, patterns of data and information, *in a short timeframe*. This is an important skill that law enforcement officers and investigators nurture. For example, when you visit an office or room that you've never been in before, take a quick look around and record your first strong impressions. What feelings are you getting? Count stuff. Look at patterns, look at contrasts, look at colors. Try to pick up everything in one or two glances around the room. Make a mental snapshot of the room and spend a few minutes impressing it in your memory. As you leave, remember the mental picture you've made of the room, the way you feel. Impress upon yourself the importance of remembering this. This picture can last for days, or years, despite the shortness of your visit. Your memory can literally retain an integrated *gestalt* of the room. Realize that what you can recall is only a small part of what went into your mind.

Sensing

The fourth area, sensing, represents the ability to take inputs from the external world through our five external senses and ensure the translation of those inputs into our mind to represent as accurate a transduction process (the transfer of energy from one form to another) as possible. The human ability to collect information through our external sensors is limited because of our physiological limitations. For example, we only see a very small part of the electromagnetic spectrum in terms of light, yet with technology we can tremendously expand the sensing capability. As humans we often take our senses for granted, yet they are highly-sensitized complex detection systems that cause immediate response without conscious thought! An example most everyone has experienced or observed is a mother's sensitivity to any discomfort of her young child. The relevance to "knowing" is, recognizing the importance of our sensory inputs, to learn how to fine tune these inputs to the highest possible level, then use discernment and discretion to interpret them.

Exercise examples cited above to increase noticing, scanning, and patterning skills will also enhance the sense of sight, which is far more than just looking at things. It includes locating yourself in position to things. For example, when you're away from city lights look up on a starry night and explore your way around the heavens. Try to identify the main constellations. By knowing their relative position, you know where you are, what month it is, and can even approximate the time of day. The stars provide context for positioning yourself on the earth.

Here are a few exercise examples for other senses. Hearing relates to comprehension. Sit on a park bench, close your eyes and relax, quieting your mind. Start by listening to what is going on around you---conversations of passersby, cars on a nearby causeway, the birds chattering, the wind rustling leaves, water trickling down a nearby drain. Now stretch beyond these nearby sounds. Imagine you have the hearing of a panther, only multidirectional, because you can move your ears every direction and search for sounds. Focus on a faint sound in the distance, then ask your auditory systems to bring it closer. Drag that sound toward you mentally. It gets louder. If you cup one hand behind one ear and cup the other hand in front of the opposite ear, you can actually improve your hearing, focusing on noises from the back with one ear and noises from the front with the other. How does that change what you are hearing?

Next time you are in a conversation with someone, focus your eyes and concentrate on the tip of their nose or the point of their chin. Listen carefully to every word they say, to the pause between their words, to their breathing and sighs, the rise and fall of their voice. Search for the inflections and subtle feelings being communicated behind what is actually being said. When people are talking, much of the meaning behind the information they impart is in their feelings. The words they say are only a representation, a descriptive code that communicates thought, interacting electrical pulses and flows influenced by an emotion or subtle feeling. By listening in this way, with your visual focus not distracting your auditory focus, you can build greater understanding of the subtleties behind the words.

There are many games that accentuate the sense of touch. An old favorite is blind man's bluff; more current is the use of blindfolding and walking through the woods used in outdoor management programs. Try this at home by spending three or four hours blindfolded, going about your regular home activities. At first, you'll stumble and bump, maybe even become frustrated. But as you continue, your ability to manage your movements and meet your needs using your sense of touch will quickly improve. You will be able to move about your home alone with relatively little effort, and you'll know where things are, especially things that are alive, such as plants and pets. You will develop the ability to *feel* their energy. Such exercises as these force your unconscious mind to create, re-create, and surface the imagined physical world. It activates the mind to bring out into the open its sensitivity to the physical context in which we live.

Patterning

The fifth area, patterning, represents the ability to review, study, and interpret large amounts of data/events/information and identify causal or correlative connections that are relatively stable over time or space and may represent patterns driven by underlying phenomena. These hidden drivers can become crucial to understanding the situation or the enemy behavior. This would also include an understanding of rhythm and randomness, flows and trends. Recall the importance of structure, relationships, and culture in creating emergent phenomena (patterns) and in influencing complex systems.

A well-known example of the use of patterning is that of professional card players and successful gamblers, who have trained themselves to repeatedly recall complicated patterns found in randomly drawn cards. To learn this skill, and improve your patterning skills, take a deck of cards and quickly flip through the deck three or four at a time. During this process, make a mental picture of the cards that are in your hand, pause, then turn over three or four more. After doing this several times, recall the mental picture of the first set of cards. What were they? Then try to recall the second set, then the third.

The secret is not to try and remember the actual cards, but to close your eyes and recall the mental picture of the cards. Patterns will emerge. After practicing for awhile, you will discover your ability to recall the patterns---as well as your ability to recall larger numbers of patterns---will steadily increase. As you increase the number of groups of cards you can recall, and increase the number of cards within each group, you are increasing your ability to recall complex patterns.

Study many patterns found in nature, art, science, and other areas of human endeavor. These patterns will provide you with a "mental reference library" that your mind can use to detect patterns in new situations. Chess experts win games on pattern recognition and pattern creation, not on individual pieces

Integrating

The last area in the cognitive capabilities is integration. This represents the top-level capacity to take large amounts of data and information and pull them together to create meaning; this is frequently called sense-making. This capability, to pull together the major aspects of a complex situation and create patterns, relationships, models, and meaning that represent reality is what enables us to make decisions. This capability also applies to the ability to integrate internal organization capabilities and systems.

While we have used the word "integrating" to describe this capability, recall that the human mind is an associative patterner that is continuously complexing (mixing) incoming information from the external environment with all that is stored in memory. Thus, while the decision-maker has an awareness of integrating, the unconscious is doing much of the work and providing nudges in terms of feelings and speculative thought. Our unconscious is forever our partner, working 24/7 for us.

These five ways of observing represent the front line of cognitive capabilities needed to assist all of us in creative and accurate situational awareness and building a valid understanding of situations. To support these cognitive capabilities, we then need processes that transform these observations and this first-level knowledge into a deeper level of comprehension and understanding.

The Cognitive Processes

Internal cognitive processes that support the capabilities discussed above include visualizing, intuiting, valuing, choosing, and setting intent. These five internal cognitive processes greatly improve our power to understand the external world and to make maximum use of our internal thinking capabilities, transforming our observations into understanding.

Visualizing

The first of these processes, visualizing, represents the methodology of focusing attention on a given area and through imagination and logic creating an internal vision and scenario for success. In developing a successful vision, one must frequently take several different perspectives of the situation, play with a number of assumptions underlying these perspectives, and through a playful trial-and-error, come up with potential visions. This process is more creative than logical, more intuitive than rational, and wherever possible should be challenged, filtered, and constructed in collaboration with other competent individuals. Often this is done between two trusting colleagues or perhaps with a small team. While there is never absolute assurance that visualizing accurately represents reality, there are probabilities or degrees of success that can be recognized and developed

Intuiting

The second supporting area is that of intuiting. By this we mean the art of making maximum use of our own intuition developed through experience, trial-and-error, and deliberate internal questioning and application. There are standard processes available for training oneself to surface intuition. Recognize that intuition is typically understood as being the ability to access our unconscious mind and thereby make effective use of its very large storeroom of observations, experiences, and information. In our framework, intuition is one of the four ways tacit knowledge expresses.

Empathy represents another aspect of intuition. Empathy is interpreted as the ability to take oneself out of oneself and put oneself into another person's world. In other words, as the old Native American saying goes, "Until you walk a mile in his moccasins, you will never understand the person." The ability to empathize permits us to translate our personal perspective into that of another, thereby understanding their interpretation of the situation and intuiting their actions. A tool that can be used to trigger ideas and dig deeper into one's intuitive capability, bringing out additional insights, is "mind mapping." Mind mapping is a tool to visually display and recognize relationships from discrete and diverse pieces of information and data (Wycoff, 1991).

Valuing

Valuing represents the capacity to observe situations and recognize the values that underly their various aspects and concomitantly be fully aware of your own values and beliefs. A major part of valuing is the ability to align your vision, mission, and goals to focus attention on the immediate situation at hand. A second aspect represents the ability to identify the relevant but unknown aspects of a situation or competitor's behavior. Of course, the problem of unknown unknowns always exists in a turbulent environment and, while logically they are impossible to identify because by definition they are unknown, there are techniques available that help one reduce the area of known unknowns and hence reduce the probability of them adversely affecting the organization.

A third aspect of valuing is that of meaning, that is, understanding the important aspects of the situation and being able to prioritize them to anticipate potential consequences. Meaning is contingent upon the goals and aspirations of the individual. It also relies on the history of both the individual's experience and the context of the situation. Determining the meaning of a situation allows us to understand its impact on our own objectives and those of our organization. Knowing the meaning of something lets us prioritize our actions and estimate the resources we may need to deal with it.

Choosing

The fourth supporting area is that of choosing. Choosing involves making judgments, that is, conclusions and interpretations developed through the use of rules-of-thumb, facts, knowledge, experiences, emotions and intuition. While not necessarily widely recognized, judgments are used far more than logic or rational thinking in making decisions. This is because all but the simplest decisions occur in a context in which there is insufficient, noisy, or perhaps too much information to make rational conclusions. Judgment makes maximum use of heuristics, meta-knowing, and verication.

Heuristics represent the rules-of-thumb developed over time and through experience in a given field. They are shortcuts to thinking that are applicable to specific situations. Their value is speed of conclusions and their usefulness rests on consistency of the environment and repeatability of situations. Thus, they are both powerful and dangerous. Dangerous because the situation or environment, when changing, may quickly invalidate former reliable heuristics and historically create the phenomenon of always solving the last problem; yet powerful because they represent efficient and rapid ways of making decisions where the situation is known and the heuristics apply.

Meta-knowing is knowing about knowing, that is, understanding how we know things and how we go about knowing things. With this knowledge, one can more effectively go about learning and knowing in new situations as they evolve over time. Such power and flexibility greatly improve the quality of our choices. Meta-knowing is closely tied to our natural internal processes of learning and behaving as well as knowing how to make the most effective use of available external data, information, and knowledge and intuit that which is not available. An interesting aspect of meta-knowing is the way that certain errors in judgment are common to many people. Just being aware of these mistakes can reduce their occurrence. For example, we tend to give much more weight to specific, concrete information than to conceptual or abstract information. (See Kahneman et al., 1982, for details.)

Verication is the process by which we can improve the probability of making good choices by working with trusted others and using *their* experience and knowing to validate and improve the level of our judgmental effectiveness. Again, this could be done via a trusted colleague or through effective team creativity and decision-making.

Setting Intent

Intent is a powerful internal process that can be harnessed by every person. Intention is the source with which we are doing something, the act or instance of mentally setting some course of action or result, a determination to act in some specific way. It can take the form of a declaration (often in the form of action), an assertion, a prayer, a cry for help, a wish, visualization, a thought or an affirmation. Perhaps the most in-depth and focused experimentation on the effects of human intention on the properties of materials and what we call physical reality has been that pursued for the past 40 years by Dr. William Tiller of Stanford University. Tiller has proven through repeated experimentation that it is possible to significantly change the properties (ph) of water by holding a clear intention to do so. His mind-shifting and potentially world-changing results began with using intent to change the acid/alkaline balance in purified water. The ramifications of this experiment have the potential to impact every aspect of human life.

What Tiller has discovered is that there are two unique levels of physical reality. The "normal level" of substance is the electric/atom/molecule level, what most of us think of and perceive as the only physical reality. However, a second level of substance exists that is the magnetic information level. While these two levels always interpenetrate each other, under "normal" conditions they do not interact; they are "uncoupled." Intention changes this condition, causing these two levels to interact, or move into a "coupled" state. Where humans are concerned, Tiller says that what an individual intends for himself with a strong sustained desire is what that individual will eventually become (Tiller, 2007).

While informed by spiritual, the embodied, intuitive and affective tacit knowledges are *local expressions of knowledge*, that is, directly related to our expression in physical reality in a specific situation and context. Connecting Tiller's model of intention with our model of tacit knowledge, it begins to become clear that effective intent relates to an alignment of the conscious mind with the tacit components of the mind and body, that is Embodied, Intuitive, and Affective tacit knowledge. We have to *know* it, *feel* it, and *believe* it to achieve the coupling of the electric/atom/molecule level and magnetic information level of physical reality.

As we use our power of intent to co-create our future, it is necessary to focus from outcome to intention, not worrying about what gets done but staying focused on what you are doing and how you "feel" about what you are doing. Are we in alignment with the direction our decisions are taking us? If not, back to the drawing board—that's looking closer at you, the decision-maker, and ensuring that your vision is clear and your intent is aligned with that vision.

In summary, the five internal cognitive processes—visualizing, intuiting, valuing, choosing and setting intent—work with the six cognitive capabilities—listening, noticing, scanning, patterning, sensing, and integrating—to process data and information and create knowledge within the context of the environment and the situation. However, this knowledge must always be suspect because of our own self-limitations, internal inconsistencies, historical biases, and emotional distortions, all of which are discussed in the third area of knowing: the Self as an Agent of Change.

The Self as an Agent of Change

The third area of the knowing framework—the self as an agent of change—is the mechanism for creating deep knowledge, a level of understanding consistent with the external world and our internal framework. As the unconscious continuously associates information, the self as an agent of change takes the emergent deep knowledge and uses it for the dual purpose of our personal learning and growth, and for making changes in the external world.

Recall that deep knowledge consists of beliefs, facts, truths, assumptions, and understanding of an area that is so thoroughly embedded in the mind that we are often not consciously aware of the knowledge. To create deep knowledge an individual has to "live" with it, continuously interacting, thinking, learning, and experiencing that part of the world until the knowledge truly becomes a natural part of the inner being. An example would be that a person who has a good knowledge of a foreign language can speak it fluently; a person with a deep knowledge would be able to think in the language without any internal translation and would not need their native language to understand that internal thinking.

In the discussion of self as an agent of change, there are ten elements that will be presented. Five of these elements are internal: know thyself, mental models, emotional intelligence, learning and forgetting, and mental defenses; and five of these elements are external: modeling behaviors, knowledge sharing, dialogue, storytelling, and the art of persuasion.

Internal Elements

Alexander Pope, in his essay on man (1732-3/1994), noted that: "Know then thyself, presume not God to scan; the proper study of mankind is man." We often think we know ourselves, but we rarely do. To really understand our own biases, perceptions, capabilities, etc., each of us must look inside and, as objectively as possible, ask ourselves, who are we, what are our limitations, what are our strengths, and what jewels and baggage do we carry from our years of experience. Rarely do we *take ourselves out of ourselves and look at ourselves*. But without an objective understanding of our own values, beliefs, and biases, we are continually in danger of misunderstanding the interpretations we apply to the external world. Our motives, expectations, decisions, and beliefs are frequently driven by internal forces of which we are completely unaware. For example, our emotional state plays a strong role in determining how we make decisions and what we decide.

The first step in knowing ourselves is awareness of the fact that we cannot assume we are what our conscious mind thinks we are. Two examples that most of us have experienced come to mind. The first is that we frequently do not know what we think until we hear what we say. The second example is the recognition that every act of writing is an act of creativity. Our biases, prejudices, and even brilliant ideas frequently remain unknown to us until pointed out by others or through conversations. Consciousness is our window to the world, but it is clouded by an internal history, experiences, feelings, memories, and desires. After awareness comes the need to constantly monitor ourselves for undesirable traits or biases in our thinking, feeling, and processing. Seeking observations from others and carefully analyzing our individual experiences are both useful in understanding ourselves. We all have limitations and strengths, and even agendas hidden from our conscious mind that we must be aware of and build upon or control.

Part of knowing ourselves is the understanding of what mental models we have formed in specific areas of the external world. Mental models are the models we use to represent our own picture of reality. They are built up over time and through experience and represent our beliefs, assumptions, and ways of interpreting the outside world. They are efficient in that they allow us to react quickly to changing conditions and make rapid decisions based upon our presupposed model. Concomitantly, they are dangerous if the model is inaccurate or misleading.

Because we exist in a rapidly changing environment, many of our models quickly become outdated. We then must recognize the importance of continuously reviewing our perceptions and assumptions of the external world and questioning our own mental models to ensure they are consistent with reality (Senge, 1990). Since this is done continuously in our subconscious, we must always question ourselves as to our real, versus stated, motives, goals and feelings. *Only then can we know who we are, only then can we change to who we want to be.*

The art of knowing not only includes understanding our own mental models, but the ability to recognize and deal with the mental models of others. Mental models frequently serve as drivers for our actions as well as our interpretations. When creating deep knowledge or taking action, the use of small groups, dialogue, etc. to normalize mental models with respected colleagues provides somewhat of a safeguard against the use of incomplete or erroneous mental models.

A subtle but powerful factor underlying mental models is the role of emotions in influencing our perception of reality. This has been extensively explored by Daniel Goleman (1995) in his seminal book *Emotional Intelligence*. Emotional intelligence is the ability to sense, understand, and effectively apply the power and acumen of emotions as a source of human energy, information, connection, and influence. It includes self-control, zeal and persistence, and the ability to motivate oneself. To understand emotional intelligence, we study how emotions affect behavior, influence decisions, motivate people to action, and impact their ability to interrelate. Emotions play a much larger role in our lives than previously understood, including a strong role in decision-making. For years it was widely held that rationality was the way of the executive. Now it is becoming clear that the rational and the emotional parts of the mind must be used together to get the best performance in organizations.

Much of emotional life is unconscious. Awareness of emotions occurs when the emotions enter the frontal cortex. As affective tacit knowledge, emotions in the subconscious play a powerful role in how we perceive and act, and hence in our decision-making. Feelings come from the limbic part of the brain and often come forth before the related experiences occur. *They represent a signal* that a given potential action may be wrong, or right, or that an external event may be dangerous. Emotions assign values to options or alternatives, sometimes without our knowing it. There is growing evidence that fundamental ethical stances in life stem from underlying emotional capacities. These stances create the basic belief system, the values, and often the underlying assumptions that we use to see the world—our mental model. From this short treatment of the concept, it is clear that emotional intelligence is interwoven across the ten elements of the self as an agent of change. (See Goleman, 1995 and 1998.)

Creating the deep knowledge of knowing through the effective use of emotional intelligence opens the door to two other equally important factors: learning and forgetting. Learning and letting go—in terms of "filing" away or putting away on the bookshelf—are critical elements of the self as an agent of change because they are the primary processes through which we change and grow. They are also the prerequisite for continuous learning, so essential for developing competencies representing all of the processes and capabilities discussed previously. Because the environment is highly dynamic and will continue to become more complex, continuous learning will be more and more essential and critical in keeping up with the world.

Since humans have limited processing capability and the mind is easily overloaded and tends to cling to its past experiences and knowledge, "letting go" becomes as important as learning. Letting go is the art of being able to let go of what was known and true in the past. Being able to recognize the limitations and inappropriateness of past assumptions, beliefs, and knowledge is essential before creating new mental models and for understanding ourselves as we grow. It is *one of the hardest acts of the human mind* because it threatens our self-image and may shake even our core belief systems.

The biggest barrier to learning and letting go arises from our own individual ability to develop invisible defenses against changing our beliefs. These self-imposed mental defenses have been eloquently described by Chris Argyris (1990). The essence of his conclusion is that the mind creates built-in defense mechanisms to support belief systems and experience. These defense mechanisms are invisible to the individual and may be quite difficult to expose in a real-world situation. They are a widespread example of not knowing what we know, thus representing invisible barriers to change. Several authors have estimated that information and knowledge double approximately every nine months. If this estimate is even close, the problems of saturation will continue to make our ability to acquire deep knowledge even more challenging. We must learn how to filter data and information through vision, values, experiences, goals, and purposes using an open mind, intuition and judgment as our tools. This discernment and discretion within the deepest level of our minds provides a proactive aspect of filtering, thereby setting up purposeful mental defenses that reduce complexity and provide conditional safeguards to an otherwise open system. This is a fundamental way in which the self can simplify a situation by eliminating extraneous and undesirable information and knowledge coming from the external world.

The above discussion has identified a number of factors that can help us achieve an appropriate balance between change and our resistance to change. This is an important attribute: not all change is for the best, yet rigidity begets antiquity. This balance is situational and comes only from experience, learning, and a deep sense of knowing when to change and when not to change the self.

This section has addressed the self as an agent of change through internal recognition of certain factors that can influence self-change. Another aspect of change is the ability of the self to influence or change the external world. This is the active part of knowing. Once the self has attained deep knowledge and understanding of the situation and external environment, this must be shared with others, accompanied by the right actions to achieve success. We live in a connected world.

External Elements

The challenge becomes that of translating knowledge into behavior, thus creating the ability to model that behavior and influence others toward taking requisite actions. Role-modeling has always been a prime responsibility of leadership in the government as well as the civilian world. Having deep knowledge of the situation the individual must then translate that into personal behavior that becomes a role model for others to follow and become motivated and knowledgeable about how to act. Effective role-modeling does not require the learner to have the same deep knowledge as the role model, yet the actions and behaviors that result may reflect the equivalent deep knowledge and over time creates deep knowledge in the learner—but only in specific situations. This is how you share the effectiveness from learning and thereby transfer implicit knowledge.

Wherever possible, of course, it is preferable to develop and share as much knowledge as possible so that others can act independently and develop their own internally and situation-driven behavior. This is the reason Knowledge Management and communities of practice and interest require management attention. Since most deep knowledge is tacit, knowledge sharing can become a real challenge.

A third technique for orchestrating external change is through the use of dialogue. Dialogue is a process described by David Bohm (1992) to create a situation in which a group participates as coequals in inquiring and learning about some specific topic. In essence, the group creates a common understanding and shared perception of a given situation or topic. Dialogue is frequently viewed as the collaborative sharing and development of understanding. It can include both inquiry and discussions, but all participants must suspend judgment and not seek specific outcomes and answers. The process stresses the examination of underlying assumptions and listening deeply to the self and others to develop a collective meaning. This collective meaning is perhaps the best way in which a common understanding of a situation may be developed as a group and understood by others.

Another way of creating change and sharing understanding is through the effective use of the time-honored process of storytelling. Storytelling is a valuable tool in helping to build a common understanding of our current situation in anticipating possible futures and preparing to act on those possible futures. Stories tap into a universal consciousness that is natural to all human communities. Repetition of common story forms carries a subliminal message, a subtext that can help convey a deep level of complex meaning. Since common values enable consistent action, Story in this sense provides a framework that aids decision-making under conditions of uncertainty.

Modeling behavior, knowledge sharing, dialogue, and storytelling are all forms of building understanding and knowledge. Persuasion, our fifth technique, serves to communicate and share understanding with others who have a specific conviction or belief and/or to get them to act upon it. To change the external environment, we need to be persuasive and to communicate the importance and need for others to take appropriate action. The question arises: When you have deep knowledge, what aspects of this can be used to effectively influence other's behavior? Since deep knowledge is tacit knowledge, we must learn how to transfer this to explicit knowledge. Nonaka and Tageuchi (1995) and Polyani (1958) have done seminal work in this area. Persuasion, as seen from the perspective of the self, gets us back to the importance of using all of our fundamental values, such as personal example, integrity, honesty, and openness to help transfer our knowing to others.

As can be seen in the discussion above, **all four forms of tacit knowledge inform knowing**. The Knowing Framework seeks to engage our senses and hone our internal processing mechanisms to take full advantage of our minds/brains/bodies. By bringing our focus on knowing, we have the opportunity to move through relational, experiential, and cultural barriers that somewhere along the course of our lives have been constructed, and sometimes self-imposed. This, however, is not the case for many of the young decision-makers moving into the workplace.

[Excerpted from Bennet and Bennet (2013)].

Appendix F
Values for Creativity

[Supports discussion of values in Chapter 9/Part II and Chapter 29/Part IV.]

$\mathbf{A}$ creative environment is fueled by the values of integrity, empathy, transparency, collaboration, learning, and contribution that foster trust and a spirit of collaborative success (Avedisian & Bennet, 2010).

Integrity is defined as "steadfast adherence to a strict moral or ethical code" (American Heritage Dictionary, 2006). A person or organization with integrity is "whole," aligning words and actions, keeping commitments, doing the right thing, and engaging in fair dealing. Empathy, discussed in Chapter 35/Part V is the act of identifying with another's struggle as if it were one's own, and is the ultimate expression of a sense of equality. "Empathy requires a porous boundary between I and thou that allows the identity of two beings to mingle in a shared mental space" (Rifkin, 2009, p. 160). Empathy asserts the unconditional value of the human person and the meaning of his growth and the growth of his fellow man. When coupled with integrity, empathy builds the foundation not for just collaboration and participation, but for true fraternity, reciprocity, and integration.

Integrity and empathy provide the pre-conditions for the effectiveness of other more operational values by creating trust and mutual respect, and providing a non-judgmental environment, all of which form the basis of communication through shared understanding. Empathy and integrity are not mutually independent. First, empathy needs to be understood, confirmed and practiced in the light of integrity. Without integrity, empathy may degenerate into sentimentality. Second, integrity is softened by empathy. Without empathy, integrity may become judgmental, and even harsh and unforgiving. Together, empathy and integrity serve as a foundation for effective teamwork and facilitating knowledge creation, sharing and leveraging, and enabling new, quick, flexible, and effective responses.

The concept of **transparency** is defined as: easily seen through or detected and free from guile; candid or open (The American Heritage Dictionary, 2000). Again, we see a level of interdependency emerging. Empathy and integrity facilitate transparency by fostering trust, while transparency, in turn, reinforces trust. Unless transparency is balanced by empathy and integrity, it could foster misunderstanding and breakdown trust and relationships rather than support them.

Transparency supports connecting with others, and when you are connecting with someone else, you are connecting with yourself. Walsch (2009) says that when you are communicating with a mind outside of your mind—moving from an internal dialogue into an external dialogue—it puts you in touch with a part of your self that is bigger than your own mind. As Walsch (2009, p. 32) explains,

> In an external dialogue, another person can bring you fresh energy, provide a different perspective. They can come to the subject with a clear head, free of the self-judgment through which you are looking at everything. They see you as you really are, proving the irony that sometimes you have to get out of yourself to get into yourself. Sometimes you have to stop looking at yourself to see yourself.

Beyond sharing documents on websites, transparency extends to openly sharing ideas, feelings, personal view points, and different levels of knowledge (Bennet and Bennet, 2008a). Applying the levels of knowledge model, transparency moves beyond surface knowledge to a focus on shallow knowledge, with the responsibility to ensure some level of understanding and meaning that makes information actionable in a changing, uncertain and complex environment. Further, by building on surface and shallow knowledge, and developing deep knowledge, decision-makers at all levels understand underlying relationships and patterns which enable them to shift their frame of reference as the context and situation shift. In this way, transparency contributes not only to better problem-solving and decision-making, but also to fostering creativity and innovation, and the sharing of expertise.

Walsch (2009) says that we are living on the edge of what he called *The Time of Instaparency*. This is a time when everything is known instantly, transparently. As he adds, "Such moment-to-moment awareness of all that's going on everywhere produces alterations in perspective that start dominoes falling all over the place" (p. 53).

Participation is a keystone for the Net Generation, who reach out and creatively engage ideas and people around the world. This participation extends to political engagement and community service. **Collaboration** means, "to work together, especially in a joint intellectual effort" (American Heritage Dictionary, 2000). In the current environment, the meaning of collaboration has extended from relatively intact internal groups at the team, unit, or company level to a fluid, changing interdependent network of diverse contributors across the internal and external environment. A knowledge worker has a new type of peer network, one that moves from autonomy to interdependence, from deference to dialogue, and from a primary focus on doing a job well to a focus on contribution to collective purposes (Heckscher, 2007, p.108-109). In this peer network, alignment around such values as collaboration, transparency, and contribution make it possible for knowledge workers to work together in environments that are open, changing, and diverse. Collaboration is a core value embraced by the Net Geners, involving engagement and participation. "Collaboration as Net Geners know it, is achieving something *with* other people, experiencing power through other people, not by ordering a gaggle of followers to do your bidding." (Tapscott, 2009, p. 163).

Closely linked to participation and collaboration, **contribution** measures success and performance in the context of helping peers and the organization move toward a common mission and strategy. Participation is the act of engagement, collaboration is how to engage, and contribution is the result of that engagement. The purpose-driven orientation of contribution is a motivating force in the lives of Net Generation knowledge workers. Through global connectivity, Net Geners share openly, engaging others ideas and contributing their ideas freely. As an operational value **learning** is integrally related to the ability to contribute. Learning in the CUCA environment means receiving, understanding, thinking critically, and learning how to adapt and apply knowledge quickly in new and unfamiliar situations.

Learning affects every other value, offering a way of practicing and applying each of the values in every aspect of work life including interactions with peers, customers, vendors, how work gets done, and how success is measured. This learning is collaborative. For example, demonstrating the interdependence between learning, empathy and collaboration, Tapscott says,

It goes without saying that collaborative learning, with its emphasis on mindfulness, attunement to others, nonjudgmental interactions, acknowledgement of each person's unique contributions, and recognition of the importance of deep participation and a shared sense of meaning coming out of embedded relationships, can't help but foster greater empathic engagement. (Tapscott, 2009, p. 607)

Bringing this conversation full circle, creativity itself could be considered an operational value in terms of the ability to perceive new relationships and new possibilities, see things form a different frame of reference, or realize new ways of understanding/having insight or portraying something. Since innovation represents the creation of new ideas and the transformation of those ideas into useful applications, the combination of creativity and contribution as operational values bring about innovation.

[Excerpted from Avedisian and Bennet, 2010]

Endnotes

22-1. Niles MacFlouer is currently developing an expanded and in-depth treatment of Quantum theory, which is expected to be available through the Ageless Wisdom Press in 2017.

23-1. Dr. William Tiller, Professor Emeritus of Materials Science and Engineering, Stanford University, is the author of *Science and Human Transformation* (Tiller, 2007), a book on esoteric concepts such as subtle energies that work beyond the four fundamental forces which he believes act in concert with human consciousness. He appeared in *What the Bleep Do We Know*? See www.tillerfoundation.com for a complete list of published material and downloadable white papers.

28-1. The KMTL Study is a 2005 research study that reached out to 34 Knowledge Management Thought Leaders located across four continents. The intent was to explore the aspects of KM that contributed to the passion expressed by these thought leaders.

28-2. CUCA represents **C**hange, **U**ncertainty, **C**omplexity and **A**nxiety. See Chapter 13/Part III.

29-1. The Monroe Institute furthers the experience and exploration of consciousness, expanded awareness and discovery of self through technology and education See www.monroeinstitute.org/

30-1. David Galenson is Professor of Economics at the University of Chicago.

References

Abraham-Hicks (2005). Excerpt from 02/29/05 workshop in San Antonio, TX. Retrieved 07/10/16 from http://abraham-hicks.us4.list-manage.com/track/click?u=1c8e6d19e03449b5d28ee9f3d&id=de13d45dd38e=d7daf54754

Abraham-Hicks (2003). Excerpt from 12/20/03 workshop in Orlando, FL. Retrieved 06/28/16 from http://abraham-hicks.us4.list-manage.com/track/click?u-1c8e6d19e03449b5d28ee9f3d&id=86b64a7019&e=d7daf54754

Alberts, D. S. and Hayes, R. E. (2005). *Power to the Edge: Command, Control in the Information Age*. Washington, D.C.: Command & Control Research Program.

AlphaDictionary (2016). Retrieved 08/28/16 from http://www.alphadictionary.com/bb/viewtopic.php?t=4675

Amabile, T. M. (1996). *Creativity in Context*. Boulder, CO: Westview.

Amabile, T. M. (1983). *The Social Psychology of Creativity*. New York: Springer.

Amen, D. G. (2005). *Making a Good Brain Great*. New York: Harmony Books.

American Heritage Dictionary of the English Language (4th ed.) (2006). Boston: Houghton Mifflin Company.

Andersson, J.L., Lilja, A., Hartvig, P., Langstrom, B., Gordh, T., Handwerker, H., et al. (1997). "Somatotopic Organization along the Central Sulcus, for Pain Localization in Humans, as Revealed by Positron Emission Tomography" in *Experimental Brain Research,* 117: 192-199.

Andreasen, N. (2005). *The Creating Brain: The Neuroscience of Genius*. New York: The Dana Foundation.

Argyris, C. (1990). *Overcoming Organizational Defenses: Facilitating Organizational Learning*. Englewood Cliffs, NJ: Prentice Hall.

Argyris, C. and Schon, D. (1978). *Organizational Learning: A Theory of Action Perspective*. Reading, MA: Addison-Wesley.

Armstrong, D.M. (1989). *Universals: An Opinionated Introduction. Boulder*, CO: Westview Press.

Atwater, F.H. (2004). *The Hemi-Sync Process*. Faber, VA: The Monroe Institute.

Augustine, J.R. (1996). "Circuitry and Functional Aspects of the Insular Lobe in Primates, including Humans" in *Brain Research Reviews, 22*, 229-244.

Avedisian, J. and Bennet, A. (2010). "Values as Knowledge: A New Frame of Reference for a New Generation of Knowledge Workers" in *On the Horizon*, Vol. 18, No. 3, 255-265.

Baird, J.D. and Nadel, L. (2010). *Happiness Genes: Unlock the Potential Hidden in Your DNA*. Franklin Lakes, NJ: New Page Books.

Barthes, R. (1985,. *In the Responsibility of Forms*, Hill and Wang, New York.

Bateson, G. (1972). *Steps to an Ecology of the Mind*. New York: Ballantine.

Begley, S., (2007). *Train Your Mind Change Your Brain: How a New Science Reveals Our Extraordinary Potential to Transform Ourselves.* New York: Ballantine Books.

Bennet, A. and Bennet, D. (2014). "Knowledge, Theory and Practice in Knowledge Management: Between Associative Patterning and Context-Rich Action" in *Journal of Entrepreneurship, Management and Innovation*, Vol. 10, Issue 1, 7-55. See www.jemi.edu.pl

Bennet, A. and Bennet, D. (2013). *Decision-Making in The New Reality.* Frost, WV: MQIPress.

Bennet, A. and Bennet, D. (2010a). "Multidimensionality: Building the Mind/Brain Infrastructure for the Next Generation Knowledge Worker" in *On the Horizon*, Vol. 18, No. 3, 240-254.

Bennet, A. and Bennet, D. (2008a). "The Depth of Knowledge: Surface, Shallow, or Deep?" in *VINE: The Journal of Information and Knowledge Management Systems,* Vol. 38, No. 4, 405-420.

Bennet, A. and Bennet, D. (2008c). "The Fallacy of Knowledge Reuse" in *Journal of Knowledge Management*, 12(5), 21-33.

Bennet, A. and Bennet, D. (2008d). "Moving from Knowledge to Wisdom, from Ordinary Consciousness to Extraordinary Consciousness" in *VINE: Journal of Information and Knowledge Systems*, Vol. 38, No. 1, 7-15.

Bennet, A. and Bennet, D. (2007b). *Knowledge Mobilization in the Social Sciences and Humanities: Moving From Research To Action.* MQIPress, Frost, WV.

Bennet, A. and Bennet, D. (2007c). "The Knowledge and Knowing of Spiritual Learning" in *VINE: The Journal of Information and Knowledge Management Systems*, 37 (2), 150-168.

Bennet, A. & Bennet, D. (2004). *Organizational Survival in the New World: The Intelligent Complex Adaptive System.* Boston, MA: Elsevier.

Bennet, A., Bennet, D. and Avedisian, J. (2015a). *The Course of Knowledge: A 21st Century Theory.* Frost, WV: MQIPress.

Bennet, A., Bennet, D. and Lewis, J. (2015c). *Leading with the Future in Mind: Knowledge and Emergent Leadership.* Frost, WV: MQIPress.

Bennet, D. (2001), "Loosening the World Knot", unpublished paper available at www.mountainquestinstitute.com

Bennet, D. and Bennet, A. (2008e). "Engaging Tacit Knowledge in Support of Organizational Learning" in *VINE: Journal of Information and Knowledge Systems,* 38(1), 72-94.

Bennet, D., Bennet, A. and Turner, R. (2015b). *Expanding the Self: The Intelligent Complex Adaptive Learning System.* Frost, WV: MQI Press.

Bennett-Woods, D. (1997). "Reflections on Wisdom", unpublished paper, University of Northern Colorado.

Bennis, Warren G., Benne, K.D., Chin, R. and Covey, K.E. (Eds.) (1976). *The Planning of Change* (3rd ed.). New York: Holt, Rinehart & Winston.

Berman, M. (1981). *The Reenchantment of the World*. Ithaca, NY: Cornell University Press.

Besant, A. and Leadbeater, C.W. (1999). *Thought-Forms*. Wheaton, IL: Quest Books.

Blair, Hugh (2015). "Readings on Sentence Structure from Hugh Blair From Lectures on Rhetoric and Belles Lettres." Retrieved 09/13/15 from http://academic.macewan.ca/einarssonr/files/2009/10/On-Sentence-Structure-by-Blair1.pdf

Blakemore, S., and Frith, Y. (2005). *The Learning Brain: Lessons for Education*. Malden, MA: Blackwell.

Boden, M. (1991). *The Creative Mind, Myths & Mysticism*. London: Basic Books.

Bohm, D. (1992), *Thought as a System*, Routledge, New York.

Bolles, E.B. (1991). *A Second Way of Knowing: The Riddle of Human Perception*. Upper Saddle River, NJ: Prentice Hall Trade.

Bower, J. L. (2000). "The Purpose of Change: A Commentary on Jensen and Senge" in Beer, Mk. and Nohria, N. (Eds.), *Breaking the Code of Change*. Boston: Harvard Business School Press, 83-95.

Bradley, F.H. (1966). *Appearance and Reality*. London: Oxford University Press.

Brown, T. (2009). *Change by Design: How Design Thinking Transforms Organizations and Inspires Innovation*. New York: HarperColllins.

Brown, M.Y. (1979). *The Art of Guiding: The Psychosynthesis Approach to Individual Counselling and Psychology*. Redlands, CA: Johnson College, University of Redlands.

Buks, E., Schuster, R. Heiblum, M., Mahalu, D and Umansky, V. (1998). "Dephasing in Electron Interference by a 'Which-Path' Detector" in *Nature* (Vol. 391) (February 26), 871-874.

Bullard, B. and Bennet, A. (2013). *REMEMBRANCE: Pathways to Expanded Learning with Music and Metamusic®*. Frost, WV: MQIPress.

Butler, J. (1906). *The Analogy of Religion, Natural & Revealed*. London: J.M. Dent & Company.

Buzsaki, G. (2006). *Rhythms of the Brain*. New York: Oxford University Press.

Byrnes, J. P. (2001). *Minds, Brains, and Learning: Understanding the Psychological and Educational Relevance of Neuroscientific Research*. New York: The Guilford Press.

Calder, A. J., Beaver, J.D., Eger, E., Jenkins, R., Winston, J., Dolan, R. J. and Henson, R.N.A. (2006). "The Neural Correlates of Eye Gaze Adaptation" in *PERCEPTION* 35, 240-24.

Campbell, D. T. (1960). "Blind Variation and Selective Retention in Creative Thought and Other Knowledge Processes" in *Psychological Review*, 67, 380–400.

Carr, N. (2003). "IT Doesn't Matter" in *Harvard Business Review* (May), 41-49.

Carrasco, M., Ling, S., and Read, S. (2004). "Attention Alters Appearance" in *Nature Neuroscience* 7, 308-313.

Carroll, S. (2016). *The Big Picture: On the Origins of Life, Meaning, and the Universe Itself*. New York: Dutton.

Carse, James P. (1986). *Finite and Infinite Games*. New York: Ballantine.

Carter, R. (2002). *Exploring Consciousness*. Berkeley: University of California Press.

Case, P. F. (2009). *Tarot Card Meanings: Fundamentals*. New Orleans, LA: Cornerstone Book Publishers.

Case, P. F. (2008). *An Introduction to the Study of the Tarot*. New Orleans, LA: Cornerstone Book Publishers.

Case, P. F. (2007). Esoteric Keys of Alchemy. Ishtar Publishing.

Christos, G. (2003). *Memory and Dreams: The Creative Human Mind*. New Brunswick, NJ: Rutgers University Press.

Clark, P.A. and Forbes, C.L. (2013). *Paul Foster Case: His Life and Works*. Fraternity o the Hidden Light.

Clavell, J. (Ed.) (1983). *The Art of War: Sun Tzu*. New York: Dell Publishing.

Clayton, V. and Birren, J.E. (1980). "The Development of Wisdom across the Lifespan: A Reexamination of an Ancient Topic" in Baltes, P.B. and Brim, O.G.J. (Eds.), *Life Span Development and Behavior*. Cambridge, MA: Academic Press, 104-135.

Pequenino, K. (2016). " Laughter to be 3D Printed and Launched into Space" in CNN Style (Arts). Retrieved 01/24/17 from www.edition.cnn.com/206/12/22/1452/eyal-gever-laughter-sculpture-in-space/index.html

Conway, J.H. and Burgiel, H. (2008). *The Symmetries of Things*. Boca Raton, FL: CRC Press.

Cooper, L.R. (2005). *The Grand Vision: The Design and purpose of a Human Being*. Ft. Collins, CO: Planetary Heart.

Cooper, R. (2005). "Austinian Truth, Attitudes and Type Theory" in *Research on Language and Computation* 5: 333-362.

Costa, J.D. (1995). *Working Wisdom: The Ultimate Value in the New Economy*. Toronto, Canada: Stoddart.

Cowley, M. (ed.) (1958). *Writers at Work: The Paris Review Interviews*. New York: The Paris Review.

Cozolino, L. J. (2006). *The Neuroscience of Human Relationships: Attachment and the Developing Social Brain*. New York: W.W. Norton.

Crandall, B. Klein, G. and Hoffman, R.R. (2006). *Working Minds: A Practitioner's Guide to Cognitive Task Analysis*. Cambridge, MA: The MIT Press.

Csikszentmihalyi, M. (1996). *Flow and the Psychology of Discovery and Invention*. New York: Harper Collins.

Csikszentmihalyi, M. (1993). *The Evolving Self: A Psychology for the Third Millennium*. New York: HarperCollins Publishing.

Csikszentmihalyi, M. and Nakamura, J. (2005). "The Role of Emotions in the Development of Wisdom" in Sternberg, R.J. and Jordan, J., *A Handbook of Wisdom: Psychological Perspectives*. New York: Cambridge University Press.

Csikszentmihalyi, M. and Csikszentmihalyi, I.S. (Eds.) (1988). *Optimal Experience: Psychological Studies of Flow in Consciousness*. New York: Cambridge University Press.

Damasio, A. R. (1999). *The Feeling of What Happens: Body and Emotion in the Making of Consciousness*. New York: Harcourt Brace & Company.

Damasio, A. R. (1994). *Descartes' Error: Emotion, Reason, and the Human Brain*. New York: G.P. Putnam's Sons.

Davenport, T.H. and Beck, J.C. (2001). *The Attention Economy*. Boston, MA: Harvard Business Review Press.

David, S. (2014). "Inclusiveness Means giving Every Employee Personal Attention." Retrieved on 10/14/16 from https://hbr.org/2014/06/inclusiveness-means-giving-every-employee-personal-attention

Davis, J. (1997). *Alternate Realities: How Science Shapes Our Vision of the World*. New York: Plenum Trade.

Davis, S. (1996). *Future Perfect*. Reading, MA: Addison-Wesley Publishing Company, Inc.

de Bono, E. (1992). *Serious Creativity: Using the Power of Lateral Thinking to Create New Ideas*. New York: HarperCollins.

de Chardin, P. Teilhard (1959). *The Phenomenon of Man*. St James Palace, London: Collins.

de Laszlo, V. (Ed.) (1958). *Psyche & Symbol: A Selection from the Writings of C.G.Jung*. New York: Anchor Books.

Delmonte, M.M. (1984). "Electrocortical Activity and Related Phenomena Associated with Meditation Practice: A Literature Review" in *International Journal of Neuroscience*, 24: 217-231.

Devlin, K.J. and Lorden, G. (2007). *The Numbers Behind Numb3rs: Solving Crime with Mathematics*. New York: Penguin Group.

de Waal, F. (2009) *The Age of Empathy: Nature's Lessons for a Kinder Society*. New York: Harmony Books.

Dictionary.com (2016). Retrieved 07/18/16 http://www.dictionary.com/browse/harmony

Dilts, R. (2003). *From Coach to Awakener*. Capitola, CA: Meta Publications.

Dobbs, D. (2007). "Turning Off Depression" in F. E. Bloom (Ed.), *Best of the Brain from Scientific American: Mind, Matter, and Tomorrow's Brain*. New York: Dana Press, 169-178.

Dreher, D. (1995). *The Tao of Personal Leadership*. New York: HarperBusiness.

Dunning, J. (2014). Discussion of consciousness via the Internet on December 13.

Eccles, R. G. and Nohria, N. (1992). *Beyond the Hype: Rediscovering the Essence of Management*. Boston: Harvard Business School Press.

Edelman, G. (1989). *The Remembered Present: A Biological Theory of Consciousness*. New York: Basic Books.

Edelman, G., and Tononi, G. (2000). *A Universe of Consciousness: How Matter Becomes Imagination*. New York: Basic Books.

Ellinor, L. and Gerard, G. (1998). *Dialogue: Rediscover the Transforming Power of Conversation*. New York: John Wiley & Sons, Inc.

Emig, J. (1983). *The Web of Meaning: Essays on Writing, Teaching, Learning and Thinking*. New Jersey: Boynton/Cook Publishers.

Encarta World English Dictionary (1999). New York: St Martin's Press.

Epstein, M. (1995). *Thoughts Without a Thinker*. New York: BasicBooks.

Ericsson, K.A., Charness, N., Feltovich, P.J. & Hoffman, R.R. (Eds.) (2006), *The Cambridge Handbook of Expertise and Expert Performance*, Cambridge University Press, New York, NY.

Erikson, J.M. (1988). *Wisdom and the Senses: The Way of Creativity*. New York: Norton.

Eysenck, H. J. (1993). "Creativity and Personality: A Theoretical Perspective" in *Psychological Inquiry*, 4, 147–178.

Finke, R. A., Ward, T. B., and Smith, S. M. (1992). *Creative Cognition: Theory, Research, and Applications*. Cambridge, MA: MIT Press.

Fischer, R. (1971). "A Cartography of Ecstatic and Meditative States" in *Science,* 174 (4012), 897-904.

Freud, S. (1908/1959). The relation of the poet to day-dreaming. In *Collected papers,* Vol. 4. London: Hogarth Press, 173-183.

Galenson, D. (2013). "The Wisdom and Creativity of the Elders in Art and Science." Blog. Retrieved 10/26/2016 from http://www.huffingtonpost.com/david-galenson/the-wisdom-and-creativity_b_2441894.html David Galenson is Professor of Economics at the University of Chicago.

Gardner, H. (2011b). *Frames of Mind: The Theory of Multiple Intelligences*. New York: BasicBooks.

Gardner, H. (2006). *Multiple Intelligences: New Horizons in Theory and Practice*. New York: Basic Books.

Gardner, H. (1993). *Multiple Intelligences: The Theory in Practice*. New York: BasicBooks.

Gazzaniga, M.S. (Ed.) (2004), *The Cognitive Neurosciences III*, The MIT Press, Cambridge, MA.

Gell-Mann, M. (1994). *The Quark and the Jaguar: Adventures in the Simple and the Complex*. NY: W.H.Freeman and Company.

Gigerenzer, G., Todd, P.M. and the ABC Research Group (1999). *Simple Heuristics that Make Us Smart*. New York: Oxford University Press. Retrieved 10/15/16 from http://library.mpib-berlin.mpg.de/ft/jc/JC_How_1999.pdf

Gladwell, M. (2005). *Blink: The Power of Thinking without Thinking*. New York: Little, Brown.

Goldberg, E. (2005). *The Wisdom Paradox: How Your Mind Can Grow Stronger as Your Brain Grows Older*. New York: Gotham Books.

Goleman, D. (1998). "What Makes a Leader?" in *Harvard Business Review*, 93-102.

Goleman, D. (1995). *Emotional Intelligence*. New York: Bantam Books.

Goleman, G.M. (1988). *Meditative Mind: The Varieties of Meditative Experience*. New York: G.P. Putnam.

Goswami, A. (2014). *Quantum Creativity: Think Quantum, Be Creative*. New York: Hay House, Inc.

Goswami, A. (2000). *The Visionary Window: A Quantum Physicist's Guide to Enlightenment*. Wheaton, Ill: Quest Books, Theosophical Publishing House

Goswami, A. (1993). The Self-Aware Universe: How Consciousness Creates the Material World. New York: Jeremy P. Tarcher.

Green, R.D. (2016). Conversation from *Huffington Post*. Retrieved 08/27/16 from http://www.huffingtonpost.com/r-kay-green/giving-back_b_3298691.html

Gruber, H. E. (1989). "The Evolving Systems Approach to Creative Work" inWallace, D.B. and Gruber, H. E. (Eds.), *Creative People at Work: Twelve Cognitive Case Studies*. New York: Oxford University Press, 3-24.

Grudin, Robert (1984). "The Ethics of Inspiration" in *The Phenomenon of CHANGE*. New York: Rizzoli for Cooper-Hewitt Museum, The Smithsonian institution's National Museum of Design.

Guilford, J. P. (1950). "Creativity" in *American Psychologist, 5,* 444–454.

Haidt, J. (2006). *The Happiness Hypothesis: Finding Modern Truth in Ancient Wisdom*. New York: Basic Books.

Hall, C.S. and Nordby, V.J. (1973). *A Primer of Jungian Psychology*. New York: New American Library; Mass Paperback Edition.

Halpern, D. F. (1996). *Thought and Knowledge: An Introduction to Critical Thinking*. Mahwah, NJ: L. Erbaum Associates

Hauck, D.W. (1999). *The Emerald Tablet: Alchemy for Personal Transformation*. New York: Penguin Group.

Hawkins, D.R. (2002). *Power VS Force: The Hidden Determinants of Human Behavior*. Carlsbad, CA: Hay House.

Hawkins, J., with Blakeslee, S. (2004). *On Intelligence: How a New Understanding of the Brain Will Lead to the Creation of Truly Intelligent Machines*. New York: Times Books.

Hawkins, D.R. (2002). *Power VS Force: The Hidden Determinants of Human Behavior*. Carlsbad, CA: Hay House.

Heckscher, C. (2007). *The Collaborative Enterprise*. New Haven, CT: Yale University Press.

Hedges, C. (2016). "In the Time of Trump, All We Have Is Each Other" in *Common Dreams:* Breaking News & Views for the Progressive Community (December 26). Truthdig.

Henry, R.C. (2005). "The Mental Universe" in *Nature*, No. 436.

Hobson, J. A. (1999). *Consciousness*. New York: Scientific American Library.

Hodges, D. (2000). "Implications of Music and Brain Research" in *Music Educators Journal, 87*(2), 17-22.

Hodgkin, R. (1991). "Michael Polanyi—Profit of Life, the Universe, and Everything" in *Times Higher Educational Supplement*, September 27, 15.

Holliday, S.G. and Chandler, M.J. (1986). *Wisdom: Explorations in Adult Competence: Contributions to Human Development*, Vol. 17, Karger, Basel.

Houston, J. (2000). *Jump Time: Shaping Your Future in a World of Radical Change*. New York: Penguin Putnam Inc.

Hume, D. (1978). Selby-Bigge, I.A. and Nidditch, P.H. (Eds.). *Treatise of Human Nature*. Oxford: Oxford University Press.

Iacoboni, M. (2008). *The New Science of How We Connect with Others: Mirroring People*. New York: Farrar, Straus & Giroux.

Ikemi, Y. and Nakagawa, S.A. (1962). "A Psychosomatic Study of Contagious Dermatitis" in *Kyoshu Journal of Medical Science* 13, 335–350.

Jackson, P.L., Meltzoff, A.N. & Decety, J. (2005). "How Do We Perceive the Pain of Others? A window into the Neural Processes Involved in Empathy" in *NeuroImage, 24*, 771-779.

Jahn, R.G. and Dunne, B.J. (2011). *Consciousness and the Source of Reality: The PEAR Odyssey*. Princeton, NJ: ICRL Press.

James, J. (1996). *Thinking in the Future Tense: A Workout for the Mind*. New York: Touchstone.

Jarvis, P. (1992). *Paradoxes of Learning: On Becoming an Individual in Society*. San Francisco, CA: Jossey-Bass.

Jeffrey, S. (2008). *Creativity Revealed: Discovering the Source of Inspiration*. Kingston, NY: Creative Crayon Publishers.

Jensen, E. (2006). *Enriching the Brain: How to Maximize Every Learners Potential*. San Francisco, CA: Jossey-Bass.

Jensen, E. (1998). *Teaching with the Brain in Mind*. Alexandria, VA: Association for Supervision and Curriculum Development.

Jevning, R., Wallace, R.K., and Beidenbach, M. (1992). "The Physiology of Meditation: A Review" in *Neuroscience and Behavioral Reviews*, 16, 415-424.

Johnson, D.L. (2007). *Your Deepest Intent*. Boulder, CO: Sounds True.

Jung, K. (1952). "Synchronicity: An Acausal Connecting Principle" in Collected Works, Vol. 8, *The Structure and Dynamics of the Psyche*, 2nd Ed. London: Routledge.

Kahneman, D. (2013). *Thinking, Fast and Slow*. New York: Farrar, Straus and Giroux.

Kahneman, D., P. Slovic and Tversky, A. (1982). *Judgment Under Uncertainty: Heuristics and Biases*. New York: Cambridge University Press.

Kammerer, P. (1919). *Das Gestex der Serie*. Stuttgart-Berlin: Deutsche Verlaga-Ansalt. Quoted in Arthur Koestler (1972). *The Roots of Coincidence*. New York: Random House.

Kandel, E. R. (2006). *In Search of Memory: The Emergence of a New Science of Mind*. New York: W.W. Norton & Company.

Kant, I. (1993) [178]. *Groundwork of the Metaphysics of Morals*. Translated by Ellington, J.W. (3rd ed.) Hackett.

Kawashima, R., Sugiura, M., Kato, T., Nakamura, A., Hatano, K., Ito, K, et al. (1999). "The Human Amygdala Plays an Important Role in Gaze Monitoring: A PET Study" in *Brain, 122*, 779-783.

Keeran, J.A. (1997-2004). "Emotive Energy" Retrieved 09/20/2016 from http://www.theoryofmind.org/unified/emotive/conclusion.html

Kelzer, K. (1987). *The Sun and the Shadow: My Experiment with Lucid Dreaming*. Virginia Beach, VA: ARE Press.

Kennedy, P. (2016). "How to Cultivate the Art of Serendipity" in *The New York Times* Sunday review (January 2, 2016). Retrieved from http://www.nytimes.com/2016/01/03/opinion/how-to-cultivate-the-art-of-serendipity.html?_r=0

Kipling, R. (1985)."Working-tools" in Ghiselin, B. (Ed.). *The Creative Process: A Symposium*. Berkeley, CA: University of California Press, 161-163. (Original article published 1937).

Kirby, J.P. and Hughes, D. (1997). *Thoughtware: Change the Thinking and the Organization Will Change Itself*. Portland, OR: Productivity Press.

Klein, G. (2003). *Intuition at Work: Why Developing Your Gut Instincts Will Make You Better at What You Do*. New York: Doubleday.

Kluwe, R. H., Luer, G., and Rosler, F. (Eds.) (2003). *Principles of Learning and Memory*. Basel, Switzerland: Birkhauser Verlag.

Koestler, A. (1975). *The Act of Creation*. London: Macmillan.

Kohut, H. (1984). *How Does Analysis Cure?* Ed. A. Goldberg & P. Stepansky. Chicago: University of Chicago Press.

Kolb, D. A. (1984). *Experiential Learning: Experience as the Source of Learning and Development*. New Jersey: Prentice-Hall.

Kostka, S. Payne, D. and Almén, B. (2013). *Tonal Harmony with an Introduction to Twentieth-Century Music*. New York: McGraw Hill.

Kramer, D.A. and Bacelar, W.T. (1994). "The Educated Adult in Today's World: Wisdom and the Mature Learner" in Sinnott, J.D. (Ed.), *Interdisciplinary Handbook of Adult Lifespan Learning*. Westport, CN: Greenwood Press.

Kurzweil, R. (1999). *The Age of Spiritual Machines*. New York: Penguin Books.

The Kybalion (1940/1912). *The Kybalion: A Study of Hermetic Philosophy of ancient Egypt and Greece.* Yogi Pub. Society.

Lakoff, G. and Johnson, M. (1999). *Philosophy in the Flesh: The Embodied Mind and Its Challenge to Western Thought.* New York: Basic Books.

Lanham, R. (1993). *The Electronic Word: Democracy, Technology, and the Arts.* Chicago: University of Chicago Press.

Laughlin, S. B. (2004). "The Implications of Metabolic Energy Requirements for the Representation of Information in Neurons" in M. S. Gazzaniga (Ed.), *The Cognitive Neuroscience III.* Cambridge, MA: The MIT Press, 187-196.

LeDoux, J. (1996). *The Emotional Brain: The Mysterious Underpinnings of Emotional Life.* New York: Touchstone.

Legge, J. (Trans) (1996). *I Ching: Book of Changes: The Ancient Chinese Guide to Wisdom and Fortunetelling.* Avenel, NJ: Random House Value Publishing, Inc.

Linden, S.J. (2003). *The Alchemy Reader: From Hermes Trismegistus to Isaac Newton.* Cambridge, UK: Cambridge University Press.

Lipton, B. and Bhaerman, S. (2009). *Spontaneous Evolution: Out Positive Future (And a Way to Get There from Here).* Carlsbad, CA: Hay House.

Llinas, R. R. (2001). *I of the Vortex: From Neurons to Self.* Cambridge, MA: The MIT Press.

Locke, J. (2016). *Essay Concerning Human Understanding*, Book III, p. 377. Retrieved 10/23/16 from http://mypages.iit.edu/~schmaus/Origins_of_Modern_Philosophy/lectures/Locke.htm

Loveridge, D.J. (1977). "Shifting Foundations: Values and Futures" in Linstone, H.A. and Simmonds, W.H.C., *Futures Research: New Directions.* Reading, MA: Addison-Wesley Publishing Company, Inc.

MacFlouer, Niles (2004-16). *Why Life Is...* Weekly radio shows: BBSRadio.com (#1-#480) and KXAM (#1-#143). Retrieved from http://www.agelesswisdom.com/archives_of_radio_shows.htm

Machlup, F. (1962). *The Production and Distribution of Knowledge in the United States.* Princeton, NJ: Princeton University Press.

Main, R. (1997). *Jung on Synchronicity and the Paranormal.* New Jersey: Princeton University Press.

Masserman J, Wechkin MS, Terris W. (1964). "Altruistic Behavior in Rhesus Monkeys" in *Am. J. Psychiatry* 121, 584–85.

Matthews, R.C. (1991). "The Forgetting Algorithm: How Fragmentary Knowledge of Exemplars Can Yield Abstract Knowledge" in *Journal of Experimental Psychology: General*, 120, 117-119.

Maturana, H. R., and Varela, F. J. (1987). *The Tree of Knowledge: The Biological Roots of Human Understanding.* Boston: Shambhala. Mavromatis, A. (1991). *Hypnagogia.* New York: Routledge.

Maunsell, J.H.R. and Treue, S. (2006). "Feature-Based Attention in Visual Cortex" in *Trends in Neuroscience* 29, 317-322.

Mavromatis, A. (1991). *Hypnagogia*. Routledge, New York, NY.

May, Rollo (1975). *The Courage to Create*. New York: Bantam.

McHale, J. (1977). "Futures Problems or Problems in Futures Studies" in Linstone, H.A. and Simmonds, W.H.C. (Eds.), *Futures Research: New Directions*. Reading, MA: Addison-Wesley Publishing Company, Inc.

McTaggart, L. (2002). *The Field: The Quest for the Secret Force of the Universe*. New York: Harper Perennial.

McWhinney, W. (1997). *Paths of Change: Strategic Choices for Organizations and Society*. Thousand Oaks, CA: SAGE Publications, Inc.

Merriam, S.B. and Caffarella, R.S. (1999). *Learning in Adulthood: A Comprehensive Guide* (2nd Ed.). San Francisco, CA: Jossey-Bass.

Merriam Webster (2016). Retrieved 06/22/2016 from www.merriam-wester.com/dictionary/faith; Retrieved 07/04/16 from http://www.merriam-webster.com/dictionary/propaganda ; Retrieved 07/06/16 from http://www.merriam-webster.com/dictionary/equal ; Retrieved 07/06/16 http://www.merriam-webster.com/dictionary/personality ; Retrieved 07/07/16 http://www.merriam-webster.com/dictionary/instinct ; Retrieved 08/26/16 http://learnersdictionary.com/definition/desire ; Retrieved 08/27/16 http://www.webster-dictionary.org/definition/Agape ; Retrieved 08/28/16 http://www.merriam-webster.com/dictionary/Quantum%20leap ; Retrieved 09/30/16 http://www.merriam-webster.com/dictionary/virtue ; Retrieved 10/01/16 http://www.merriam-webster.com/dictionary/sympathy ; Retrieved 10/01/16 http://www.merriam-webster.com/dictionary/serendipity ; Retrieved 11/07/16 http://www.merriam-webster.com/dictionary/karma

Michael, D. N. (1977). "Planning's Challenge to the Systems Approach" in Linstone, H.A. and Simmonds, W.H.C., *Futures Research: New Directions*. Reading, MA: Addison-Wesley Publishing Company, Inc.

Middlebrook, P.N. (1974). *Social Psychology and Modern Life*. New York: Alfred A. Knoph.

Miniter, R. (2005). *Disinformation: 22 Media Myths that Undermine the War on Terror*. Washington, D.C.: Regnery Publishing.

Minsky, M. (2006). *The Emotion Machine: Commonsense Thinking, Artificial Intelligence, and the Future of the Human Mind*. New York: Simon and Schuser.

Mulhall, D. (2002). *Our Molecular Future: How Nanotechnology, Robotics, Genetics, and Artificial Intelligence will Transform Our World*. Amherst, NY: Prometheus Books.

National Research Council. (2000). *How People Learn: Brain, Mind, Experience, and School*. Washington, DC: National Academy Press.

Nelson, A. (2004). "Sophia: Transformation of Human Consciousness to Wisdom", unpublished paper, Fielding Graduate University, Santa Barbara, CA.

Nelson, R.D. (1994). "Effect Size Per Hour: A Natural Unit for Interpreting Anomalous Experiments" in Princeton Engineering Anomalies research, School of Engineering/Applied Science, PEAR *Technical Note* 94003 (September).

Nelson, R.D. (1997). "Wishing for Good Weather: A Natural Experiment in Group Consciousness" in *Journal of Scientific Exploration*, 11(1), 47-58.

Nelson, R.D., Bradish, G.J., Dobyns, Y.H., Dunne, B.J. and Jahn, R.G. (1996). "FieldREG Anomalies in Group Situations" in *Journal of Scientific Exploration*, 10(1): 111-41.

Nelson, R.D., Jahn, R.G., Dunne, B.J., Dobyns, Y.H. and Bradish, G.J. (1998). "FieldREGII: Consciousness Field Effects: Replications and Explorations" in *Journal of Scientific Exploration* 12(3), 425-54.

Nonaka, I. and Takeuchi, H. (1995). *The Knowledge-Creating Company: How Japanese Companies Create the Dynamics of Innovation*. New York: Oxford University Press.

Norton Simon Museum (2016). "The Triumph of Virtue and Nobility Over Ignorance." Retrieved 10/14/16 from https://www.nortonsimon.org/collections/browse_title.php?id=F.1972.26.P

Nussbaum, S.W. (2000). "Profundity with panache: the unappreciated proverbial wisdom of sub-Saharan Africa" in Brown, W.S. (Ed.), *Understanding Wisdom: Sources, Science and Society*. Philadelphia, PA: Templeton Foundation Press.

Omnes, R. (1999). *Understanding Quantum Mechanics*. Princeton, NJ: Princeton University Press.

Pearl, J. (1984). *Heuristics: Intelligent Search Strategies for Computer Problem Solving*. Boston: Addison-Wesley Longman Publishing Co.

Peat, F.D. (1988). *Synchronicity: The Bridge Between Matter and Mind*. New York: Bantam Books.

Pert, C. B. (1997). *Molecules of Emotion: A Science Behind Mind-Body Medicine*. New York: Touchstone.

Pelegrinis, T.N. (1980). *Kant's Conceptions of the Categorical Imperative and the Will*. Hyderabad, India: Zeno Publishers

Perkins, D. N. (1995). *Outsmarting IQ: The Emerging Science of Learnable Intelligence*. New York: Free Press.

Poincaré, H. (2001). *The Value of Science: Essential Writings of Henri Poincaré*. New York: Random House (Modern Library Science).

Polanyi, M. (1967). *The Tacit Dimension*. New York, NY: Anchor Books.

Polanyi, M. (1958). *Personal Knowledge: Towards a Post-Critical Philosophy*. Chicago: University of Chicago Press.

Pope, A. (1732-3/1994). Essay on Man and Other Poems. Dover.

Planck, M. (1920). "The Genesis and Present State of Development of the Quantum Theory" (Nobel Lecture, June 2).

Popp, F.A. (2002). "Biophotonics: A Powerful Tool for Investigating and Understanding Life" in Durr, H.P., Popp, F.A. and Schommers, W. (Eds.), *What is Life? Scientific Approaches and Philosophical Positions* (Series on the Foundations of Natural Science and Technology). Singapore: World Scientific.

Portante, T. and Tarro, R. (1997). "Paying Attention" in *Wired Magazine* (September).

Pribram, K.H. (1991). *Brain and Perception: Holonomy and Structure in Figural Processing.* Hillsdale, NJ: Lawrence Erlbaum.

Pribram, K.H. (Ed.) (1993). *Rethinking Neural Networks: Quantum Fields and Biological Data,* Proceedings of the First Appalachian Conference on Behavioral Neurodynamics. Hillsdale, NJ: Lawrence Erlbaum.

Pribram, K.H. (1998). "Autobiography in Anecdote: The Founding of Experimental Neuropsychology" in Bilder, R. (Ed.), *The History of Neuroscience in Autobiography.* San Diego: California Academic Press, 306-49.

Prinz, W. (2005). "An Ideomotor Approach to Imitation" in Hurley, S. and Chater, N., Perspectives on Imitation: *From Neuroscience to Social Sciene Vol. 1: Mechanisms of Imitation and Imitation in Animals.* Cambridge, MA: MIT Press., pp. 141-56.

Reber, A.S. (1993). *Implicit Learning and Tacit Knowledge: An Essay on the Cognitive Unconscious.* New York: Oxford University Press.

Rifkin, J. (2009). The *Empathic Civilization: The Race to Global Consciousness in a World in Crisis.* New York: Penguin Group.

Riggio, R.E. (2015). "Are You Empathic? 3 Types of Empathy and What They Mean". Retrieved 09/14/15 from https://www.psychologytoday.com/blog/cutting-edge-leadership/201108/are-you-empathic-3-types-empathy-and-what-they-mean

Riordan, C.M. (2014). "Diversity Is Useless Without Inclusivity". *Harvard Business Review.* Retrieved on 10/14/16 from https://hbr.org/2014/06/diversity-is-useless-without-inclusivity

Ritchey, D. (2003). *The H.I.S.S. of the A.S.P.: Understanding the Anomalously Sensitive Person.* Terra Alta, WV: Headline Books, Inc.

Ritsema, R. and Karcher, S. (Trans) (1995). *I Ching: The Classic Chinese Oracle of Change (The First Complete Translation with Concordance).* New York: Barnes & Noble, Inc.

Rizzolatti, G. (2006, November). "Mirrors in the Mind" in *Scientific American.*

Roberts, J. (1994). *The Nature of Personal Reality.* New Jersey: Amber-Allen Publishing.

Rock, A. (2004). *The Mind at Night: The New Science of How and Why We Dream.* New York: Perseus Books Group.

Rowan, J. (1990). *Subpersonalities: The People Within Us.* New York: Routledge.

Ross, P. E. (2006b). "The Expert Mind" in *Scientific American,* (August), 64-71.

Russell, P. (2007). *The Awakening Earth: The Global Brain.* Edinburgh: Floris Books.

Salk, J. (1973). *The Survival of the Wisest*. New York: Harper & Row.

Schacter, D. L. (1996). *Searching for Memory: The Brain, the Mind, and the Past*. New York: Basic Books.

Scott, C. (2016a). *Life Bites*. Frost, WV: MQIPress.

Searle, J.R. (1983). *Intentionality: An Essay in the Philosophy of Mind*. Cambridge, England: Cambridge University Press.

Senge, P.M., Scharmer, C.O., Jaworski, J. and Flowers, B.S. (2004). *Presence: Exploring Profound Change in People, Organizations and Society*. New York: Random House, Inc.

Senge, Peter (1990). *The Fifth Discipline*. New York: Doubleday.

Sheldrake, R. (1989). *The Presence of the Past: Morphic Resonance and the Habits of Nature*. New York: Vintage Books.

Silverman, D. P. (ed.) (1997). *Ancient Egypt*. New York: Oxford University Press.

Simonton, D. K. (1999). "Talent and Its Development: An Emergenic and Epigenetic Mode" in *Psychological Review*, 106, 435–457.

Singer, T., Seymour, B., O'Doherty, J., Kaube, H., Dolan, R.J. & Frith, C.D. (2004). "Empathy for Pain Involves the Affective but Not Sensory Components of Pain" in *Science, 303*, 1157-1162.

Smith, H. (1986) (reissued 1993). *Forgotten Truth*. New York: Harper.

Smith, M.K. (2003). "Michael Polanyi and Tacit Knowledge" in *The Encyclopedia of Informal Education*, 2, www.infed.org/thinkers/Polanyi.htm

Snow, C.P. (1959/1961). *The Two Cultures and the Scientific Revolution*. The Rede Lecture. New York: Cambridge University Press.

Sternberg, R.J. (2003). *Wisdom, Intelligence, and Creativity Synthesized*. Cambridge: Cambridge University Press.

Sternberg, R.J. (Ed.) (1990). *Wisdom: Its Nature, Origins, and Development*. Cambridge, MA: Cambridge University Press.

Stocker, G. (1998). "InfoWar" in Stocker, G. and C. Schöpf, *Infowar*. New York: SpringerWien.

Stonier, T. (1997). *Information and Meaning: An Evolutionary Perspective*. London: Springer-Verlag.

Stonier, T. (1992). *Beyond Information: The Natural History of Intelligence*. London: Springer-Verlag.

Stonier, T. (1997). *Information and Meaning: An Evolutionary Perspective*. London: Springer-Verlag.

Tallis, F. (2002). *Hidden Minds: A History of the Unconscious*. New York: Arcade.

Tapscott, D. (2009). *Grown up Digital*. McGraw Hill, New York.

Tchaikovsky, P.I. (2016). *The Life and Letters of Pete Ilich Tchaikovsky*. Toronto: University of Toronto Press. Retrieved 09/22/16 from https://archive.org/stream/lifelettersofpet00chaiuoft/lifelettersofpet00chaiuoft_djvu.txt

Templeton, Sir John (2002). *Wisdom from World Religions: Pathways Toward Heaven on Earth*. Philadelphia, PA: Templeton Foundation Press.

Thera, N. (1962). *The Heart of Buddhist Meditation*. New York: Samuel Weiser.

Thuan, T.X. (2001). *Chaos and Harmony*. New York: Oxford University Press.

Tiller, W. (2007). *Psychoenergetic Science: A Second Copernican-Scale Revolution*. DVD from www.illerfoundaion.com

Torrance, E. P. (1974). *Torrance Tests of Creative Thinking*. Lexington, MA: Personnel Press.

The Urantia Book (1955). Chicago: URANTIA Foundation.

Vaillant, G.E. (2012). *Triumphs of Experience*. Self-published.

Vinge, V. (1993). "The Coming Technological Sigularity: How to Survive in the Post-Human Era". (Paper presented to the Vision-21 Symposium sponsored by NASA's Lewis Research Center and the Ohio Aerospace Institute, March 30-31, 1993). Retrieved from www.rohan.solsu.edu/faculty/vinge/isc/siguarity.htl (July 7, 2001).

von Foerster, H. (1977). "Objects: tokens for (eigen-) behaviors" in Inheler, B., Gracia, R., and Voneche, J. (Eds.), *Hommage a Jean Piaget: Epistemologie Genetique et Eqilibration*. Delachaux et Niestel.

Wade, D. (2006). *Symmetry: The Ordering Principle*. New York: Walker Publishing Company.

Walker, A. (2011). "Creativity Loves Constraints: the Paradox of Google's Twenty Percent Time" in *Ephemera* 11, (4), 369-386.

Wallas (1926). *The Art of Thought*. London; Johnathan Cape [republished in 1931].

Walsch, N.D. (2009). *When Everything Changes, Change Everything: In a Time of Turmoil, A Pathway to Peace*. Ashland, OR: EmNin Books.

Warmington and Rouse (1984). Great Dialogues of Plato.

West, M.A. (1980). "Meditation and the EEG" in *Psychological Medicine*, 10: 369-375.

Weyl, H. (1952). *Symmetry*. Princeton, NJ: Princeton University Press.

Wilber, K. (1993). *The Spectrum of Consciousness*. Wheaten, IL: Quest Books.

Willis, A. (2012). *Achieving Balance*. Great Britain: Manicboy Publishing.

Wilson, E. O. (1998). *Consilience: The Unity of Knowledge*. New York: Alfred A. Knopf.

Wing, R.L. (Trans) (1986). *The Tao of Power: Lao Tzu's Classic Guide to Leadership, Influence, and Excellence*. New York: Doubleday.

Writing: The Nature, Development and Teaching of Written Communication (Vol. II) (1982). Lawrence Erlbaum Associates.

Wycoff, J. (1991). *Mindmapping: Your Personal Guide to Exploring Creativity and Problem-Solving*. New York: The Berkley Publishing Group.

Zey, M.G. (2000). *The Future Factor: The Five Forces Transforming Our Lives and Shaping Human* Destiny. New York: McGraw-Hill.

Zull, J. E. (2002). *The Art of Changing the Brain: Enriching the Practice of Teaching by Exploring the Biology of Learning*. Sterling, VA: Stylus.

Index

About the Mountain Quest Institute

MQI is a research, retreat and learning center dedicated to helping individuals achieve personal and professional growth and organizations create and sustain high performance in a rapidly changing, uncertain, and increasingly complex world. Drs. David and Alex Bennet are co-founders of MQI. They may be contacted at alex@mountainquestinstitute.com

Current research is focused on Human and Organizational Systems, Change, Complexity, Sustainability, Knowledge, Learning, Consciousness, and the nexus of Science and Spirituality. MQI has three questions: The Quest for Knowledge, The Quest for Consciousness, and The Quest for Meaning. **MQI is scientific, humanistic and spiritual and finds no contradiction in this combination**. See www.mountainquestinstitute.com

MQI is the birthplace of Organizational Survival in the New World: The Intelligent Complex Adaptive System (Elsevier, 2004), a new theory of the firm that turns the living system metaphor into a reality for organizations. Based on research in complexity and neuroscience—and incorporating networking theory and Knowledge Management—this book is filled with new ideas married to practical advice, all embedded within a thorough description of the new organization in terms of structure, culture, strategy, leadership, knowledge workers and integrative competencies.

Mountain Quest Institute, situated four hours from Washington, D.C. in the Monongahela Forest of the Allegheny Mountains, is part of the Mountain Quest complex which includes a Retreat Center, Inn, and the old Farm House, Outbuildings and mountain trails and farmland. See www.mountainquestinn.com The Retreat Center is designed to provide full learning experiences, including hosting training, workshops, retreats and business meetings for professional and executive groups of 25 people or less. The Center includes a 26,000 volume research library, a conference room, community center, computer room, 12 themed bedrooms, a workout and hot tub area, and a four-story tower with a glass ceiling for enjoying the magnificent view of the valley during the day and the stars at night. Situated on a 430 acres farm, there is a labyrinth, creeks, four miles of mountain trails, and horses, Longhorn cattle, Llamas and a myriad of wild neighbors. Other neighbors include the Snowshoe Ski Resort, the National Radio Astronomy Observatory and the CASS Railroad.

About The Organizational Zoo Ambassadors Network

The Organizational Zoo Ambassadors Network (OZAN) is an international group of professionals interested in using The Organizational Zoo concepts as part of their capability development programs. Zoo Ambassadors have been trained in the application of OZAN Tools and approaches. They freely share their experiences through an international network which interacts primarily through a wiki supplemented by occasional face to face events and some on-line learning modules. See http://www.organizationalzoo.com/ambassadors/

About Quantra Leadership Academy

Quantra Leadership Academy (aka QLA Consulting) is a transformational leadership and personal development training company run by Dr. Theresa Bullard**. QLA is dedicated to helping individuals and organizations innovate their way of thinking to achieve breakthrough results.** There is one question that lies at the foundation of QLA: *What is your potential?* When you tap into your potential, greatness happens, you experience breakthroughs, "Ah-ha" moments occur, and you get into "The Zone" of peak performance. It is our passion to help you access your full potential, sustain what you achieve, and be able to refuel whenever you want. When you get to the point where you can do this on demand that is when you become a self-transforming agent of change. QLA shows you how to get there and gives you tools to accelerate your progress. By blending science, consciousness studies, and mental alchemy, or the art and science of transforming your mindset, we help you **reach your potential** and become more successful in essential areas of your work and life. *To help you* **access more of your potential,** *we offer a progression of transformative tools and trainings that integrate Quantum principles, cutting-edge methods, and ancient wisdom for using your mind more creatively and effectively.* For more info: www.QLAconsulting.com

About the Authors

Dr. Alex Bennet, a Professor at the Bangkok University Institute for Knowledge and Innovation Management, is internationally recognized as an expert in Knowledge Management and an agent for organizational change. Prior to founding the Mountain Quest Institute, she served as the Chief Knowledge Officer and Deputy Chief Information Officer for Enterprise Integration for the U.S. Department of the Navy, and was co-chair of the Federal Knowledge Management Working Group. Dr. Bennet is the recipient of the Distinguished and Superior Public Service Awards from the U.S. government for her work in the Federal Sector. She is a Delta Epsilon Sigma and Golden Key National Honor Society graduate with a Ph.D. in Human and Organizational Systems; degrees in Management for Organizational Effectiveness, Human Development, English and Marketing; and certificates in

Total Quality Management, System Dynamics and Defense Acquisition Management. Alex believes in the multidimensionality of humanity as we move out of infancy into full consciousness.

Dr. David Bennet's experience spans many years of service in the Military, Civil Service and Private Industry, including fundamental research in underwater acoustics and nuclear physics, frequent design and facilitation of organizational interventions, and serving as technical director of two major DoD Acquisition programs. Prior to founding the Mountain Quest Institute, Dr. Bennet was CEO, then Chairman of the Board and Chief Knowledge Officer of a professional services firm located in Alexandria, Virginia. He is a Phi Beta Kappa, Sigma Pi Sigma, and Suma Cum Laude graduate of the University of Texas, and holds degrees in Mathematics, Physics, Nuclear Physics, Liberal Arts, Human and Organizational Development, and a Ph.D. in Human Development focused on Neuroscience and adult learning. He is currently researching the nexus of Science, the Humanities and Spirituality.

Dr. Arthur Shelley is a capability development and knowledge strategy consultant with over 30 years professional experience. He has held a variety of professional roles including managing international projects in Australia, Europe, Asia and USA and has facilitated professional development program with organisations as diverse as NASA, Cirque du Soleil, World Bank, government agencies and corporates. He has facilitated courses in Masters programs on Executive Consulting, Leadership, Knowledge Management, Applied Research Practice and Entrepreneurship in face to face, blended and on-line modes. Arthur is the author of three books: *KNOWledge SUCCESSion (2017) Being a Successful Knowledge Leader (2009)*; *The Organizational Zoo, A Survival Guide to Workplace Behavior (2007)*. In 2014 he was awarded with an Australian Office of Learning and Teaching citation for "Outstanding contributions to student learning outcomes". Arthur is a regular invited speaker and workshop facilitator at international conferences to discuss his writing or to share experiences as the former Global Knowledge Director for Cadbury Schweppes. He is founder of The Organizational Zoo Ambassadors Network (a professional peer mentoring group), creator of the RMIT University MBA mentoring program and co-facilitator of the Melbourne KM Leadership Forum. Arthur has a PhD in Project Management, a Master of Science in Microbiology/Biochemistry, a Graduate Certificate in Tertiary Learning and Teaching and a Bachelor of Science. Arthur may be reached at arthur.shelley@rmit.edu.au

Dr. Theresa Bullard combines a Ph.D. in Physics with a life-long path of embracing the new paradigm of Science and Consciousness. Her passion and ability to bridge these worlds are her strengths and distinguish her as an exceptional teacher, speaker, leader and change-agent. Theresa is the founder of QLA Consulting Inc., President of the Board of Directors of Mysterium Center, an International Instructor with the Modern Mystery School, and co-founder of the Universal Kabbalah Network. She has over 15 years of experience in science research, international speaking, and transformational training. Author of *The Game Changers: Social Alchemists in the 21st Century*, along with several guided meditation albums and audio tools for accessing Quantum conscious states, her mission is to help individuals and organizations thrive in a changing world. Theresa may be contacted at Theresa@Quantumleapalchemy.com

Dr. John Lewis is a speaker, business consultant, and part-time professor on the topics of organizational learning, thought leadership, and knowledge & innovation management. John is a proven leader with business results, and was acknowledged by Gartner with an industry "Best

Practice" paper for an innovative Knowledge Management implementation. He is a co-founder at The CoHero Institute, creating collaborative leadership in learning organizations. John holds a Doctoral degree in Educational Psychology from the University of Southern California, with a dissertation focus on mental models and decision making, and is the author of *The Explanation Age*, which Kirkus Reviews described as "An iconoclast's blueprint for a new era of innovation." John may be contacted at John@ExplanationAge.com

Other Books by MQI Press (www.MQIPress.net)

MQIPress is a wholly-owned subsidiary of Mountain Quest Institute, LLC, located at 303 Mountain Quest Lane, Marlinton, West Virginia 24954, USA. (304) 799-7267

Other Bennet eBooks available from in PDF format from MQIPress (US 304-799-7267 or alex@mountainquestinstitute.com) and Kindle format from Amazon.

The Course of Knowledge: A 21st Century Theory

by Alex Bennet and David Bennet with Joyce Avedisian (2015)

Knowledge is at the core of what it is to be human, the substance which informs our thoughts and determines the course of our actions. Our growing focus on, and understanding of, knowledge and its consequent actions is changing our relationship with the world. Because **knowledge determines the quality of every single decision we make**, it is critical to learn about and understand what knowledge is. **From a 21st century viewpoint,** we explore a theory of knowledge that is both pragmatic and biological. Pragmatic in that it is based on taking effective action, and biological because it is created by humans via patterns of neuronal connections in the mind/brain.

In this book we explore *the course of knowledge*. Just as a winding stream in the bowls of the mountains curves and dips through ravines and high valleys, so, too, with knowledge. In a continuous journey towards intelligent activity, context-sensitive and situation-dependent knowledge, imperfect and incomplete, experientially engages a changing landscape in a continuous cycle of learning and expanding. *We are in a continuous cycle of knowledge creation such that every moment offers the opportunity for the emergence of new and exciting ideas, all waiting to be put in service to an interconnected world.* Learn more about this **exciting human capacity**! AVAILABLE FROM AMAZON in Kindle Format. AVAILABLE FROM MQIPress in PDF.

Expanding the Self: The Intelligent Complex Adaptive Learning System

by David Bennet, Alex Bennet and Robert Turner (2015)

We live in unprecedented times; indeed, turbulent times that can arguably be defined as ushering humanity into a new Golden Age, offering the opportunity to embrace new ways of learning and living in a globally and collaboratively entangled connectedness (Bennet & Bennet, 2007). In this shifting and dynamic environment, life demands accelerated cycles of learning experiences. Fortunately, we as a humanity have begun to look within ourselves to better understand the way our mind/brain operates, the amazing qualities of the body that power our thoughts and feelings, and the reciprocal loops as those thoughts and feelings change our physical structure. This emerging knowledge begs us to relook and rethink what we know about learning, providing a new starting point to expand toward the future.

This book is a treasure for those interested in how recent findings in neuroscience impact learning. The result of this work is an expanding experiential learning model call the Intelligent Complex Adaptive Learning System, adding the fifth mode of social engagement to Kolb's concrete experience, reflective observation, abstract conceptualization and active experimentation, with the five modes undergirded by the power of Self. A significant conclusion is that should they desire, adults have much more control over their learning than they may realize. AVAILABLE FROM AMAZON in Kindle Format. AVAILALBE FROM MQIPress in PDF.

Decision-Making in The New Reality: Complexity, Knowledge and Knowing

by Alex Bennet and David Bennet (2013)

We live in a world that offers many possible futures. The ever-expanding complexity of information and knowledge provide many choices for decision-makers, and we are all making decisions every single day! As the problems and messes of the world become more complex, our decision consequences are more and more difficult to anticipate, and our decision-making processes must change to keep up with this world complexification. This book takes a consilience approach to explore decision-making in The New Reality, fully engaging systems and complexity theory, knowledge research, and recent neuroscience findings. It also presents methodologies for decision-makers to tap into their unconscious, accessing tacit knowledge resources and increasingly relying on the sense of knowing that is available to each of us.

Almost every day new energies are erupting around the world: new thoughts, new feelings, new knowing, all contributing to new situations that require new decisions and actions from each and every one of us. Indeed, with the rise of the Net Generation and social media, a global consciousness may well be emerging. As individuals and organizations we are realizing that there are larger resources available to us, and that, as complex adaptive systems linked to a flowing fount of knowing, we can bring these resources to bear to achieve our ever-expanding vision of the future. Are we up to the challenge? AVAILABLE FROM AMAZON in Kindle Format. AVAILABLE FROM MQIPress in PDF.

Leading with the Future in Mind: Knowledge and Emergent Leadership

by Alex Bennet and David Bennet with John Lewis (2015)

We exist in a new reality, a global world where the individuated power of the mind/brain offers possibilities beyond our imagination. It is within this framework that thought leading emerges, and when married to our collaborative nature, makes the impossible an everyday occurrence. *Leading with the Future in Mind*, building on profound insights unleashed by recent findings in neuroscience, provides a new view that converges leadership, knowledge and learning for individual and organizational advancement.

This book provides a research-based *tour de force* for the future of leadership. Moving from the leadership of the past, for the few at the top, using authority as the explanation, we now find leadership emerging from all levels of the organization, with knowledge as the explanation. The future will be owned by the organizations that can master the relationships between knowledge and leadership. Being familiar with the role of a knowledge worker is not the same as understanding the role of a knowledge leader. As the key ingredient, collaboration is much more than "getting along"; it embraces and engages. Wrapped in the mantle of collaboration and engaging our full resources—hysical, mental, emotional and spiritual—we open the door to possibilities. We are dreaming the future together. AVAILABLE FROM AMAZON in Kindle Format. AVAILABLE FROM MQIPress in PDF.

Other books available from the authors and on Amazon..

The Game Changers: Social Alchemists in the 21ˢᵗ Century

by Theresa Bullard, Ph.D. (2013), available in hard and soft formats from Amazon.

Just about everywhere we look right now change is afoot. What is all this change about? Why now? And how do we best adapt? Many have called this time a "quickening", where the speed with which we must think, respond, and take action is accelerating. Systems are breaking down, people are rising up, and there is uncertainty of what tomorrow will bring. This book is dedicated to times such as these, times of great transformation. It can be seen as a companion guide on how to navigate the tumultuous tides of change. It aims to put such current events into a possible context within the evolutionary and alchemical process that humanity is going through. In it, author, physicist, and change-agent, Theresa Bullard, Ph.D., discusses emerging new paradigms, world events, future trends, and ancient wisdom that help reveal a bigger picture of what is happening. She offers insights and solutions to empower you, the reader, to become a more conscious participant in these exciting times of change. With this knowledge you will be more equipped to harness the *opportunities* that such times present you with. AVAILABLE FROM AMAZON in Kindle Format ... Paperback

The Organizational Zoo: A Survival Guide to Work Place Behavior

by Arthur Shelley (2006), available in hard and soft formats from Amazon.

Organizational Zoo is a fresh approach to organizational culture development, a witty and thought-provoking book that makes ideal reading for students and management. When you think of your organization as containing ants, bees, chameleons, and other creatures on through the alphabet, your work world becomes more manageable. Discover the secret strengths and weaknesses of each distinct animal so that you can communicate more productively—or manipulate more cunningly. Your choice! AVAILABLE FROM AMAZON in Paperback

The Explanation Age

by John Lewis (2013) (3rd Ed.), available in hard and soft formats from Amazon.

The technological quest of the last several decades has been to create the information age, with ubiquitous and immediate access to information. With this goal arguably accomplished, even from our mobile phones, this thought-provoking book describes the next quest and provides a blueprint for how to get there. When all organizational knowledge is framed as answers to our fundamental questions, we find ubiquitous and visual access to knowledge related to who, where, how, etc., yet the explanations are still buried within the prose. The question of "why" is arguably the most important question, yet it is currently the least supported. This is why business process methodologies feel like "box-checking" instead of "sense-making." This is why lessons learned are not actually learned. And this is why the consequential options and choices are captured better within a chess game than within the important decisions faced by organizations and society. With implications for business, education, policy making, and artificial intelligence, Dr. Lewis provides a visualization of explanations which promotes organizational sense-making and collaboration. AVAILABLE FROM AMAZON in Paperback

KNOWledge SUCCESSion: Sustained Capability Growth Through Strategic Projects

by Arthur Shelley (2016), available in hard and soft formats from Amazon.

KNOWledge SUCCESSion is intended for executives and developing professionals who face the challenges of delivering business benefits for today, whilst building the capabilities required for an increasingly changing future. The book is structured to build from foundational requirements towards connecting the highly interdependent aspects of success in an emerging complex world. A wide range of concepts are brought together in a logical framework to enable readers of different disciplines to understand how they either create barriers or can be harvested to generate synergistic opportunities. The framework builds a way to make sense of the connections and provides novel paths to take advantage of the potential synergies that arise through aligning the concepts into a portfolio of strategic projects. AVAILABLE FROM AMAZON. Kindle Format ... Paperback

Knowledge Mobilization in the Social Sciences and Humanities: Moving from Research to Action

by Alex Bennet and David Bennet (2007), available in hard and soft formats from Amazon.

This book takes the reader from the University lab to the playgrounds of communities. It shows how to integrate, move and use knowledge, an action journey within an identified action space that is called knowledge mobilization. Whether knowledge is mobilized through an individual, organization, community or nation, it becomes a powerful asset creating a synergy and focus that brings forth the best of action and values. Individuals and teams who can envision, feel, create and apply this power are the true leaders of tomorrow. When we can mobilize knowledge for the greater good humanity will have left the information age and entered the age of knowledge, ultimately leading to compassion and—hopefully—wisdom. AVAILABLE FROM AMAZON. Kindle Format ... Paperback AVAILABLE FROM MQIPress in PDF and Softback.

Being a Successful Knowledge Leader: What Knowledge Practitioners Need to Know to Make a Difference.

by Arthur Shelley (2009). AVAILABLE FROM AMAZON. Paperback

Being a Successful Knowledge Leader explores the challenges of leading a program of knowledge-informed change initiatives to generate sustained performance improvement. The book explores how to embed knowledge flows into strategic development cycles to align organizational development with changing environmental conditions. The high rate of change interferes with the growth of organizational knowledge because what is relevant only generates a competitive advantage for a short time. Also, the people who possess this knowledge are more mobile than previously. Combined, these factors can have a detrimental impact on performance and need to be mitigated against to ensure capabilities are built rather than diluted overtime. The characteristics for success that a knowledge leader needs to possess are explored from a unique perspective to stimulate creative thinking around how to develop and maintain these in emergent times.

Organizational Survival in the New World: the Intelligent Complex Adaptive System

   by Alex Bennet and David Bennet (Elsevier, 2004), available in hard and soft formats from Amazon.

In this book David and Alex Bennet propose a new model for organizations that enables them to react more quickly and fluidly to today's fast-changing, dynamic business environment: the Intelligent Complex Adaptive System (ICAS). ICAS is a new organic model of the firm based on recent research in complexity and neuroscience, and incorporating networking theory and Knowledge Management, and turns the living system metaphor into a reality for organizations. This book synthesizes new thinking about organizational structure from the fields listed above into ICAS, a new systems model for the successful organization of the future designed to help leaders and managers of knowledge organizations succeed in a non-linear, complex, fast-changing and turbulent environment. Technology enables connectivity, and the ICAS model takes advantage of that connectivity by fostering the development of dynamic, effective and trusting relationships in a new organizational structure. AVAILABLE FROM AMAZON in Kindle Format ... Hardback ... Paperback

Other MQIPress books available in PDF format at www.MQIPress.net (US 304-799-7267 or alex@mountainquestinstitute.com) and Kindle format from Amazon.

REMEMBRANCE: Pathways to Expanded Learning with Music and Metamusic®

   by Barbara Bullard and Alex Bennet (2013)

Take a journey of discovery into the last great frontier—the human mind/brain, an instrument of amazing flexibility and plasticity. This eBook is written for brain users who are intent on mining more of the golden possibilities that lie inherent in each of our unique brains. Begin by discovering the role positive attitudes play in learning, and the power of self affirmations and visualizations. Then explore the use of brain wave entrainment mixed with designer music called Metamusic® to achieve enhanced learning states. Join students of all ages who are creating magical learning outcomes using music and Metamusic.® AVAILABLE FROM AMAZON in Kindle Format.

The Journey into the Myst (Vol. 1 of The Myst Series)

by Alex Bennet and David Bennet (2012)

 What we are about to tell you would have been quite unbelievable to me before this journey began. It is not a story of the reality either of us has known for well over our 60 and 70 years of age, but rather, the reality of dreams and fairytales." This is the true story of a sequence of events that happened at Mountain Quest Institute, situated in a high valley of the Allegheny Mountains of West Virginia. The story begins with a miracle, expanding into the capture and cataloging of thousands of pictures of electromagnetic spheres widely known as "orbs." This joyous experience became an exploration into the unknown with the emergence of what the author's fondly call the Myst, the forming and shaping of non-random patterns such as human faces, angels and animals. As this phenomenon unfolds, you will discover how the Drs. Alex and David Bennet began to observe and interact with the Myst. This book shares the beginning of an extraordinary *Journey into the Myst*. AVAILABLE FROM AMAZON in Kindle Format. AVAILABLE FROM MQIPress in PDF.

Patterns in the Myst (Vol. 2 of The Myst Series)

by Alex Bennet and David Bennet (2013)

The Journey into the Myst was just the beginning for Drs. Alex and David Bennet. Volume II of the Myst Series brings Science into the Spiritual experience, bringing to bear what the Bennets have learned through their research and educational experiences in physics, neuroscience, human systems, Knowledge Management and human development. Embracing the paralogical, patterns in the Myst are observed, felt, interpreted, analyzed and compared in terms of their physical make-up, non-randomness, intelligent sources and potential implications. Along the way, the Bennets were provided amazing pictures reflecting the forming of the Myst. The Bennets shift to introspection in the third volume of the series to explore the continuing impact of the Myst experience on the human psyche. AVAILABLE FROM AMAZON in Kindle Format. AVAILABLE FROM MQIPress in PDF.

The Profundity and Bifurcation of Change Part I: Laying the Groundwork

by Alex Bennet and David Bennet with Arthur Shelley, Theresa Bullard and John Lewis

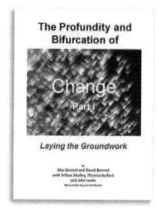

This book lays the groundwork for the **Intelligent Social Change Journey** (ISCJ), a developmental journey of the body, mind and heart, moving from the heaviness of cause-and-effect linear extrapolations, to the fluidity of co-evolving with our environment, to the lightness of breathing our thought and feelings into reality. Grounded in development of our mental faculties, these are phase changes, each building on and expanding previous learning in our movement toward intelligent activity. As we lay the groundwork, we move through the concepts of change, knowledge, forces, self and consciousness. Then, recognizing that we are holistic beings, we provide a baseline model for individual change from within.

The Profundity and Bifurcation of Change Part II: Learning from the Past

by Alex Bennet and David Bennet with Arthur Shelley, Theresa Bullard and John Lewis

Phase 1 of the Intelligent Social Change Journey (ISCJ) is focused on the linear cause-and-effect relationships of logical thinking. Knowledge, situation dependent and context sensitive, is a product of the past. **Phase 1 assumes that for every effect there is an originating cause.** This is where we as a humanity, and as individuals, begin to develop our mental faculties. In this book we explore cause and effect, scan a kaleidoscope of change models, and review the modalities of change. Since change is easier and more fluid when we are grounded, we explore three interpretations of grounding. In preparation for expanding our consciousness, a readiness assessment and sample change agent's strategy are provided. (Release 01/15/17)

The Profundity and Bifurcation of Change Part III: Learning in the Present

by Alex Bennet and David Bennet with Arthur Shelley, Theresa Bullard and John Lewis

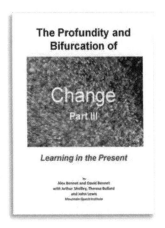

As the world becomes increasingly complex, Phase 2 of the Intelligent Social Change Journey (ISCJ) is focused on **co-evolving with the environment**. This requires a deepening connection to others, moving into empathy. While the NOW is the focus, there is an increasing ability to put together patterns from the past and think conceptually, as well as extrapolate future behaviors. Thus, we look closely at the relationship of time and space, and pattern thinking. We look at the human body as a complex energetic system, exploring the role of emotions as a guidance system, and what happens when we have stuck energy. This book also introduces Knowledge Capacities, different ways of thinking that build capacity for sustainability.

The Profundity and Bifurcation of Change Part IV: Co-Creating the Future

by Alex Bennet and David Bennet with Arthur Shelley, Theresa Bullard and John Lewis

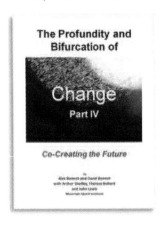

As we move into Phase 3 of the Intelligent Social Change Journey (ISCJ), **we fully embrace our role as co-creator**. We recognize the power of thought and the role of attention and intention in our ever-expanding search for a higher level of truth. Whether we choose to engage it or not, we explore mental discipline as a tool toward expanded consciousness. In preparing ourselves for the creative leap, there are ever-deepening connections with others. We now understand that the mental faculties are in service to the intuitional, preparing us to, and expanding our ability to, act in and on the world, living with conscious compassion and tapping into the intuitional at will.

The Profundity and Bifurcation of Change Part V: Living the Future

by Alex Bennet and David Bennet with Arthur Shelley, Theresa Bullard, John Lewis and Donna Panucci

We embrace the ancient art and science of Alchemy to **explore the larger shift underway for humanity** and how we can consciously and intentionally speed up evolution to enhance outcomes. In this conversation, we look at balancing and sensing, the harmony of beauty, and virtues for living the future. Conscious compassion, a virtue, is introduced as a state of being connected to morality and good character, inclusive of giving selfless service. We are now ready to refocus our attention on knowledge and consciousness, exploring the new roles these play in our advancement. And all of this—all of our expanding and growth as we move through the Intelligent Social Change journey—is giving a wide freedom of choice as we approach the bifurcation. What will we manifest? (Release 03/01/17)

Available in PDF format from <u>www.MQIPress.net</u>

Available in Kindle format from <u>www.amazon.com</u>

Made in the USA
Middletown, DE
19 November 2020